Business and the European Community

Related titles in the series

Advertising
Business and Commercial Law
The Business Environment
Business French (book/cassette pack)
Business German (book/cassette pack)
Business Italian (book/cassette pack)
Business Studies
Commerce
Economics
English for Business
Management Theory and Practice
Marketing
Office Procedures
Organizations and Management

Business and the European Community

Keith Perry BA, MA, MA(Econ), ARHistS

MADE SIMPLE
BOOKS

Made Simple
An imprint of Butterworth-Heinemann Ltd
Linacre House, Jordan Hill, Oxford OX2 8DP

ℜ A member of the Reed Elsevier plc group

OXFORD   LONDON   BOSTON
MUNICH   NEW DELHI   SINGAPORE   SYDNEY
TOKYO   TORONTO   WELLINGTON

First published 1994

British Library Cataloguing in Publication Data
Perry, K.
  Business and the European Community
  I. Title
  341.2422

ISBN 0 7506 1569 9

Typeset by Scribe Design, Gillingham, Kent
Printed in Great Britain by Clays, St Ives plc

Contents

Preface

'A frog placed in water which is gradually heated to boiling point will not jump out as long as the rate of change is below the frog's noticeable difference threshold. The result is a boiled frog, even though the frog appears to have had the option of jumping out of the pan at any time' (Professor K Weick 1983).

The reader will easily derive the message in Professor Weick's analogy. Since 1985 the European Community has been changing inexorably, and businesses in the EC and across the world that do not react in a positive way will be boiled alive!

The EC is the largest trading bloc in the world and is becoming increasingly influential in a number of policy areas. As the single market advances, as competition policy gains more authority, as Community funding for R and D and structural improvements in Europe increases, so the EC will impinge more and more on the individual business, in whatever sector that business operates. Clearly business people need to know how the EC operates, how they can exploit opportunities and face threats from within it and indeed how they can influence its decisions.

It is the chief aim of this book to explain the importance of the Community framework and the main EC policies and how businesses can respond to them. As such the book will be of interest to the general reader, as it covers many aspects of the development and nature of the Community. However, it is chiefly pointed towards students pursuing studies leading to undergraduate, professional or GCE A Level examinations, especially those engaged in business studies. It will also be of assistance to managers, in particular those expanding their existing qualifications through day release courses, so that they may more keenly appreciate the increasingly competitive environment in the European Community and thus be more able to frame appropriate and effective strategic responses.

I gladly express my thanks to those at Butterworth-Heinemann, with whom I have been associated in this project, especially Jacquie

Shanahan and Alison Boyd. I am grateful also to the library staff at Bournemouth University for their usual courteous and friendly help.

Several individuals merit special gratitude. I thank Professor Michael Bond, Dean of the Dorset Business School for his moral and practical support. Ralph Tomlinson, FCMA, MIAM, MBIM, and Daniele Overath, Director of Interel, provided much valuable advice and current material. Roger Day of British Aerospace is also thanked for providing a role model of modern British entrepreneurship from Accrington to the Moscow Underground.

My deepest debt of gratitude is to my wife Joan. Her life has become increasingly stressful as she has successfully pursued her own career in a difficult business sector yet she has always given unfailing encouragement and practical assistance. Those mixed blessings, my three daughters, must also be thanked for conspiring on most occasions to render good cheer when the task of completing this book taxed the spirits!

Keith Perry

1
The origins and evolution of the European Community

The founding of the European Community

The idea of a united Europe is many centuries old; indeed such an aim cannot be much less old than the practice of war, for the interest shown in this aim has been most intense after periods of particularly destructive warfare.

Thinkers in the early Middle Ages looked for inspiration to the great days of the Roman Empire, to the empire of Charlemagne in the early ninth century or even to the idea of a Catholic Europe with the Pope, in the words of F H Hinsley, as 'the court of moral appeal'. Following the French Wars of 1792 to 1815, Victor Hugo at the third Universal Peace Congress in 1849 looked forward to a United States of Europe similar to the United States of America. Then the day would dawn, he said, 'when cannonballs and bombs would give way to votes, with universal suffrage of the peoples, when two immense communities, the United States of America and the United States of Europe will be seen holding hands across the sea'.

The First World War, with its totally new scale of senseless slaughter, led to renewed consideration of the European idea. The outstanding figure in the interwar years was Count Coudenhove-Kalergi. His impeccable international outlook is understandable when it is recalled that his father, who was of Greek and Dutch extraction, was an Austro-Hungarian diplomat and that his mother was Japanese. The Count started a Pan-European Union, which had the support of several major politicians, including Aristide Briand. Briand who was the first to coin the phrase 'common market' was French foreign minister in the 1920s, and in 1929 he put forward a scheme for a European Union to the League of Nations. It was, however, rather vague and was received with considerable reservation in most countries. The onset of the Great Depression, the rise of Nazism and the death of Briand himself in 1932 ensured its complete failure.

It was the impact of the Second World War that really stimulated genuine moves towards European integration. The War led to the impoverishment of the continent, destroyed its political system and led to a collapse of all civilized standards. Thus bold new solutions were taken on board; it was now widely believed that Europe could only be rebuilt by a co-operative effort in a period where the nation state on its own had proved ineffective in defending its people from foreign invasion and exploitation.

Much credit should be given to the European Resistance movements for bringing the European idea to the top of the political agenda. As Vaughan has stressed, 'The Resistance movement which began in Italy was not only an opposition (to Fascism); it was also pro Europe, revolutionary in many ways, often federalist and thus immensely positive. The ferment of ideas it produced was perhaps the greatest single intellectual landmark in the history of European integration; it provided Europeans with a European ideology'. Thus while fighting for their lives against Fascism, Resistance members through pamphlets and newspapers emphasized the need for a postwar United States of Europe with one government, one federal army and one court. Many Resistance fighters became prominent in national and European Community affairs after 1945, and even in the 1990s this group included the President of France, François Mitterrand.

After the Second World War ended, the creation of new institutions was accelerated not only by the fear of a future revived Germany but also by the prevalent apprehension about the intentions of Russian Communism under Stalin. The West feared both the sheer military might of Russia and the kind of subversion seen in the Communist take-over of Czechoslovakia in 1948. The presence of large Communist parties in both Italy and France made the threat only too real. Integration was also encouraged by United States pressure in favour of a united Europe. The Americans believed that such a Europe would be prosperous, thus providing both a barrier to Communism and a market for American exports and investment.

Solid support for European initiatives came from a group of dedicated European-minded politicians whose experience and background made them loathe the internecine warfare in Europe since 1914. Three of the men in the vanguard of the movement were devout Catholics – Konrad Adenauer, the anti-Prussian Mayor of Cologne, who became Chancellor of West Germany, Alcide de Gasperi, a deputy of the Vienna Diet while Austria-Hungary was fighting Italy in the First World War, and Prime Minister of Italy after 1945, and Robert Schuman, a German national during the First World War and then a French foreign minister after the return of Alsace-Lorraine to France in 1919.

Special mention should, however, be made of Jean Monnet, who was to earn the title 'Father of Europe'. Born in 1888 at Cognac, he began his working life in his father's brandy business but became an important French diplomat in both world wars in addition to being Deputy Secretary-General of the League of Nations in the interwar years. By 1949 he was a power behind the scenes in French political life, as he was in charge of economic planning and the distribution of American funds through Marshall Aid.

What worried Monnet, as the Cold War intensified, was the division of Europe into two camps and the problem of reinstating Germany safely within the European family of nations. As a blueprint for a united Europe, he suggested to the British in March 1949 the formation of a common market in coal and steel (later called the Schuman Plan, because Schuman as French foreign minister formally proposed it). Having enjoyed working with the British in both wars, he viewed Britain and France as natural partners and expected the British to reciprocate. To his consternation the British poured cold water on the scheme and Monnet realized that Europe would have to go on without Britain. In June 1950 he told Stafford Cripps, the Labour Chancellor of the Exchequer:

'My dear friend, you know how I've felt about Britain for 30 years. There is no question about that. I hope with all my heart that you will join from the start. But if you don't, then we will go ahead without you; and because you are realists you will adjust to the facts when you see that we've succeeded'.

Six West European States (France, West Germany, Italy, the Netherlands, Belgium and Luxembourg) did not share Britain's reservations, and in 1951 the Treaty of Paris established the European Coal and Steel Community (ECSC). It was a true forerunner of the later European Community in the sense that it aimed at the creation of a common market and also that the institutions created to run it were a model for the later Community institutions. The new organization was successful in achieving its objectives, and much of its success was due to Monnet himself as President of the High Authority (the executive authority of the ECSC). He was already 63 years old but he set a pace of work exhausting to colleagues half his age, e.g. forcing them to work through August, the traditional holiday month, in 1952. As Monnet put it, 'L'Europe ne se fera pas dans les bôites de nuit'. Such an example was not only exhausting but exhilarating for his colleagues, who deeply respected their leader because, though he was a slavedriver, he never sought the limelight for himself.

It should be stressed that while he possessed a genuine European vision, Monnet also had a shrewd sense of French interests. For example, French economic progress was threatened by coal short-ages as West Germany expanded its steel production and needed its coal for that purpose. A common market in coal enabled the French to continue coal purchases from West Germany. Yet, in Alan Milward's words, the Treaty of Paris 'ended 80 years of bitter and deadly dispute between France and Germany and made the reconstruction of Europe possible'.

To build on the ECSC and prepare the way for a wider union, Monnet founded his Action Committee for the United States of Europe in 1955. In effect he used his vast contacts to create a powerful pressure group that could galvanize national governments, parliaments and publics across Western Europe into appreciating the need for a wider and closer union. His organization included important politicians and trade unionists from across the political spectrum and from all West European states.

Developments soon followed. In 1955 delegates from the member states of the ECSC met at Messina and agreed to form the European Economic Community (EEC). The constitution and programme were worked out in the next 18 months, largely through the genius of the Belgian minister Paul-Henri Spaak in forcing through decisions. In March 1957 the Treaty of Rome, setting up the EEC, was ready for signature. It established a customs union of the six countries concerned, pledged to reduce and by 1969 abolish all tariffs on their mutual trade.

The objectives of the Treaty of Rome

For much of its history, coverage of the European Community in the media became obsessed by economic issues such as farm prices and the Community budget. As a result it has been all too easy to forget that political motives were perhaps stronger than economic motives in the creation of the Community. An early President of the Commission, Dr Walter Hallstein, once said, 'We are not in business at all; we are in politics'.

Incorporated into the Rome Treaty were three major political objectives: political unity, peace and democracy.

Political unity

Although since 1957 the Community has been primarily concerned with economic integration, the ultimate aim of the founding fathers was that close economic ties would eventually lead to political unity. The Treaty of Rome pointed to a determination 'to lay the foundations of an ever closer union among the peoples of Europe'. It was believed at the time that the development of economic ties would lead naturally and inevitably towards the goal of political union, but in fact the very successes of the Community helped to perpetuate the national attitudes it was supposed to replace. As Stanley Henig explained,

> The achievements of the European Community have in practice strengthened rather than weakened the nation state. Certainly they have not publicly demonstrated the need for it to wither away as the central repository of popular political allegiance. This is perhaps the greatest irony in the development of European integration.

In other words the development of the Community and its policies seemed to go hand in hand with a weakening rather than a strengthening of the vision of a politically united Europe. Only after 1985 did the drive for more political unity recover any momentum.

Peace

The Community was created partly as an instrument for the cementing of peace in Europe. The signatories to the Rome Treaty promised to 'strengthen the safeguards of peace and liberty', and called upon the peoples of Europe who shared their ideal to join in their efforts. Such concern for peace was only natural, given the bitter enmities engendered in Europe by two world wars. It is in this context that we can appreciate the importance of the creation of the ECSC in 1951. Its greatest achievement was to make war between France and Germany virtually impossible by the building of a common market in coal and steel. The European Community was able to build on the ECSC, and it is easy to forget that the Community has contributed to European peace since 1957, a period in marked contrast to the 30 years before 1945, in which there were two terrible wars.

It has of course been argued that war was no longer an instrument of policy for solving differences between the states of Western Europe and that a period of peace would have ensued from the 1950s with or without the existence of the European Community. But at the very least the Community offered a forum within which conflicts between member states could be resolved peacefully – 'jaw jaw not war war'. In the past the absence of such an appropriate forum for conciliation allowed international disputes to escalate into war.

Democracy

The number of states in the world that are parliamentary democracies is, and always has been, small. Only a minority of states in the

United Nations may be called democracies in any meaningful sense, and of these a significant proportion are members of the European Community. An important aim of the Community has been the strengthening of democracy in Europe and indeed the wider world. The founding fathers hoped that the development of the Community into a parliamentary democracy would strengthen democracy among its member states. The Treaty of Rome pointed to the pooling of Community resources as having as its aim 'peace and liberty'. In his memoirs Jean Monnet emphasized that 'the essential thing is gradually to create among Europeans the broadest common interest, served by democratic institutions to which the necessary sovereignty has been delegated'. Thus one of the chief motives for welcoming new states into the Community, especially in the 1980s and 1990s has been the belief that Community membership would buttress the rather frail democracy in the states of Southern and Eastern Europe.

Naturally, then, the Community had to make some effort to be a democratic organization. From the start work began on the development of a European Parliament, and, as a democracy implies participation, it has always been one of the guiding principles of European decision-making that there would be consultations with interest groups such as producers, consumers, workers and traders. Eventually the Economic and Social Committee (ECOSOC) was created to represent such groups. Nevertheless the powers of these bodies remained so weak and the power of unelected bodies such as the Commission so strong that there remained 'a democratic deficit' in Community affairs.

The Treaty of Rome also pointed to four major economic objectives: negative integration, positive integration, improvement of living standards, and the encouragement of trade with overseas countries.

Negative integration

The removal of barriers to the free movement of goods, services, persons and capital is called negative integration. Article 3 of the Treaty of Rome called for 'the elimination, as between member states, of customs duties and of quantitative restrictions in regard to the import and export of goods, as well as of all other measures having equivalent effect; the establishment of a common customs tariff and of a common commercial policy towards third countries'. Such arrangements were to be accomplished within 12 years, starting 1 January 1958 with the Common External Tariff (CET) being set at the level of the average of tariffs in force on imports from the outside world.

The creation of the Common External Tariff and the elimination of intra-Community tariffs were both achieved 1½ years ahead of schedule. The aim of this progressive removal of tariffs and other barriers to trade, and the creation of a customs union, was to reconcile conflicting economic interests and to promote a common economic prosperity. It was hoped that such co-operation would prevent the recurrence of the economic nationalism of the interwar years. After the Wall Street Crash of 1929 individual states had increased tariffs and quotas, actions that had aggravated the world slump by reducing world trade by nearly 70 percent in the 1930s.

However, the Treaty of Rome emphasized that another important Community objective was 'the elimination, as between members states, of obstacles to freedom of movement for persons, services and capital'. The aim here was to give a national of any member state an absolute right to enter another member state for the purpose of working or doing business, and with the additional right of being employed on the same terms as workers of the host country.

In practice the removal of barriers to the free movement of goods, services, persons and capital was to prove more difficult than the founding fathers had perhaps appreciated. The long road towards the Single Market will be analysed in Chapter 3.

Positive integration

The Community wished to go further than a customs union with a free internal market. In the words of A M El Agraa, 'The EEC is a common market aspiring to become a complete economic and political union'. It has always aimed at economic union, at what is sometimes called positive integration. The Treaty of Rome was less specific here but the objective was the development of co-ordinated or harmonized Community policies that would, in certain fields, replace national policies. Article 3 of the Treaty pointed, for example, to the establishment of common policies in the spheres of agriculture, transport and balance of payments control.

The only form of positive integration on which the Rome Treaty was specific was the Common Agricultural Policy (CAP). Its aims as stated in Articles 38–47 of the Treaty of Rome were to increase agricultural productivity, to ensure a fair standard of living for farmers, to stabilize markets, to assure availability of supplies and to ensure a reasonable price for consumers (see Chapter 6).

Interestingly the Treaty of Rome did not put forward the concept of monetary union as an explicit objective, and it was only accepted as such in 1969. The other striking omission from the Rome Treaty was that of industrial policy, which only became significant in the late 1970s.

Improvement of living standards

Because Europe reflects world trends in its disparities of wealth, the founders of the Community attempted to bring in machinery to provide all its citizens with a fair share of wealth. The Rome Treaty provided for a Social Fund, set up in 1958 to retrain workers from declining industries. Its scope was widened after 1972 through pressure from the West German Chancellor, Willy Brandt, so that it could deal with other social problems – migrant workers, women and the young. With the later horrendous rise in Community levels of unemployment, the emphasis was laid increasingly on help for the young unemployed.

The Community was also pledged under the Rome Treaty to reduce differences between the various regions of the Community. The task became more urgent after 1957, because the prosperity gap in the Community widened. By the early 1980s the inhabitants of the Community's ten poorest regions earned on average a quarter of the amount enjoyed by their counterparts in the ten richest areas. At the beginning of the 1970s the ratio was less than 3 to 1. Only in 1974, however, did the Community agree to set up a European Regional Development Fund (ERDF) to tackle its regional problems. For many years it had an insufficient share of the Community budget to implement its policies, a situation that was to change markedly after 1988.

The encouragement of trade with overseas countries

Article 3 of the Rome Treaty stated that Community activities should include 'the association of overseas countries and territories with a view to increasing trade and to promoting jointly economic and social development'. Under Article 113 the Commission was given the responsibility, once authorized by the Council of Ministers, to negotiate trade treaties with non-Community countries. The Commission carried out this task effectively, so that nearly every country in the world has some kind of trading link with the Community. A particularly important development was the creation of the Lomé Conventions, from 1975 onwards, with the countries in Africa, the Caribbean and the Pacific (the ACP countries).

The Community record in the encouragement of global trade was, however, to be a mixed one. Trade problems were to develop, especially with Japan and the United States. At times trade disputes, particularly with the Americans, threatened to provoke a trade war and block the process of liberalizing world trade through the General Agreement on Tariffs and Trade (GATT). Among a number of issues exacerbating relations with the US were crucial disputes over steel and agriculture (see Chapter 11).

The evolution of the European Community after 1957

All the major West European powers except one joined the Community at its inception. Britain had refused to sign the Rome Treaty, fearful of losing its independence. Her rather disdainful diplomacy (which actually made the six founder members more determined to succeed in the great venture) seemed designed to minimize the importance of the new institution. British ministers did not believe that the new undertaking would work, and set up a small free trade area. In 1959 the European Free Trade Area (EFTA) was created, comprising Britain, Sweden, Norway, Denmark, Austria, Switzerland and Portugal. The Community states saw the new organization almost as a rival, which it was perhaps meant to be.

An appreciation of psychological factors is essential if we are to understand British attitudes in the immediate postwar years. F N Northedge refers to 'the notorious emotional detachment of the British people from mainland Europe', a detachment that perhaps prevented a proper appreciation of national interests. To the British, Europeans were foreigners who ran their affairs badly, e.g. allowing the spread of Fascism, and who dragged honest Britain into costly and risky wars. The British survival during the Second World War heightened what has been termed 'the Channel Complex'. In her finest hour Britain had stood alone. She had been undefeated, she had escaped occupation and she emerged from the war with renewed pride in her national virtues and institutions. The continental countries of Western Europe, on the other hand, had just passed through the worst ordeal in their history, and the common experience of Nazi occupation made it imperative for them to develop some form of European unity from the ruins.

In government circles the belief that Britain could still maintain a world role died hard. As Winston Churchill phrased it in 1950, Britain stood at the intersection of three overlapping circles – the English-speaking world, the Commonwealth and Europe. It was by her position within all three that she might still play a unique world role. Therefore, as Uwe Kitzinger explains, 'none of these three bonds, and certainly not that with Europe, could afford to be tightened to the extent that they might damage the other two'.

To put it bluntly, Europe was by far the least important of the three overlapping circles to Britain in the immediate postwar years. There was still considerable belief in the idea of the Commonwealth and in the 'special relationship' with the United States of America. It should also be remembered that the British standard of living in the late 1940s and early 1950s was far superior to that of the Continent and therefore there seemed little to be gained from integration with nations suffering economic difficulties and political instability. Finally, given the three major wars between France and

Germany since 1870, the British could not believe in the feasibility of any genuine Franco-German rapprochement.

British politicians were soon forced by events to reconsider this rather arrogant attitude. The European Community represented a market of 200 million people, and, contrary to British expectations, began to forge ahead economically while Britain stagnated. Enjoying internal tariff cuts of 30 per cent by 1960, the EEC countries succeeded in raising industrial output by more than 50 per cent between 1954 and 1960, while Britain's industrial output rose by only 20 per cent in the same period. This EEC performance appeared to be attracting American investment that had previously gone to Britain. Before the EEC came into existence, over half of American investment in Europe was in Britain; by 1960 this percentage had fallen to 41 per cent. The small EFTA market of 95 million people, over half of whom were British, was clearly no substitute for the EEC market, which might provide UK industry with the required salutary shock through greater competition and with greater opportunities in a large market.

However, in the 1950s political considerations were the controlling ones among most British politicians. It seemed clear that the EEC could become a third superpower and that non-membership would lead to Britain's political insignificance. Such worries were reinforced by the decline of the so-called 'special friendship' with the USA. The limitations of this relationship had been cruelly demonstrated by the Suez disaster of 1956, when Britain, in collusion with France and Israel, invaded Egypt in an attempt to retain control over the Suez Canal, only to be forced, primarily by American pressure, to call for a ceasefire after 1 day's fighting. Similarly, the rapid decolonization of the late 1950s and early 1960s demonstrated that the second of Churchill's overlapping circles – the Commonwealth and Empire – was also declining as a major influence in British foreign policy. Such realities provoked a major debate on the issue of Europe in 1960, and the government of Harold Macmillan was converted into opening negotiations with the Six in August 1961.

British membership was to be delayed until 1973, and for this the British themselves must take some blame. By haggling over the terms of entry for 16 months, they created an impression of a reluctant applicant. But the main factor obstructing British membership was the inflexible opposition of the French President, Charles de Gaulle, who vetoed the whole issue both in 1963 and 1967. Born in 1890, midway in the period between the Franco–Prussian War and the First World War, de Gaulle was moved by the fallen greatness of France and the absolute necessity of restoring it. He was sceptical of a supranational body like the EEC and believed in close ties with Adenauer's West Germany. He was profoundly opposed to any Anglo-Saxon influence in Europe, and believed that Britain in the

Common Market would be a kind of American Trojan horse. In addition, as Guy de Carmoy has stressed, 'Britain's presence would alter the balance of power within the enlarged Community. France would no longer have the freedom of action she enjoyed in an institution where she held the political reins and Germany was content to follow her lead'. By 1967 three other countries (Ireland, Denmark and Norway) were also applying for Community membership, and de Gaulle was concerned to retain French dominance. In 1966 he remarked to George Brown, Deputy Leader of the Labour Party, on the impossibility of two cocks (France and Britain) living in one farmyard with ten hens. Brown recorded de Gaulle as saying that 'he had had a lot of trouble getting the five hens to do what France wanted, and he wasn't going to have Britain coming in and creating trouble all over again, this time with ten'.

Only with the accession to the French presidency of Georges Pompidou in 1969 did a more favourable consideration of British membership become possible. Coming from peasant and banking stock, the new president had a keen eye for French interests, but he was not hostile to Britain.

The new British Prime Minister in 1970 was Edward Heath, a man with genuine and fervent European attitudes. He had made his maiden parliamentary speech in 1950, attacking the failure of the then Labour government for failing to give the Schuman Plan proper consideration. His travels in Europe in his youth and his experiences as a lieutenant-colonel in the Second World War helped to form his commitment to Europe, and in the 1950s he took a far more European line than his leaders. Heath saw integration as a means of avoiding war, but, as Uwe Kitzinger has explained, there was a more positive side. Heath believed that European countries did some things better than Britain, and he anticipated that if Britain joined Europe she would gain economically and culturally. He was also a most stubborn individual in pursuit of his major political objective – British membership of the Community.

Accordingly the Community opened negotiations in 1979 with Britain, Ireland, Denmark and Norway. The discussions were not always easy, but private Anglo–French talks led to a solution of six issues – Britain's budget contribution, sterling, her application of Community preference, New Zealand dairy produce, cane sugar and fish. Eventually the Treaty of Accession was signed and came into effect on 1 January 1973. Ireland and Denmark joined Britain as new members of the Community, but the Norwegian people rejected membership in a referendum.

Thus was solved the first enlargement of the Community, but the remaining years of the 1970s were difficult. The startling rise in oil prices in 1974 pushed Community economies into recession, and in 1975 the Community suffered its first negative rate of growth, which resulted in a decline in living standards in some member states. At the same time the number of unemployed rose from 5 million in 1977 to 10 million in 1982. Nevertheless the Community was still regarded by non-members as a club worth belonging to, and the 1980s saw the accession of three states to full membership – Greece in 1981 and Spain and Portugal in 1986.

Some progress was also made on key areas such as economic and monetary issues. At a summit meeting at The Hague in 1969 the Six decided that the Community should transform itself into an Economic and Monetary Union (EMU), although only in 1979 was a more modest scheme in the shape of the European Monetary System (EMS) implemented. Regional problems were addressed by the establishment of the European Regional Development Fund (ERDF) in 1975, and in the same year an attempt to create a new relationship with the Third World was forged by the signing of the first Lomé Convention.

There were a number of institutional developments. Meetings of the heads of state were formalized and given the title of the European Council. The European Parliament, initially elected by national parliaments, became directly elected by the people. However, the main advance was in the field of political co-operation. By the 1980s the perception that the Community should have a greater world role led to a search for a common foreign policy, sometimes called political co-operation. The basic arrangements for political co-operation had been created by the Luxembourg Report of 1970, which agreed that foreign ministers should meet at least every 6 months for discussons on foreign policy matters. The report also created the basic bureaucratic machinery, as it set up a committee of senior officials (political directors) from the member states' foreign offices. The committee began to meet monthly to prepare the ground for meetings of the foreign ministers so that the Community could react more rapidly and in a more united fashion. The country occupying the Presidency of the Council of Ministers (which rotates from one member state to another every 6 months on the alphabetical principle) had to ensure that political co-operation worked smoothly. In the view of Douglas Hurd, the system worked well because the change of presidency led to new ideas being presented every 6 months.

In 1981 the foreign ministers in the London Report stated their determination to strengthen political co-operation, and consequently the 1980s did see a more co-ordinated Community response on crises in the Middle East, on the need to give assistance to the economies of Eastern Europe, and diplomatic and commercial support for Britain in her war with Argentina in 1982. The level of agreement reached should not be overstated. In many areas no common Community line was adopted. In the words of Douglas Hurd, close

Community co-operation on international issues still only amounted to 'islands of agreement amid a sea of matters where there is still no European line'. In 1990 the Community showed a market lack of unity during the Gulf crisis and in 1992 over the tragedy of Yugoslavia. Only slowly was the Community losing its reputation as an 'economic giant and a political dwarf'.

The single market and European union

The issue of the Community's relative economic decline continued to be the main concern of most political leaders. In particular the failure to create a genuine internal market was deemed to be a major cause of slow growth in most Community economies. In 1985 the new President of the European Commission, Jacques Delors, appointed Lord Cockfield to write a White Paper, 'Completing the Internal Market', in which a list of 300 necessary reforms were suggested.

To expedite the implementation of such an ambitious body of reform, the Member States signed the Single European Act (SEA) in 1986, and the treaty came into effect in July 1987. The principal purpose of the act, in the words of Josephine Steiner, was to 'eliminate the remaining barriers to the single internal market within the deadline of 31 December 1992'. The SEA extended the sphere of Community competence and introduced a number of procedural changes designed to accelerate Community decision-making. In particular, in Article 100A, which was added to the Rome Treaty, there was to be an increase in the number of areas in which voting could be taken by qualified majority (see Chapter 2). This meant that the majority of the legislation required to complete the internal market would be enacted by qualified majority. Without such a reform it is hard to see how the single market programme would ever have gathered any momentum, given early problems in the Community decision-making procedure.

It may well be that the signatories to the SEA committed themselves implicitly to a good deal more than they were committing themselves to explicitly. The Treaty of Rome had called for internal free trade and the free movement of services, workers and capital within the European Community. The SEA reaffirmed these original goals, defining the internal market as 'an area without frontiers in which the free circulation of goods, services, persons and capital is ensured'. However, the SEA went considerably further than the Rome Treaty in its commitment to complete European Union; its amendments to the Rome Treaty permitted the member states to go further than a single market and establish a fuller economic and monetary union, creating in effect a United States of Europe.

Such implications worried the British government, which argued that the commitment to economic and monetary union was not legally binding but merely a pious hope. In the British view the SEA was only the necessary framework for the achievement of the main goal – the completion of an open, liberalized and deregulated European market, providing for the free movement of factors of production and the extension of competition which alone would stimulate European business so that it could compete globally with Japanese and American rivals. In contrast to this minimalist view was an alternative perception held by other member states such as France and West Germany – that the SEA resulted from a determination of most member states to increase the scope and pace of European integration.

The goal of European integration was seen as more urgent following the revolutionary changes in Eastern Europe in 1989. The collapse of Communism within the Soviet Union led to the incorporation of East Germany into the Community when German reunification was formally concluded in October 1990. Other states were freed from Soviet control and sought closer relations with the Community. Czechoslovakia, Hungary and Poland all signed association agreements with the Community at the end of 1991 with a view to the establishment of free trade within 10 years.

The reunification of Germany and the possibility that new states could accede to full membership brought to a head a crucial question in Community policy-making. Would the Community increase the number of states rapidly (as the British wanted) and achieve a widening of the Community or should such a widening be delayed until fuller political and economic union was achieved? During 1989 and 1990 the President of the Commission, Jacques Delors, forced a concentration on this problem, fearful that Germany's preoccupation with the incorporation of East Germany and the pressures from applicant states would distract attention and commitment from the goal of 'an ever closer union'. The year 1991 saw intense discussion of a possible Treaty of Political Union. Finally at Maastricht in December 1991 the heads of government of the member states of the Community agreed to a draft treaty establishing, in the words of the preamble, 'a European Union ... an ever closer Union among the peoples of Europe where decisions are taken as closely as possible to the citizens'.

The Maastricht Summit laid down a timetable for movement towards economic and monetary union that could by 1999 create a single currency for those member states that could meet quite stringent conditions in terms of budget deficits and rates of inflation. The treaty extended the Community's commitment to joint policies in the fields of defence and security, stipulating unanimity in the Council of Ministers for the adoption of policies but allowing for qualified majority on the actions required to implement them. The text included a commitment to NATO as the basis for European defence and associated the Western European Union – the European alliance linked to NATO – closely with the conduct of defence policy (see Chapter 15).

Further reading

Camps, M, *Britain and the European Community*, OUP, London, 1964.

Camps, M, *European Unificiation in the Sixties*, OUP, London, 1967.

George, S, *Britain: An Awkward Partner in the EC*, OUP, Oxford, 1990.

Laqueur, W Z, *The Rebirth of Europe*, Penguin, Harmondsworth, 1982.

Mayne, R, *The Recovery of Europe*, Harper and Row, New York, 1970.

Pinder, J, *The European Community: The Building of a Union*, OUP, Oxford, 1991.

Vaughan, R, *Twentieth Century Europe: Paths To Unity*, Croom Helm, London, 1979.

Questions

1 Why was the movement for European unity particularly strong in the years after 1945?
2 Critically examine the reasons for British reluctance to join the EEC in 1957.
3 Account for the Macmillan government's decision to apply for membership of the EEC in 1961.
4 Why was British membership of the EEC delayed until 1973?
5 Account for the drive towards more integration in the EC during the 1980s.

2
The Community institutional framework

The European Community functions in accordance with a constitution enshrined in a series of basic treaties that define the powers of the main institutions and their relationship with the member governments. The Treaty of Paris, establishing the European Coal and Steel Community (ECSC), was signed in 1951, and was followed by two separate Treaties of Rome (March 1957), which established the European Atomic Energy Community (EURATOM) and the European Economic Community (EEC). It was agreed to create a single Assembly, Court of Justice and Economic and Social Committee for all three Communities.

In April 1965 it was further agreed by a Treaty signed in Brussels to create a single Council of the European Communities, replacing the Special Council of Ministers of the ECSC, the Council of the EEC and the Council of EURATOM. A Commission of the European Communities was to replace the High Authority of the ECSC, the Commission of the EEC and the Commission of EURATOM, a single Audit Board being created for all three Communities. This so-called Merger Treaty came into force in 1967, and the term European Community was increasingly used to refer to the unified Communities.

The fifth major treaty – the Treaty of Brussels of 1972 – brought about the enlargement of the Community from six members to nine, with 1975 seeing important decisions concerning direct elections to the European Parliament. In 1987 the Single European Act widened the use of qualified majority voting (QMV) by the Council of Ministers, while the European Parliament gained extra powers. The Maastricht Treaty in 1991 added to the powers of the European Parliament and the European Court (see final chapter).

The European Council

At their meeting in Paris in 1974 the Community heads of government decided to meet three times a year under the name of the

European Council with a view to making more rapid progress in Community policy, particularly in the field of political co-operation. These meetings have become formally organized, with the Commission being represented at the European Council by the President of the Commission and one of the vice-presidents, while heads of government are accompanied by their foreign ministers. There had been occasional summit meetings in the past, the first major one being The Hague Summit of 1969, in which the Six recommitted themselves to the Community.

When Giscard d'Estaing advanced the idea of a European Council in 1973, the hope was that the summits would be occasions for tranquil reflection on the longer term issues facing the Community. In practice the government leaders have rarely found time at their meetings to discuss long-term strategy, free from the pressure of detailed decision-making. In fact the European Council has become the Community's highest court of appeal and its supreme decision-making institution. It has had to arbitrate on major disputes, such as Britain's net financial contribution to the Community budget and farm price increases, which are technically complicated issues.

There are two chief reasons for this development. First, there have been more serious disputes among the member states in recent years owing to the worsening economic climate. Second, as other Community institutions have personnel who have lacked the political influence in their own countries to force through any solutions to the problems dealing with major issues, they are then forced to pass the problem over to the European Council.

Difficult questions have led to acrimonious meetings of the European Council, particularly in the long disputes over Britain's contributions to the Community budget. An unfortunate feature is that the summits have become media circuses with more than 1,000 journalists from the press, radio and television in attendance. The pressure on the national leaders to be seen to be taking a 'strong' line is therefore great, and some have been unscrupulous about using press leaks and 'off the record' comments as part of their tactics in Community disputes. Nevertheless the European Council has proved itself capable of reaching constructive decisions on the future of the EC, e.g. on the Single Market and European Monetary Union (EMU).

The Council of Ministers

The Council is the principal decision-making body of the European Community, and the only institution that directly represents the governments of the member states. The Council takes the final decisions on policy for the Community on the basis of proposals from the Commission, after taking into account the opinions of the European Parliament and the Economic and Social Committee. Normally the Council cannot enact any measure without a Commission proposal. There are now three separate procedures by which such a proposal may become law (see Community law and the legislative process, p.29).

The office of President of the Council is held for a term of 6 months by each member state in turn. It has become the practice for each member to try and establish a particular style of work and to single out certain matters to which it wishes to give priority. Given that the chairman can influence Council business, the President may exercise an important, if temporary, influence.

For major decisions the Council consists of the foreign ministers of the member states, but on a day to day basis membership depends upon the subject before the Council, and as Community affairs have developed, so a wider range of national ministers has attended to Council business. Three groups of ministers meet most frequently – those for foreign affairs, agriculture and finance. This large number of ministers has created difficulties for member governments, because if Community issues are handled by various politicians, it becomes more difficult to see their European policy as a coherent whole. There is even a danger that a national minister in pursuit of a Community policy may distance himself from his own national colleagues. The greater specialization of the Council creates problems, because as individual issues become compartmentalized, so it becomes more difficult to negotiate package deals acceptable to all parties. The Council of Agricultural Ministers in particular appears to have developed an independent existence of its own.

Under the Rome Treaties the Council may take decisions in any one of three ways: by unanimity, by simple majority or by qualified majority. On matters regarded by a member state as being of vital interest, it has been until recently the Council's practice to proceed only on the basis of unanimity. Some Council decisions have therefore to be taken by unanimous vote, but abstention by one member state does not invalidate an otherwise unanimous vote.

In practice many issues are settled on the basis of consensus. In order to improve the work of the Council, the heads of government agreed at the Paris Summit of 1974 that the practice of requiring unanimity for agreement on issues that were not of vital concern should be abandoned. Decisions on most matters are taken by majority vote, often by the system of 'qualified majority'. The vote is weighted, giving a total of seventy-six, of which fifty-four are required for a 'qualified majority'. Germany, France, Italy and Britain have ten votes each, Spain eight votes, Belgium, the Netherlands, Portugal and Greece five votes each, Ireland and Denmark three each and Luxembourg two. This means that the five large countries cannot force a decision on the seven smaller ones and that any three large countries can block a decision.

The Council tends to leave much of the details to COREPER (see below) and concerns itself with major political issues. Unfortunately, as with the European Council, members have had to put up with excessive pressure from the media and national groups, e.g. the French farmers, which often lobby violently. Meetings of the Council attract much media publicity and are portrayed by the media in terms of victory or defeat for national interests. The problem is made worse by Council ministers themselves leaking information to the press to gain a political advantage. As a result, agreements have become more and more difficult to achieve.

Decision-making is in any case difficult without the problems pointed to above. Ministers who are dealing with delicate problems already have too much business and can only attend part-time to Community affairs. Consequently until the late 1980s there was often a time-lag in reaching a decision, and the Council became a major bottleneck preventing the efficient expediting of Community business. Fortunately the 1987 Single European Act appears to have accelerated the process by which qualified majority voting will be increasingly used.

The Committee of Permanent Representatives

As the Council of Ministers only met at intervals and in any case faced acute problems in expediting Community business, it was decided in 1965 to set up the Committee of Permanent Representatives (generally referred to as COREPER after the French acronym). It is an organization of senior officials who prepare Council meetings and handle business between Council meetings. It meets regularly either to consider matters referred back to it by the Council of Ministers because ministers have been unable to reach agreement, or to give a preliminary view to ministers on Commission proposals formally submitted to the Council but for which its timetable has left no time for discussion. In 1966 COREPER gained fresh influence when it was agreed that the Commission would work through it to make contact with national governments before deciding on the exact form of any intended proposal.

The importance of this institution has grown since 1965, because through its links with both the Commission and the Council of Ministers, it has a part in all the major stages of Community policy-making from early discussions to the final Council decision-making and it forms an essential link between the Commission and the national governments. Many decisions are now made by COREPER in advance of a Council meeting, the Council merely giving formal assent.

The permanent representatives therefore have considerable importance. They have assistance from specialist subordinate committees, they hold ambassadorial rank and are effectively the member states' ambassadors in Brussels. Thus they act as the deputies to the ministers and in that capacity may attend Council meetings.

The European Commission

The Commission, which is based in Brussels, consists of seventeen members – two each from Britain, France, Germany, Spain and Italy, and one each from Belgium, Denmark, Ireland, Luxembourg, the Netherlands, Portugal and Greece. These seventeen commissioners are chosen by agreement between the governments of the member states normally for a period of 4 years with renewable appointments. Both the President and the five vice-presidents are chosen from the seventeen for a 2-year renewable period. In practice an individual can expect two terms as president and several have been – like Roy Jenkins, President 1977–80, and Jacques Delors, President from 1985 on – significant in national politics and able to meet the Council ministers on a more or less equal footing.

Under the terms of the Treaties, the members 'shall be chosen on the grounds of their general competence' and according to Article 10 of the Merger Treaty 'in the general interests of the Communities be completely independent in the performance of their duties . . . neither seek nor take any instructions from any government or any other body and refrain from any action incompatible with their duties'. They must also when taking up their office as commissioners 'give a solemn undertaking that, both during and after their term of office, they will respect the obligations arising therefrom'. Thus, though he is initially appointed by the national government, the commissioner does not represent that government nor is he allowed to be influenced by it. He is, in theory, supposed to be completely independent, a servant of the Community rather than the national interest.

The Commission heads an administration of about 15,000 international civil servants organized in twenty-three directorates-general, each responsible to one of the commissioners. Each commissioner has responsibility for one or more Community policies, and in practice is given a large measure of influence in framing policy. Nevertheless, despite this division of responsibilities, the Treaty of Rome set up the Commission as a collegiate institution, and therefore all important measures, including proposals to the Council, have to be adopted by the commissioners as a body.

Unlike the Council, however, the Commission uses majority voting as the only way of dealing with the large volume of work. In practice only important matters, particularly politically delicate issues, are discussed by the commissioners themselves at their weekly meetings. More routine proposals are usually dealt with by 'written procedure'. The proposals are circulated to each member of the Commission, and if no objections are raised within a specified period, they are adopted automatically.

Commissioners have help from two sources: (1) a *chef de cabinet*, a French phrase meaning a small personal staff, which includes an assistant normally of the same nationality as themselves, (2) the Commission staff of the particular general directory they head. Their work can be complex, because Commission proposals have to be integrated into twelve national economies and there is of course the problem of using nine official languages. As a result, half the Commission staff are translators, and many are from Belgium, Italy, France or Luxembourg, as it is in these states that most of the institutions are based. However, the general directories are composed of staff from all the twelve nationalities in the Community, and care is taken to prevent any national viewpoint becoming too dominant by ensuring that the holders of the highest posts are drawn from several member states and that each director (the head of the general directory) is of a different nationality from the Commissioner to whom he or she is responsible.

The Commission has four main roles:

1 It acts as a Community watchdog. As the guardian of the Treaties, the Commission has the function of ensuring that member states abide by their obligations. It can investigate circumstances where a breach of obligations is suspected, either by a member state or a firm, and issue a reasoned opinion. If matters are not set right within a stated period, the Commission can refer the matter to the European Court of Justice. The Commission has few direct sanctions but it can fine firms for breaches of the rules, especially the rules relating to fair competition. In practice member states usually in the long run accept their obligations to abide by Community decisions.

2 The Commission's main function is that of initiator of policy. The Treaty of Rome was never a full guide to future policy, and therefore the Commission has a great deal of influence in shaping Community developments. The directorate making a proposal will enter into discussion with government departments and other interested groups before the proposal is formulated. It is then discussed with COREPER, the European Parliament, and the Economic and Social Committee before it reaches the Council of Ministers.

3 The Commission administers policies previously agreed by the Council or derived directly from the provisions of the Treaties. It administers the funds of the common programmes that account for most of the Community budget. It is particularly occupied in the running of the Common Agricultural Policy, because of the daily management of the markets that are necessary.

4 Operating upon a mandate from the Council, the Commission negotiates on behalf of the Community in certain external matters. Under Article 113 of the Rome Treaty it has negotiated trade agreements with foreign countries. Important examples of this function are the Lomé Conventions the Commission agreed with African, Caribbean and Pacific States (ACP) from 1975 on. In fact the Commission has negotiated treaties with many areas of the world, including the states of the European Free Trade Area (EFTA). Eastern Europe, North Africa and the Middle East. Commission representatives were also responsible for negotiating on behalf of the EC in the Uruguay Round of the GATT (see Chapter 11).

The Commission suffers from an invidious reputation: it is supposed to be bursting at the seams with too many interfering bureaucrats. In fact the Commission has a staff that is really quite small relative to its considerable responsibilities, and while it may on occasions commit absurdities in the search for harmonized policies, most stories about it are simply untrue. This shortage of personnel, combined with the Commission's low level of popularity, has created stress for the EC's bureaucrats. A 1992 report revealed that nearly 40 per cent of former EC employees had to retire early for psychological or psychiatric reasons. The main factors put forward as causing this were press criticism, the lack of a social life and the strain of working in a foreign language away from home. Commission staff tend to become trapped in their jobs, disliking the work but unable to give up the high salaries and attendant perks such as freedom from taxation.

Despite this negative image, the Commission did an immense amount to relaunch the EC in the 1980s, and much credit must be given to the President of the Commission from 1985, Jacques Delors. Born in 1925, he became an academic high flyer and later worked in the Banque de France and as a professor at the Ecole Nationale d'Administration. In the 1970s he became prominent in political life and was Economics Minister in Mitterrand's government from 1981 to 1984. A man of real drive and ability, Delors inspired both respect and fear in his Commission colleagues but, under his aegis the EC moved ahead on enlargement and the single market programme. At the same time he succeeded in putting both the Social Charter and European Monetary Union at the top of the political agenda.

Nevertheless Delors has had his critics. At times he has been accused of lacking impartiality where French interests have been concerned, the implication being that he has had his eye on becoming French president when Mitterrand retires. More fundamentally he has been accused of moving too rapidly towards European union. *The Sunday Times* in June 1992 described him as 'a Utopean socialist to his bone marrow. His goal is a nuclear-armed, pan-European, socialist super-state, commanded from Brussels'. Whether such comments are just is debatable; what is not is the danger that the pace of the march towards a federal Europe could provoke some kind of nationalistic backlash in the member states. The Danish rejection of the Maastricht Treaty in the referendum of June 1992 was evidence of such a reaction.

The Court of Auditors

The Court is made up of independent experts appointed by member governments. It is a recent creation, beginning work in 1977 when the European Parliament demanded a closer audit of the Community budget. The Parliament hoped that the Court of Auditors could monitor expenditure much more thoroughly than in the past, checking on the use made of Community revenue by member states and the Commission and on their methods of collecting duties and levies. Thus it is the Community's financial watchdog.

At times the Court has been able to compliment the Commission on its activities but it has certainly not been afraid to bark. It has criticized the Commission on aspects of its food aid to developing countries, claiming that one firm that had made deliveries of dubious quality continued to be awarded contracts. It has continually called on the Commission to develop a system of accounts that is more complete and more informative. It has particularly condemned the Commission's record in dealing with fraud in the Common Agricultural Policy and has indeed helped to uncover these frauds in the first place. In its 1982 report the Court, for example, pointed out that the Commission had recovered only £1 million out of £12 million in farming subsidies fraudulently claimed. The Court also singled out the building of a fitness centre for the free use of Commission staff in Luxembourg, claiming that this had not been properly authorized. Despite its efforts, however, fraud has continued to swallow up a significant percentage of the EC Budget. According to a report in 1989 by Piet Dankert, a former President of the European Parliament, fraud was consuming 10 per cent of Community funds.

The European Parliament

Origins

The European Assembly, as it is called in the Treaties, has its origins in the Assembly of the Coal and Steel Community established in 1951. When the Treaties of Rome were signed in 1957, that assembly was merged with the two assemblies of the EEC and EURATOM, thus creating one assembly. Until the enlargement of the Community in 1973, the assembly (now known as the European Parliament) consisted of 142 delegates chosen by the respective national parliaments from their own members. When Denmark, Britain and Ireland joined the Community in 1973, the Parliament was enlarged to 198 delegates.

At the Copenhagen Summit of 1974 it was decided to hold direct elections to the European Parliament, and these were held for the first time in June 1979. Currently the 518 European members of Parliament (MEPs) represent the member states in the following proportions: Britain, Germany, France and Italy have 81 members; Spain 60 members; the Netherlands 25 members; Greece, Portugal and Belgium 24 members; Denmark 16 members; Ireland 15 members; and Luxembourg 6 members.

The Powers of the European Parliament

The European Parliament acts as a consultative body on most Community affairs, and in recent years its power has grown. It has, in theory, the power to dismiss the Commission, though in practice perhaps this is of little value, as to do so would bring the Community to a halt and the Parliament has no right to appoint a new Commission. However, it might continue to dismiss Commissions of which it disapproved until it obtained a satisfactory one. A vote of censure can also be a way of expressing Parliamentary opinions on a Community policy so that the Commission or other institutions may amend it.

The Parliament has also become more effective in using its power verbally or in writing to keep the Commission and Council of Ministers on their toes. It considers and gives opinions on the Commission's proposals before they are examined in the Council, and although not obliged to do so, the Commission does often change its proposals on parliamentary advice. It also receives and comments on reports from the other two bodies. Since 1974 the foreign ministers have been meeting four times a year with the political committee of the European Parliament to discuss foreign policy issues.

An important development in the Parliament's power occurred in 1970, when it was agreed that if the Community were to become independent in financial matters, then some kind of parliamentary control over Community revenue should be established: now a draft budget has to be prepared by the Commission and then sent to the Council of Ministers for approval. It is then discussed by the Parliament. To understand the Parliament's budgetary control it is necessary to explain that the budget is made up of compulsory and non-compulsory expenditure. Compulsory expenditure (about 80 per cent of the total budget) may be amended by Parliamentary majority, but the Council can reject any changes proposed here. The Parliament has more real control over non-compulsory expenditure, because it can suggest changes in this section up to a certain limit, and though the Council may amend the decision, the Parliament must receive the total draft budget back and at this point can reject the Council's amendments in the non-compulsory section. If there is considerable disagreement, the Parliament has the right to reject the draft budget entirely and demand a new one.

The European Parliament is run by a bureau comprising the president and twelve vice-presidents who are elected by secret ballot to serve for 2½ years. The main task of the bureau is to draw up the draft agenda for each parliamentary session. The Parliament also elects five quaestors, who deal with administrative and financial matters of concern to the European Members of Parliament. They too are elected for 2½ years.

The Parliament has eighteen specialized permanent committees, each dealing with particular areas of the Community's activities, e.g. agriculture and regional policy. The membership of the committees broadly reflects the political and national balance of the House as a whole. The committees usually meet in Brussels so that they can make easier contact with the Council and the Commission. Their work comprises the detailed examination and amendment of draft laws.

Problems

Given the political will, the Parliament could become one of the most important Community institutions in the next decade. However, it does face a number of severe problems, five in particular:

1 In the direct elections of 1979 each country was entitled to use its own electoral system but for the future elections it was hoped to adopt a uniform system. However, though other member states use some form of proportional representation, Britain still adheres to its first past the post system.

2 Because of the need for interpretation into several languages, debates in the European Parliament lack the cut and thrust of the better sessions in national parliaments. The language barrier is in fact a major obstacle to European unity. A number of suggestions have been made to improve the problem – that everyone should speak French or English, that there should be official languages (all nine) but certain working languages (the four chief ones) or that interpretation be given in only two or three. All ideas, however, come up against the same stumbling block; it is politically unacceptable that those speaking minority languages should be put at a disadvantage in the work of the Parliament. The enlargement of the Community to include Portugal and Spain has made the problem even more insoluble.

3 At present the Parliament meets in Strasbourg and Luxembourg; the Parliament's secretariat is based in Luxembourg while most meetings of the Parliament's committees are held in Brussels. This three-site mode of operation imposes an absurd strain on conscientious European Members of Parliament, who already have a large constituency in which they wish to spend time, who will have to attend sessions of the Parliament in Strasbourg and Luxembourg and who may also be members of specialist committees meeting in Brussels.

4 The Parliament now possesses more moral and practical authority than ever before. Nevertheless it still has insufficient power to be a fully effective instrument of democratic control, and certainly the Council of Ministers has little sympathy for the pretensions of the Parliament, because the ministers see it as a threat to national sovereignty. Thus the EC suffers from what has been termed 'a democratic deficit', and this can only be solved by giving the European Parliament a bigger share in decision-making with the Council of Ministers.

5 Finally, it has to be admitted that the work of the Parliament is treated with overwhelming apathy or hostility by the publics in the Community. It has received bad publicity, particularly over its overseas expenses, like the Great Bogota Scandal in 1982 when thirty-eight MEPs visiting South America took fifty-eight interpreters with them. It is still condemned as a talking shop without influence, and Walter Ellis of the *Financial Times* once described the MEPs as walking down the corridors of weakness. Again, this argument may be countered by pointing to the growing powers of Parliament under the co-operation procedure.

The Economic and Social Committee (ECOSOC)

This body was created by the Rome Treaty with advisory status and its role is to represent various categories of economic and social life in the Community, such as employers, unions, farmers, the self-employed and the general public. Members are appointed by the Council from national lists, each member being appointed for four years and acting in a personal capacity. There are 189 members in all, 24 each from France, Germany, Italy and the United Kingdom; 21 from Spain; 12 each from Belgium, Portugal, the Netherlands and Greece; 9 each from Denmark and Ireland; and 6 from Luxembourg. In practice members come from three main groups – employers, unions and those representing the general interest.

The opinion of the Committee is sought on all major policies by the Council and Commission and particularly on issues relating to transport, agriculture, harmonization and the free movement of workers. However, it has not really had an effective voice in Community affairs for a number of reasons. First, it only has a consultative role and its opinions can be ignored by the more powerful institutions within the Community. Second, the varied membership makes it difficult to produce a single point of view except of a very general and bland nature. Sometimes it has to produce a series of reports reflecting the differences of opinion. Third, often reports appear too late to be useful because of the search for agreement. Fourth, members of the Committee have too many commitments in their home countries and the amount of time they are able to spend on Committee affairs is therefore limited. Senior trades union officials, for example, are unlikely to make regular appearances at meetings of the Committee.

On the other hand, the views of the Committee can be useful to the Commission and to the Council in their policy-making, and its work does help quite a large number of influential individuals and their assistants to familiarize themselves with the workings of the Community. It should be pointed out that ECOSOC has had the power since 1972 to issue its 'own initiatives' opinions on matters of concern, and in the 1980s it became a less passive body, roundly criticizing the failure of the Commission and Council of Ministers to take action over unemployment and environmental problems.

In addition to ECOSOC, there are more than seventy consultative bodies helping the Community's work, such as the Consultative Committee for the coal and steel industry and the Standing Committee on Employment.

The European Court of Justice

The European Community is such a complex body that a court is necessary for several reasons. It must ensure that the institutions of the Community act in a constitutional way, fulfilling their Treaty obligations, but it also has to ensure the observance of Community rules by member states, firms and individuals within the Community. For these reasons the European Court of Justice was established by Article 136 of the Treaty of Rome. It is based in Luxembourg and is not to be confused with the International Court of Justice at The Hague or the European Commission on Human Rights. It operates independently of all other Community institutions and is the supreme arbiter of Community law. Article 193 of the Treaty of Rome stipulates that 'member states undertake not to submit a dispute concerning the interpretation or application of this Treaty to any method of settlement other than those provided for therein'. This clause effectively prevents other international tribunals being brought into Community affairs.

The thirteen judges who hold office for 6 years are drawn one from each member state and are assisted by six advocates-general who are responsible for the preliminary investigation of a matter and for submitting a reasoned opinion to the judges to help them to come to a decision. The deliberations of the judges are kept secret. Their judgment, with reasons, is given publicly in open court but there is only one judgment: no dissenting judgments are given. Whatever differences of view there may have been among the judges are therefore concealed and subsequently no judgment can be weakened by the charge that it is only a majority view.

The Court will hear cases brought by the Commission against member states or against the Council, cases brought by member states against each other or against the Council or Commission or by a person against a Community decision that affects him. The Court can enforce penalties for the infringement of the regulations. It is also responsible for the interpretation of the Treaty of Rome and subsequent legislation. Curiously, there has not been a great deal so far that the Court can do to enforce a judgment. However, member states and Community institutions have in practice always complied with its judgments. It seems unlikely that any defiance of the Court will take place, because the Court has been given so central a place in the Community structure that such defiance would be tantamount to a fundamental breach of the Treaty itself.

The Court has successfully disposed of a large number of cases since it was set up, despite the complexity of many of them. The three fields of Community activity that created most work for the Court were agriculture, competition policy and social security for migrants, areas where the member states had pre-existing policies of their own and where the integration of two sets of law was difficult. Indeed the universal application of Community law is a slow business, since it must be incorporated into twelve different legal systems.

Through its judgments the Court of Justice is contributing to the emergence of a veritable European law applicable to all Community institutions, member states, national courts and individuals, with the authority of the Court's judgments in the field of Community law surpassing that of national courts. In cases of non-application of Community law by the Council or member states the Court has been approached for help by individuals and upheld important principles contained in the Treaties, e.g. equal pay for men and women.

The number of cases on which the court has had to pass judgment has risen remorselessly, with, for example, 600 cases in 1989. The huge growth in the workload led in 1989 to the creation of a lower court, the Court of First Instance, thus establishing a two-tier system. The lower court deals mainly with complaints by individuals against institutions, competition cases and disputes between the Commission and its staff.

The workload is one reason for cases on average taking about 2 years to be resolved. Another reason for delay in enforcing rulings has been inadequate sanctions. However, under the Maastricht Treaty the court will be able to fine governments that fail to comply with its rulings.

If fully implemented, Maastricht would increase the court's power by bringing new areas of work within the scope of EC law, expanding the court's brief in fields such as consumer protection and the environment. Lord Denning, former Master of the Rolls, in 1992 likened this spread of Community competence to a strong tide: 'It flows into the estuaries and up the rivers. It cannot be held back'.

Community law and the legislative process

Community law is either embodied in the Treaties themselves and is called the primary legislation of the European Community or it is derived from the Treaties and referred to as secondary legislation. Some Community law may have direct internal effect as law in the member states from the Treaties, though to a considerable extent the Treaties only laid out the basic framework of Community law and left the Community institutions to work out the details later.

The Community makes use of five kinds of legal instruments – regulations, directives, decisions, recommendations and opinions. Regulations have direct internal effect on the member states. They are legally binding and must be applied directly, like national laws. They prevail over national law if any conflict arises between the two. Directives are equally binding on member states as regards the aim to be achieved but it is left to the national authorities as to how these aims are to be carried out. Decisions are usually concerned with specific problems rather than with the Community as a whole. They are binding in every respect on those to whom they are addressed. When a decision is addressed to a government of a member state, it imposes binding obligations but does not have direct internal effect as law in the member state; when a decision is addressed to individuals, it does have direct internal effect in relation to the individuals to whom it is addressed and is binding on the party concerned. Recommendations and opinions have no binding force.

Community law in the fields covered by the Treaties takes precedence over the national law of the member states, and in the case of conflict with national law Community law is supreme.

The procedures for preparing and adopting Council instruments have become more complex in recent years. Until the passing of the Single European Act in 1987, a process called the *consultation procedure* was the only one followed. Here the Commission in creating a policy prepared a draft proposal that it sent to the Council and usually to the European Parliament and ECOSOC as well. The draft proposal was also considered in the Committee of Permanent Representatives by one of its specialist committees. The Parliament, after debating and voting on the proposal, sent its opinion to the Commission and Council as did ECOSOC, including amendments.

Only when the above opinions had been received could the Council take a decision. However, the key feature of the consultation procedure was that neither the Council nor the Commission was obliged to take any notice of the views of the Parliament.

Such a situation left the European Parliament (EP) without much influence on legislation and requiring more of the real rights of a true parliament. As Juliet Lodge has affirmed, 'There is no substitute for genuine entrenched power'. The *co-operation procedure*, introduced in the Single European Act, was a significant step in this direction. With the co-operation procedure a Commission proposal goes to the EP (for a first reading) and ECOSOC in the same way as under the consultation procedure. The EP may reject, accept or amend the proposal or withhold or give its opinion. It may persuade the Commission to amend the proposal according to its wishes or withdraw it before a vote is taken. After the EP has given the opinion in the first reading, the proposal, with the Commission's views on the EPs opinion, goes to the Council, which may deliberate but may not act until the EP's views are known. The Council then adopts a 'common position' by qualified majority voting and transmits it to the EP. Both Council and Commission are obliged to inform the EP of the reasons that led to their decision. The EP now can debate the common position in a second reading and has 3 months within which to accept, reject, or re-submit amendments on, the proposal. At this stage the Commission may also amend the proposal if it wishes. The proposal then goes back to the Council, which has 3 months to take a final decision; if it fails to reach a decision in that period, the proposal lapses.

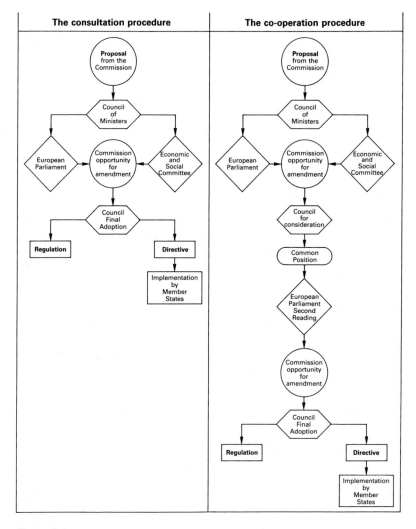

Figure 2.1

The Council may adopt the proposal often on the basis of qualified majority voting. However, in certain circumstances it has to use
the unanimity rule. These circumstances are (*a*) when the Council
wishes to amend a proposal on its own initiative, (*b*) when the
Council decides to adopt amendments proposed by the EP but
rejected by the Commission, (*c*) when the Council decides to adopt
a common position the EP has rejected, and (*d*) when the Council

wishes to override a proposal which the EP has adopted by an absolute majority (260 votes) at the second reading.

The EP has been critical of the co-operation procedure partly because it was initially applied to only ten articles of the Rome Treaty, e.g. issues such as the free movement of labour. In fact two-thirds of the proposals in the 1985 Commission White Paper on the Internal Market fell under the co-operation procedure, so that the EP was fully involved in this area. To exploit its new role it needed to streamline its organization to ensure mobilizing the 260 MEPs required to pass amendments. In practice the co-operation procedure has given the EP an enhanced role. Rather than risking the complete defeat of a proposal that the unanimity requirement poses, the Council in recent years has taken on board many of the EP's amendments, thereby making it a much more active partner in the decision-making process.

Nevertheless the continuing lack of real democratic accountability was criticized in the run-up to the Maastricht Summit in December 1991, because the EP could still not make its own proposals and its wishes could be ignored when the Council reached unanimity on a proposal. Therefore at Maastricht a further move was made to tilt power away from the Commission and Council and towards the EP – the *co-decision procedure*. If within the co-operation procedure the Council does not approve a proposal, the proposal will pass to a new 'conciliation committee' instead of being allowed to lapse as in the past. Council and EP will be equally represented on the Committee. They may agree to a solution, which must then be approved by QMV in Council and by a simple majority in the EP. If the conciliation committee cannot find a solution, the EP has the ultimate right to reject the proposal by absolute majority. This important parliamentary right to veto is to be extended to crucial issues such as internal market legislation, consumer protection, health, education and the environment. It is also worth emphasizing that the Commission plays no part in the later stages of the co-decision procedure.

The EP will gain other powers from the Maastricht Treaty, e.g. the right to approve a new Commission and its president, and the right to request the Commission to submit a proposal on a particular question where the EP decides by an absolute majority (260) of MEPs that new legislation is required. Parliament would also gain the power to investigate alleged contraventions of Community law off its own bat, and would be able to appoint an ombudsman to receive complaints from EC citizens. Clearly the EP's role in decision-making is steadily growing.

Conclusion: the problem of 'lourdeur'

In the words of Stanley Henig, 'The European Community has not always lived up to the hopes and expectations of its founders, but it remains nonetheless unique amongst regional and international organisations'. There is no case in recorded history of separate nation states giving over so many powers to central institutions. The Community offers a relatively civilized and relatively efficient forum for carrying out a range of tasks affecting inter-state relations. Much of the work is detailed and mundane. As a Community official told Stanley Henig, 'The Community is an extremely boring place'. The average Commission official is likely to be considering the minutiae of, say, the price of imported olives rather than grand strategy. Nevertheless this work is necessary, and if it were not done by the Community, it would have to be done by other national or international organizations. And if the charge is true that the Community works slowly in evolving policies, then the same charge can often be levelled at national governments.

It should be remembered that the central Community institutions are only partly independent of the national institutions. Of the major central institutions, the Council is state-dominated and both the Commission and the Court personnel are state-appointed. The Community's own financial resources are strictly limited. Whether the developing powers of the European Parliament or the future enlargement of the Community will affect the institutions remains to be seen. The European Parliament could conceivably become a real curb on executive power in the Community.

However, increased Parliamentary power and the growing number of members states could make decision-making in the Community even more difficult. The problem of 'lourdeur' or weighing down of institutions would be aggravated, because there would be more institutions and more countries to consult in every decision-making process and the whole process could grind to a halt. Another problem contributing to 'lourdeur' is siting. It is an administrative nonsense for the Commission to be based mostly in Brussels but partly in Luxembourg, and for Parliament to have three sites. The Community needs a capital proper. Decision-making, anyway, has been made more difficult by the recession, which has added vigour to a new form of lobbying – Euro-lobbying. Powerful interest groups such as COPA (The Committee of Agricultural Organizations) put pressure on the Council and the Commission and create the wrong atmosphere for cooperative decision-making.

The final factor contributing to 'lourdeur' is of course language. The Community has nine official languages – Danish, Dutch, English, French, German, Greek, Italian, Spanish and Portuguese. Translators now have to cope with as many as seventy-two language pairs, since each of the nine official languages may have to be translated into any of the other eight. As a result the institutions now generate between them more than a million pages of translation a year, and over 40 per cent of Community administrative costs are made up by translating and interpreting with their back-up services.

This problem is not merely a financial one. As the number of languages grows, so do the pressures on efficiency. It is easy to find good translators to work with language pairs such as French or German but there are not enough qualified translators to do the same between, say, Greek and Danish. The result is that the work of the institutions suffers because essential documents have not been circulated in time for meetings, which have then to be postponed. Computer-based technology, e.g. research into a European machine translation system, has only partly solved this problem.

Further reading

Corbett, R and Jacobs, F, *The European Parliament*, Longmans, London, 1991.

Keohane, R and Hoffmann, S, *The New European Community Decision-Making and Institutional Change*, Westview Press, London, 1992.

Kirchner, E J, *Decision-Making in the European Community*, Manchester University Press, Manchester, 1992.

Nugent, N, *Government and Politics of the European Community*, Macmillan (Second Edition), 1991.

Wood, A, *The Times Guide to the European Parliament*, Times Books, London, 1989.

Questions

1 What are the chief functions of the European Commission?
2 Explain how a Commission proposal becomes part of Community law.
3 To what extent have recent changes improved the Community's decision-making process?
4 In what ways may the 1991 Maastricht Treaty influence institutional issues within the EC?
5 Have the increased powers of the European Parliament solved the Community's 'democratic deficit'?

3
The genesis of the single market programme

The hopes of the founding fathers

The founding fathers of the European Community were imbued with a sense of the need for supranational solutions for a Europe destroyed by war and Fascism. For them long-term political objectives were probably more important than economic questions. However, as is clear from the Spaak Memorandum of 1956, economic development was seen as a vital precursor of political union. For that necessary economic development, a model existed for the new United States of Europe to follow. In the words of Owen, 'the founding fathers looked across the Atlantic to the USA – the world's largest integrated common market – and judged that the size of American markets had fostered the development of large-scale production technologies which in turn were partly responsible for American productivity levels being the highest in the world'.

Consequently the Rome Treaty is extremely specific on the creation of the internal market, especially in Article 3, which lays down the key objectives of the Community and in particular spells out the 'four freedoms' – the free movement of goods, persons, services and capital. Article 3(a) calls for 'the elimination, as between member states, of customs duties and of quantitative restrictions on the import and export of goods and of all other measures having equivalent effect', while Article 3(c) requires 'the abolition as between member states, of obstacles to the free movement of persons, services and capital'. In order to facilitate free movement, Article 3(h) requires 'the approximation of the laws of the member states to the extent required for the proper functioning of the common market' – the necessary harmonisation of member states' laws – and Article 3(f) calls for 'the institution of a system ensuring that competition in the Common Market is not distorted'.

Thus the Common Market envisaged by the founding fathers would include in addition to product market integration, the integration of services markets and of the markets for factors such as labour, financial capital, entrepreneurial and management resources and technological knowledge. In the words of Jacques Pelkmans it would be a common market 'wherein all private economic agents are free to trade, to invest, to offer services, to work and to pay or purchase wherever they prefer. It is essential that all the economic freedoms, normally enjoyed in a national market, extend to the total area of the group'.

Since 1957 economists have attempted to delineate the economic advantages of such market integration. One of its main champions has been John Pinder, who exploited two terms – negative integration, which consists of the removal of discrimination, and positive integration, which consists of the formation of common policies. The end of negative integration is a common market that, as a result of the liberalization of trade and the consequent factor movements, will result in an optimum allocation of resources. This would happen as a result of several mutually reinforcing 'dynamic' effects, the first being the stimulation of competition. The effect of market enlargement on the productive efficiency of firms has been emphasized by politicians like Harold Macmillan who referred to *'the bracing cold shower'* of competition. According to this view industrial structures undergo a change and national monopolies become Community oligopolies, while the situation for established oligopolies becomes more fluid with a reduction in the feasibility of oligopolistic collusion.

Dennis Swann refers to the possibility of a psychological change resulting from enhanced competition. Before the formation of the Common Market, relations between competitors in the small national markets may have been personal and friendly. However, when trade liberalization occurs, firms in one national market will seek to grow not at each other's expense but at the expense of producers in other national markets with whom relations are impersonal. Producers from these other national markets will tend to behave likewise. Consequently every firm will become aware of the fact that its own national market can no longer be regarded as secure and will look less favourably on the preservation of less efficient compatriots. Thus a sustained drive for efficiency becomes necessary for survival. The stimulation of competition forces through greater specialization in production, because the exposure of previously protected high-cost producers in some economies to low-cost producers in others will cause them either to reduce their costs or reallocate production to other lines.

The creation of a large market will also have an effect on the rate of growth by way of its impact on the inducement to invest, not only as regards indigenous firms but also foreign investment. The infiltration of American investment was encouraged by the larger market or the prospect thereof, and such investment brought with it more aggressive business strategies and better management techniques.

Above all, economists have stressed the opportunities a larger market gives for the fuller exploitation of economies of large-scale production. National markets may not be big enough to enable firms to expand sufficiently to achieve the minimum optimal scale, and such a scale of plant or firm may require the sales areas of the large Community market. The larger market may also enable firms to expand and mount the R and D necessary to compete with overseas rivals, and the scene becomes set for self-sustaining growth. The employment of labour and capital would be concentrated on those activities that secured the highest rate of return, increasing the competitiveness of the member states not only in the internal market but in the market of non-member states.

Such was the theory, but the evolution of the Community since 1957 saw the maintenance of a large gap between theory and practice. As Pelkmans observed in 1986, the Community was 'far removed from a true common market'.

Progress towards a true internal market, 1957–85

The Rome Treaty called for an end to tariffs and quotas on trade between member states in Articles 9 and 30 respectively. Under Article 8 the Common Market was to be progressively established during a transitional period of 12 years but in fact a faster timetable proved possible. Despite the existence of tariffs and quotas and the fact that the Community was entering uncharted waters in seeking integration, duty and quota-free movement of goods between member states was achieved by stages by 1 July 1968, 18 months ahead of schedule.

Given that governments and pressure groups usually combine to obstruct such developments, this relatively trouble-free experience of the Community warrants some explanation. Hine points to six factors that account for the rapid progress. First, the development of the rival grouping, EFTA, was a spur to the Community to maintain an equivalent pace of trade liberalization. Second, the rapid economic growth of the 1960s absorbed resources released from firms unable to meet foreign competition. Third, much of the increased specialization was intra-industry in nature. Therefore, rather than whole industries contracting, adjustments to produce ranges tended to occur *within* industries. Fourth, tariff cuts stimulated exports as well as imports, so that the net effect on balance of payments and employment was small. Fifth, the level of protection in the Community was already low following work in the OECC to abolish quotas and after negotiations through GATT to cut tariffs. Therefore the removal of remaining restrictions had no dramatic effects.

Hine's final reason is a much less positive one. He rightly points to the replacement of tariff by non-tariff barriers by 1970. To a considerable extent there was a change in the nature of protection rather than a decrease in its level. Nevertheless the favourable experience of the six founder member states in establishing a customs union ahead of schedule was reflected later in the 5-year transition period given to new members in 1973 and to Greece in 1981 and the 7-year period given to Spain and Portugal in 1986.

The abolition of tariffs and quotas represented the removal of an institutional barrier to trade but market integration also required that action be taken against private firms that attempted to prevent the interpenetration of national product markets through various restrictive practices. To counter such practices the Community developed a competition policy that is one of its more tough and effective policies (see Chapter 5).

The abolition of tariffs and quotas and the creation of a vigorous competition policy were two real achievements but progress in other areas affecting the internal market was much more modest. In Articles 67–73 the Rome Treaty called for the abolition of controls on capital movements and the harmonization or elimination of factors distorting the allocation of capital between member states. However, member states were in practice tempted to exercise control over capital movements, preferring to keep capital at home for modernization of the economy, or, in the case of West Germany, to prevent the inflow of capital because it might create inflationary pressure or strengthen the already strong mark.

Therefore in 1960 and 1962 the Community brought in two directives in an attempt to loosen up capital movements. The directives divided transactions into four categories. List A related to direct investment and capital movements concerned with trade in goods, areas where free movement of capital was required as a result of the Rome Treaty provisions on non-capital issues like the right to establishment, e.g. the foreign worker's need to repatriate his earnings. List B concerned operations in securities dealt with on stock exchanges. Non-residents were enabled to acquire securities other than bonds, but, as with List A member states, could introduce controls in special circumstances. List C dealt with the issue of securities on capital markets, while List D covered movements of short-term capital between banks, e.g. the purchase of Treasury bills and the opening of bank accounts in other Community countries.

The progress here was limited. Lists A and B were freed unconditionally (except for the special circumstances clause) but capital movements in List C were only conditionally freed, i.e. the directives merely required that the liberalization achieved by 1960 should not be reversed except under the exceptional circumstances provision. This meant that countries that had not liberalized by 1960 were under no obligation to do so. As for List D, there was no obligation to liberalize whatsoever.

In 1981 the Commission admitted that liberalization had not proceeded much beyond the level provided for in the directives of 1960 and 1962. However, as Swann explains, the development of the Eurocurrency market has made such lack of progress less important. Even if a state restricts its own nationals in their purchase of another member state's currency, it has less objection to its nationals borrowing Eurodollars in order to finance a transaction in another member state because such an option does not weaken its exchange rate, unlike the purchase of another member state's currency. In addition, some member states made substantial progress unilaterally on liberalizing capital movements, e.g. the UK abolished all remaining exchange controls in the first years of the Thatcher government. To an extent the problem was less one of deficient law and more in the fact that Community residents wishing to transfer capital between member states did not make full use of the existing provisions of Community law to assert their rights in the question.

Nevertheless, despite few Community moves, some measure of free movement of capital was attained. The same cannot be said for the free movement of labour and services, despite these areas receiving more Community attention. Article 48 of the Rome Treaty required that free movement of labour be achieved before the end of the transition period and banned discrimination based on nationality in regard to employment, remuneration and conditions of work, and this was established in theory in stages between 1961 and 1968.

Complete freedom of movement could, however, only become a reality if certain problems were overcome. Workers would need to be informed of job opportunities in other member states and would require their social security rights to be transferable. It was true that the Commission adopted in 1972 its *Système européen de diffusion des offres et demandes d'emploi et de compensation international (SEDOC)*, a system with a register of jobs and a coding to establish true comparability between jobs, but it did not have much impact in establishing a European job market. In 1980 it offered 25,000 jobs to British people and only achieved a 10 per cent matching rate.

Problems also existed over the transferability of social security rights. The Rome Treaty did lay down that migrant workers from all member states were eligible for the same social security benefits as national workers. Periods of employment and insurance completed in member states were aggregated for the purpose of calculating benefit, and at any time the beneficiary could transfer the benefits from one member state to another. In 1970 the Council of Ministers extended these principles to self-employed insured persons.

However, a mere framework of law giving Community nationals equal rights in issues of jobs and social security did not guarantee effective free movement of labour. Of 6 million migrant workers in the Community in 1982, 4.5 million came from third countries. Only Italy and Ireland were large suppliers of migrant labour, with figures of 700,000 and 400,000 respectively.

Similar limitations clouded the efforts to effect free movements for the professions and freedom to provide services. The founding fathers did appreciate that particular problems arose when a profession was subject to regulation and could be practised only by the gaining of a diploma or similar professional qualification. Under these circumstances free movement required a system that prevented the host member state from stipulating that the qualifications must have been obtained in that member state, i.e. the holder of qualifications that entitled the pursuit of an activity in one member state must be given the right, in principle, to follow it in any other member state.

Therefore Article 57(1) of the Rome Treaty provided for the mutual recognition of professional qualifications in order to make it easier for persons to take up and pursue activities as self-employed persons. Article 56(2) also provided for the co-ordination of the provisions laid down by law, regulation or administrative action in the member states concerning the taking up and pursuit of activities. This enabled the Council to adopt mandatory guidelines as to the training requirements laid down under national law.

The directives adopted up to 1985 in order to achieve mutual recognition of professional qualifications showed four different patterns:

1 For some activities the Council adopted transitional measures. Pending the mutual recognition of diplomas, production of a certificate establishing that the activity was lawfully carried out in the country of origin allowed freedom to provide the service in other member states. This was applied to travel and insurance agents. If the activity was carried out for 1 to 4 years, that had to be acceptable as sufficient evidence of professional ability by the host member state.

2 For some activities the Council adopted a directive on the co-ordination of training requirements as well as a directive on mutual acceptance of professional qualifications. Such directives were adopted for doctors in 1975, for nurses responsible for general care in 1977, for dentists and vets in 1978, for midwives in 1980 and for pharmacists in 1985.

3 In 1985 the Council adopted a single directive for the mutual recognition of national qualifications for training and excluded any requirements on co-ordination of training. This group was limited to architects.

4 In 1977 the Council adopted a directive to help the legal profession to exercise its right to provide services. It left until a later

date the detailed measures needed to facilitate effective exercise of the right of establishment. There was no co-ordination whatso-ever of training requirements and the directive did not provide the real recognition of profession qualifications.

A mere listing of these approaches is misleading in the sense that it does not convey how painfully slow the progress was. The methods employed led to huge delays between the date when the Commission put forward a draft and the date when the Council actually adopted it – 8 years for doctors, 18 years for architects and 14 years for pharmacists. Such figures take no account of the period required for implementing the directives.

The other crucial issue worthy of notice is that freedom to provide many services was still only partly won. Unsatisfactory progress was evident, for example, in the freedom to provide services in shipping, inland transport, insurance and mortgage credit.

Nevertheless it may be tentatively asserted that the development of the internal market, for all its limitations, helped the economic growth of the Community up to 1985. Certainly there was an impres-sive growth in trade between member states (some of which of course would have occurred with or without the existence of the EC). By 1980 trade in manufactures between the Six was almost $200 billions, a sixfold increase in money terms over the 1970 level and a threefold increase in real terms. Intra-Community trade was by 1980 equivalent to 30 per cent of the Six's manufacturing output, compared to 20 per cent in 1970.

A J Marques Mendes concluded in 1986 that Community integra-tion had played a major role in the economic growth achieved, estimating that in 1981 the GDP was 5.9 per cent higher than it would have been without integration. He pointed to export growth (much of it to other EC countries) as the main driving force, such export growth being encouraged by the trade liberalization of the 1960s and the 1973 enlargement.

Both Owen and Hine have stressed that increased economies of scale have been realized in the larger market. Owen in 1976 pointed to the economies being at plant level, rather than in the growth in size of the whole firm. In his 1983 work he cited three European industries – cars, trucks and white goods – as examples of industries where successful firms were those that had achieved the lowest costs as a result of superior scale. Changes in technology and production management had raised the minimum efficient scale and only as a result of the large internal market could European firms achieve their optimum size.

As Hine explains, there was a tendency before the Community was formed for each firm within its protected national market to make a full range of products at relatively high cost. The arrival of tariff-free trade then forced firms to concentrate on their more successful product lines and manufacture these on a more substantial scale to meet export demand. Trade between Community countries intensified and became increasingly intra-industry in nature. More specialized production and longer production runs enabled costs to be reduced.

Thus the progress towards a true internal market was significant, particularly in the field of product market integration. Unfortunately the pace of that progress slowed in the 1970s and prospects for future advance were clouded by a growing climate of protectionism.

The crucial obstacles to market integration in the 1980s

The quarter of a century to 1970 had seen an almost uninterrupted reduction of barriers to trade in Europe. There was an almost universal acceptance that trade and restrictions on it were subject to international rule. However, since then the governments of the mature industrial economies have turned increasingly to protection and a unilateral approach, with the spawning of insidiously opaque non-tariff barriers, which were more difficult to regulate and could be a much more absolute control of trade than tariffs.

Even in 1970 the rise of NTBs was seen as serious and R E Baldwin explained their rise as a consequence of 'the increased international interdependence that improvements in transportation and communications have brought about and from the successful removal of many measures that directly impede trade'. Martin Wolf points to two distinct forces that combined to increase protectionism in Europe. The first was euphoria. Governments in their desire to increase economic growth were encouraged to take a more interventionist path by the success of apparently interventionist countries like France and Japan. The second was anxiety. 'Evidence of the arteriosclerosis of the market was mounting in one country after another, the problem apparently originating in the labour markets.' The result was a rise in inflation, a decline in corporate profitability and reduced investment. The economic environment then further worsened as a result of the 1973 oil crisis, which by reducing effective demand and increasing inflation contributed to the stagflation of the 1970s. After the second oil price shock of 1979, European governments followed more contractionary policies, which arguably exacerbated the unemployment situation. By 1987 unemployment in the Community had reached 16.2 millions (11.7 per cent of the labour force). The temptation for governments to intervene so as to protect domestic employment became irresistible. Hager pointed in 1981 to more than 400 cases of suspect or downright illegal barriers to trade among EC member states and estimated that the rate had risen fourfold in 6 years. Thus the new protectionism was mainly government-induced, was only partly directed at non-member states, and as such threatened further development of the internal market.

Of the many obstacles affecting the Community's internal market, seven were particularly prominent: (*a*) frontier obstacles, (*b*) fiscal issues, (*c*) public procurement discrimination, (*d*) technical barriers to trade, (*e*) state subsidies, (*f*) barriers to the free movement of labour and (*g*) trademarks.

Frontier delays

Most aggravating and arguably the most unnecessary of all obstacles was the frequency of frontier delays. Lorry drivers taking a commercial load from Rotterdam to Naples could spend 10 hours of the 26-hour journey wasting time at customs posts. Dutch lorry drivers claimed that they needed 300 rubber stamps on their documents to drive their Gouda cheese into France. One reason for this state of affairs was the failure to harmonize customs procedures and the lack of co-ordination in the opening hours of adjacent customs posts. Dover, for example, was usually opened 24 hours a day, while Calais closed from Saturday afternoon to midnight on Sunday. Unfortunately Article 27 of the Rome Treaty was very casual on this issue, making approximation of customs procedures a non-binding recommendation.

The delays were exacerbated by the complex documentation procedures whereby lorry drivers were required to have 70–80 different pieces of paper to show customs officers. As a result the average frontier delay was 80 minutes, with delays of up to 10 hours on the Franco–Italian border.

A more insidious reason for the delays may have been the dishonesty of customs officials who created delays in order to boost their earnings by allowing lorries to clear customs only when drivers had paid a bribe in the form of cigarettes or whisky. Small wonder that in 1984 exasperated French lorry drivers blockaded French roads near the Italian border in protest at the long delays at customs posts. Such impatience had much in common with the annoyance of the coachman of the *ancien régime* in France having to stop at tolls and customs on the provincial borders, paying gabelle for the importation of salt from Normandy to Brittany. The transport of air freight presented a similarly distasteful picture.

Fiscal issues

Taxes had similar effects to tariffs on the international flow of goods and services, and could therefore constitute a non-tariff distortion of international trade. Consequently the Rome Treaty in Articles 95–100 provided for the harmonization of taxation in terms of structure and rates of tax. Article 99 referred to the harmonization of indirect taxation and Article 100 to the harmonization of corporation tax.

Most of the progress on the harmonization of indirect taxation was over value added tax (VAT), which the Community adopted as its turnover tax in two 1967 directives. By 1985 further directives had harmonized methods of calculating VAT in the Community.

However, serious differences remained between the member states, and the Commission in its 1985 White Paper pointed to three questions needing to be addressed. First, the common base or coverage differed considerably between member states in some areas, in particular food, fuel and transport. In Ireland and the UK, food, for example, was zero rated. Second, the number of rates, for seven out of nine member states imposed VAT at a reduced rate in addition to a standard rate and three of these states also imposed a higher rate. Third, the level of the standard rate of VAT varied between 12 per cent and 23 per cent in nine member states.

Progress was even slower over excise duties. As Swann explains, the Commission has rightly disliked variations on goods like oil in the member states. 'In so far as this product is an input in the production of other goods and services, a distortion of competition is created through the differential effects on costs of production . . . '

In addition, differences in excise rates on products in each member state was used as an indirect form of protection. The 1978 case of Denmark v the Commission exemplified this. Denmark had been applying a higher excise duty on spirits that it did not produce itself than on spirits that it did produce, such as aquavit. The British were similarly placed in their application of a lower duty on beer than wine, though in this case there were genuine difficulties on how the incidence of the duty was to be calculated.

Wide variations existed in the Community over which products should be subject to excise duty. Member states agreed on excise duties on tobacco, alcoholic beverages and hydrocarbon oils but there was a wide variation of practice over wine. No duty was levied on wine in Italy or Greece, and only on sparkling wine in Germany and imported wine in Luxembourg. Some countries did not levy excise duties on certain oils; in Belgium no duty was levied on heavy fuel oil, domestic heating oil and lubricants.

In addition, the level of excise duty varied considerably. The spread of duty on a packet of twenty cigarettes in 1985 was from 1.28 ECU in Greece to 1.96 ECU in Denmark. The heaviest tax on beer, wines and spirits was to be found in Denmark, Ireland and the UK.

In the area of direct taxation any distorting effect on trade was less easy to justify. Direct taxes were levied on factor payments such as wages at the end of the production process and therefore should

Table 3.1 Community VAT rates, March 1985 (%)

	Lower	*Standard*	*Higher*
Belgium	6 and 17	19	25
Denmark		22	
Germany	7	14	
France	5.5 and 7	18.6	33.3
Ireland	10	23	
Italy	2 and 9	18	38
Luxembourg	3 and 6	12	
Netherlands	5	19	
UK		15	

Source: Completing the Internal Market, COM(85)310, 14 June 1985, p.49.

not affect the price mechanism directly or cause a barrier to trade. However, this was not necessarily true of taxes on profits. If such corporation taxes were shifted forward on to the consumer (with the producer thus seeking to maintain his level of post-tax profits), then firms in high corporation tax countries would tend to raise their prices more than those in low tax countries, and a non-tariff barrier would be created. Even if tax was not shifted forward on to consumers, capital would be misallocated, as it would tend to flow to low-tax countries until the returns net of tax were equalized. Therefore, though less urgent an issue than indirect taxation, the harmonization (or approximation) of direct taxation was desirable in the long run, but the Community has yet to address the issue.

Fiscal harmonization in general was a difficult problem with which to grapple, inevitably so given the diversity and complexity of the economic systems within the Community. National tax systems differed widely in 1957 both in terms of structure and rates. The proportion of total revenue raised from indirect taxation varied from 27 per cent in the Netherlands to 58 per cent in Ireland between 1960 and 1973.

In addition, harmonization of taxes would remove one of the major weapons of demand management policy to the Community level. To member states, the loss of fiscal independence in pursuit of the goal of distortion-free trade has seemed somewhat idealistic. Community VAT rates are shown in Table 3.1.

Public procurement discrimination

The public sector – central and local government and nationalized bodies – is a major spender in the economic systems of the member states. The Commission reported in 1986 that such public spending on goods and services totalled c. 200 billion ECU, about 9 per cent of the Community's GDP. Unfortunately this spending was highly discriminatory in nature in the sense that institutions in the public sector adopted 'buy national' attitudes. Such behaviour was contrary to Article 7 of the Rome Treaty, which prohibits discrimination on grounds of nationality, and Articles 30 and 34 which prohibit quantitative restrictions or measures having equivalent effect.

Consequently Community directives were adopted to combat the problem. Since 1978 public supply contracts of 200,000 ECU or over are supposed to be advertised throughout the Community in the official journals, except for those concerned with transport services, water, energy or telecommunications. Other exceptions were made for security and artistic or technical reasons, or where articles were manufactured for research. Tenders were to be accepted (subject to proof of competence) from the lowest or otherwise most effective bidder, irrespective of nationality, within the EC.

Public works contracts required common procedures, established in 1971 for advertising and awarding public sector construction contracts of which the estimated cost was a million ECU or more. Exceptions included certain industrial and nuclear installations, transport, water and energy services. Contracts were to be awarded on the same criteria as for public supply contracts.

These directives in fact had little impact. The economic recession encouraged the use of national rather than Community suppliers. There were too many excluded sectors as shown above, and some countries followed the tactic of publishing details in the official journal in a long specification unfamiliar to foreign firms. Another tactic was project splitting, a device to ensure that the value of the individual project was below the minimum figure required by the directives. Sometimes the bid times allowed by the directives were too short to allow foreign participation. According to figures published by the Commission, in 1982 every single penny of central government supply spending in Italy went to Italian suppliers. The figures for France, West Germany and the UK were 99.91 per cent, 99.7 per cent and 98.3 per cent respectively.

Technical barriers to trade

The problem of public procurement was closely related to that of technical barriers to trade. Many of the items bought by public authorities were subject to varying national standards, and these differences in national standards prevented trade in many products even when the Community directives on procurement were followed. Trade in advanced technological goods was particularly hit because the purchase of computers in a number of member states was at the discretion of public authorities, and until some kind of agreement on harmonization was reached, a non-discriminatory procurement policy was meaningless.

The classic example of the technical barrier to trade was the case of Cassis de Dijon. The German company Rewe-Zentral A G sought to import into West Germany the French blackcurrent liqueur Cassis de Dijon, and requested an authorization from the West German Administration for Spirits. The latter informed Rewe that West German law forbade the sale of liqueurs with less than 32 per cent alcohol content. Since the Cassis had an alcohol content of only 15–20 per cent, it could not be imported. Rewe contested the matter in the German courts, and the case was referred to the European Court of Justice, which declared that the West German law was a measure of the kind prohibited under Article 30 of the Rome Treaty, i.e. that the minimum alcohol content rule had in this particular case the effect of a zero import quota.

The German government had defended the minimum alcohol content on the grounds of protection of the consumer, but in a most significant ruling the Court observed that such an end could equally be served by merely requiring suppliers to indicate on the label the actual alcoholic content. In addition, it stressed that any product legally made and sold in one member state must in principle be admitted to the market of any other member state.

Such technical barriers could prevent a firm exporting at all to another member state if the product concerned did not meet the standards of the importing country. Alternatively, the exporter might have to modify the specification of the commodity to make it acceptable to other countries, but, in so doing, the ability to generate economies of scale was reduced. Delays would then occur as the commodity was 'inspected' for conformity to the importing country's standard; thus extra costs were imposed on the producer of a 'lead and lags' nature.

Articles 100–102 of the Rome Treaty conferred a general power to harmonize rules so as to prevent any distortion of competition in the Common Market, and over the years the Commission laboured on with a small staff to push through harmonization directives. By 1981 nearly 200 directives aimed at eliminating technical barriers to trade had been adopted, about 150 of them applying to industrial products and the remainder to foodstuffs.

However, progress was disappointingly slow. The major reason for this was the enormous burden of work required to harmonize standards. In certain cases the standards conformed to those issued by the International Standards Organization (ISO), while similar European bodies dealt with cases not covered by ISO. These included the European Standards Co-operating Committee or

Comité Européen de Normalisation (CEN), and more specialist standards authorities like Comité Européen de Normalisation Electrotechnique (CENELEC) for electrical products. But so much consultation was needed with other Community institutions, member governments, consumer organizations and industry-based pressure groups that the pace was slow indeed.

A further difficulty was the type of harmonization to be achieved. Harmonization measures fell into either the 'total' or 'optional' categories. Total harmonization required all the products covered by a particular directive to conform to the standards set out in the directive. This necessitated the abolition of national standards and therefore legislative action by member governments, whereas 'optional' harmonization permitted the parallel existence of Community and national rules.

There were also difficulties over which standard to adopt in any particular field. No country wanted to accept a reduction of its standards through the harmonization process. Therefore the Community standard tended to converge on the highest standard already in existence among the member states, but this imposed significant financial burdens on poorer member states caused by some redesigning of the capital stock. Consequently total harmonization measures met with resistance from countries with lower standards and inertia in countries where standards were already high.

Finally the pace of technical change presented a problem for the harmonization process in two ways. First, directives became outdated by the time that they were adopted and, second, directives once adopted rapidly became obsolescent as the products to which they referred were replaced by new ones.

State subsidies

State subsidies distorted competition within the Community by giving an unfair advantage to domestic producers when they exported to other member states or sought to compete against imports coming from producers located in other member states. As Alan Dashwood has explained, Community machinery to supervise such subsidies had a two-fold function – to remove an impediment to the free play of competition and to help the co-ordination of national policies that were liable to conflict – with the result that state aid became more expensive and less effective or that difficulties were exported from one member state to another.

The groundwork for such supervision was laid down in Article 92(1) of the Rome Treaty, which declared as incompatible with the Common Market state aids that distorted competition between member states. In Articles 92(2) and 92(3) respectively two categories of exception were allowed – aid of a social character and aid to promote the welfare of disadvantaged regions. Article 93 empowered the Commission to review state aid and if necessary amend it or abolish it.

In practice the Commission was unable to stem the tide of state subsidies, as was illustrated by two types of state aid – the sectoral and the regional. Excessive amounts of regional aid given by governments meant that the various regions of the Community competed with each other to attract footloose investment capital, and schemes became more costly as a result of competitive outbidding. The consequence was not an increase in the flow of investment but reciprocal neutralization, with unjustified profits for the beneficiary enterprise. Many regional subsidies appeared not to be genuinely regional in motivation but, in Denton's words, 'merely camouflage for other motives for subsidisation', in particular as a device to attract foreign investment within national borders. That much of this state aid was wasteful is evident if the Delorean and Caterpillar cases in the UK are recalled. Yet the problem was a difficult one, because it was recognized from the formation of the Community that it was essential to redistribute some of the gains of wider competition to areas made worse off, and the Community promoted its own regional development programme. Despite this, member governments jealously guarded their sovereignty to carry out national regional aid schemes.

Sectoral aids were also a minefield. The Commission in 1972 took a strict line on such subsidies, but it was forced to soften its approach in the wake of the 1973 oil crisis. The escalation of state aid in industries like shipbuilding throughout the world left member states aware that their own industries could well become uncompetitive if they did not provide financial assistance.

The Commission had to bow to realities, and it evolved what has been called the compensatory justification criterion. If the Commission used its discretionary power not to raise objections to an aid proposal, the aid was to contain a compensatory justification taking the form of a contribution by the beneficiary of the aid towards the fulfilment of Community objectives under Article 92. For example, steel firms in receipt of state aid had to engage in restructuring plans to restore competitiveness and financial viability.

Perhaps this was merely the Commission putting a gloss on its inability to check such subsidies, given the high rates of unemployment in the Community and the secrecy practised by member governments. In reality progress on the reduction of state aids could only occur when the economic outlook improved and governments ceased to be obsessed by unemployment statistics.

Barriers to free movement of labour

Various obstacles to labour mobility can be classified as natural, i.e. those associated with geographical distance; social, stemming mainly from difficulties in social integration, and artificial, arising because of the existence of national frontiers. It follows then that there are factors at work blocking labour mobility for which the Community cannot be blamed. Laid-off workers are unlikely to find work elsewhere in Europe because their sector of business is probably similarly depressed in other member states. Most workers feel that it is better to stay at home where the language, customs and welfare systems are familiar. The possession of a council house impedes mobility but so does the private possession of a property, given the considerable cost of moving house and the difficulty of selling in depressed areas. Other constraints include the disruption of children's education, the loss of friends and family roots. Thus the differentials in rewards or other incentives to move have to be very considerable to induce international movement.

However, the Community can be condemned for not doing more up to 1985 to loosen up Europe's inflexible labour markets, which had become a major cause of the Community's high unemployment. Member states won exceptions to the rule on free movement of labour, e.g. the exclusion of foreigners from public administration. One may also castigate particularly administrative obstacles, because Europeans moving from one country to another were caught in a bureaucratic jungle of byzantine proportions. This situation was far removed from the original brave hopes of the founding fathers, with their vision of a fluid jobs market running from Sicily to Schleswig-Holstein. In practice the Community was still balkanized into closed-off national job markets, owing to the immense bureaucratic and economic obstacles.

Trademarks

By 1985 there were 1.8 million trademarks in the Community, a quarter of which were alarmingly similar to each other but related to entirely different products. This caused confusion for exporters and constituted a barrier to trade, with resulting limitation on consumer choice. Trademarks, like patents, are property rights that can be invoked to inhibit the free movement of goods, as the 1983 case of Theodor Kohl K G versus Ringelhan and Rennett S A and Ringelhan Oberhasen demonstrated.

The West German firm Ringelhan and Rennett was a well known supplier of pharmaceutical equipment and its products carried the symbol 'r and r' until it went into liquidation in 1982. A French subsidiary of the company continued to produce goods carrying the symbol 'r and r', and a competitor, Theodor Kohl, objected to these products being imported into West Germany on the grounds that the trademark 'r and r' might mislead customers into thinking that the products had been manufactured by the original German firm. In the end the case went from the German courts to the European Court, which ruled that a ban on imports from the former French subsidiary would offend against Article 30 of the Rome Treaty prohibiting quantitative restrictions.

The Commission set up a working group in 1981 to tackle the whole problem, with the idea of creating a Community system of trademark law and a Community trademark office but interested parties have ensured that progress in this area was slow. Meanwhile trademarks and patents have added to the army of non-tariff barriers.

The effect of non-tariff barriers

The massed ranks of NTBs, often not transparent, created an atmosphere of uncertainty for intra-Community business. It was particularly serious at a time when gloom over Eurosclerosis was so prevalent. There were indeed a number of worrying symptoms of European decline. Pelkmans particularly highlighted the Community's declining share of the world's exports of manufactures, its rapidly growing deficit in information technology goods and the penetration of the internal market by Japanese and American rivals as evidence of the Community's growing lack of competitiveness. Though market fragmentation was only one of several possible causes, it seems likely that it was a significant contributory factor.

There was little hard evidence on the costs of market fragmentation, some of which may be unquantifiable anyway. However, Jacques Pelkmans, anticipating the later Cecchini Report, made a valuable contribution in 1986 towards an overview with some statistical underpinning. He pointed to a number of direct costs, some of which could be roughly quantified. The cost of frontier delays was estimated by the Commission in 1983 to be some 12 billion ECU, equivalent to between 5 per cent and 10 per cent of the actual value of the goods traded. Another major cost was that of adapting products to conform with the technical regulations that differ among member states. As Pelkmans explained, 'the costs of such technical barriers do not consist of the costs of the adaptation itself, but also of the efficiency loss of limiting scale economies or affecting basic designs'. Discriminating public procurement was, in Pelkmans' view, costing about 40 billion ECU a year, if it was assumed that preference for domestic suppliers incurred an average price increase of 10 per cent on procurement expenditure by member states of 400 billion ECU a year. State subsidies amounted to some 32 billion ECU in 1981, much of it wasted in propping up ailing enterprises and perpetuating chronic over-capacity in some industries.

The indirect costs of market fragmentation consisted in the reduction of the competitiveness of European industry both within the internal market and in the world market. Here Pelkmans distinguished between low, medium and high technology goods. In low technology industries like textiles the costs lay in the slowing down in the adjustment process caused by a combination of external protection, e.g. the MFA, and state subsidies. Medium technology products were held back from access to other member states' markets by technical barriers to trade and state aids, while high technology products suffered similar difficulties but in addition had to endure discriminatory public procurement. For the latter two groups there was a loss of technical economies of scale and a reduction in the R and D base.

Pelkmans also analyzed twenty-eight high technology sectors (an area where the Community performance was generally poor) and found that in only eleven were there few barriers to trade. Out of twenty of these sectors that achieved very modest success, seventeen also suffered from low levels of intra-Community trade, the low levels being partly due to deficiencies in the internal market.

Pelkmans concentrated on product market integration, but to the costs of market fragmentation for goods must also be added the costs of failure to effect the other three freedoms. Again, the task of quantifying this was great, but the kind of loss was demonstrated in one service sector, insurance, by Chapatte. In 1980 total Community insurance premium income was estimated to be \$118 billion, with insurance premiums from domestic business representing 4–6 per cent of the GNP of the member states. However, if there had been true freedom to provide cross-frontier services, the whole Community could have benefited. Competitive insurers would have been able to expand on a Community scale without incurring the costs of establishment. Community insurers would then have been more competitive and able to export their services more successfully to the rest of the world. Manufacturers and business in general would have benefited from a wider range of insurance cover and more competitive premiums and able to reduce their costs. Consumers would have benefited both from cheaper goods and from the improved insurance facilities.

Such an analysis may sound idealistic, but, given the growing importance of the tertiary sector in economic life, it reinforced the view of Pelkmans that completion of the internal market was essential for Community economic growth. Significantly the Commission in its 1985 White Paper contrasted the creation of the 5 million Community jobs in the services sector between 1973 and 1982 with the 6.7 millions and 13.4 millions in Japan and the USA respectively.

The Community strikes back: the Commission white paper of 1985

The problem of the internal market was only one of many issues facing the Community in the 1980s and was to an extent dwarfed by the debates over the CAP, the budget and enlargement. Yet the patent failure to achieve one of the Community's most basic objectives became a source of increasing concern, as evidenced by a number of Commission statements on the internal market in 1984.

In February the Community published '*Evaluating the Functioning of the Internal market*', in April came '*Checks and Formalities Relating to Intra-community Trade in Goods*', and in June '*Consolidating the Internal Market*'. The first of these in a broad brush approach pointed to the importance of the internal market, alleged considerable progress but lamented existing obstacles such as frontier controls and lack of fiscal harmonization. It emphasized the need for technical harmonization and a proper transport policy. The second document gave an exhaustive survey of the excessive frontier formalities and suggested such solutions as the Single Administrative Document (SAD). The third document admitted a loss of momentum in the integration process and examined the main requirements of a consolidation programme for the internal market.

In the past such declarations might have been dismissed as more pious statements of intent, but a change in attitudes was taking place at Commission and governmental level, perhaps prompted by the deep recession of 1980–81 and the waste of money on ailing industries. These declarations were, however, merely forerunners for a bold Commission initiative – its white paper of June 1985 proposing a 7-year plan to 'complete' the internal market by 1992. It was a landmark in Community affairs of the 1980s because it was comprehensive, much more candid than most Commission statements and set a detailed double calendar, one for Commission proposals and one for Council decisions.

In the white paper the Commission exhorted the Community to pledge itself to the completion of a fully unified internal market by 1992, declaring that 'the time for action has come'. It proposed measures classified under three headings: (*a*) the removal of physical barriers to trade, (*b*) the removal of technical barriers and (*c*) the removal of fiscal barriers.

The removal of physical barriers

The Commission pointed to a double reason for removing physical barriers. Their removal was necessary for political reasons, because to the ordinary citizen the barriers were 'the obvious manifestation of the continued division of the Community'. In addition, they were an unnecessary burden on industry, adding to costs and damaging competitiveness. Therefore the Commission declared that it wanted to do away with internal frontier controls in their entirety.

Under this category, then, the Commission was aiming at the abolition of customs posts, immigration controls and national passports. It envisaged simpler documentation through the SAD, and the shifting of the collection of VAT away from frontiers to inland tax offices. There would be an end to quotas and health checks on animals and plants, such checks becoming the responsibility of the exporting member state. As far as individuals were concerned, a common passport would be implemented with a need for common roles concerning extradition.

The removal of technical barriers

Under the removal of technical barriers the Commission now supported the general principle that 'if a product is lawfully manufactured and marketed in one member state, there is no reason why it should not be sold freely throughout the Community'. The principle should apply not only to goods but also to services and people.

As the Commission admitted, such a new approach would require radical changes of attitude. Previously it had used Article 100 of the Rome Treaty in an effort to create a common market through harmonization of technical standards, but this had given rise to long delays because of the unanimity required in Council decision-making. Therefore the Commission now proposed that for a wide range of products it would concentrate on obligations of performance rather than technical construction. Products would be harmonized under Article 100 according to essential health and safety requirements, conformity with which would provide freedom of circulation throughout the Community. The technicalities of achieving the obligation would be left to standardization bodies such as CEN and CENELEC or appropriate national organizations.

The change would mean that for a particular sector of industry, a 'general reference to standards' directive would replace 100 detailed technical directives subject to constant amendment because of the pace of technical change, i.e. national standards once vetted by the Commission would be valid throughout the Community. A number of industries, such as information technology, would benefit from the new approach, especially as since 1983 member states had had to notify the Commission in advance of all technical specifications they intended to introduce on their own territory. The new information procedure had come into force on 1 January 1985 but the Commission wanted it to cover more industrial products.

The Commission's declarations were less convincing over public procurement. It admitted that existing provisions were not working, promised to open discussions with member states with a view to applying the directives to energy, transport, water and telecommunications, and laid down 1988 as a date for Council action in this vexed area.

On the question of the right of establishment for the professions and the freedom to provide services the Commission admitted that swift action was needed to open up the whole market for services, both traditional ones such as banking and new areas such as information marketing. For the professions it suggested a new method to assess comparability of vocational training qualifications, with the introduction of a European vocational training card to serve as proof that the holder had been awarded a specific qualificiation. For services the Commission wanted minimal co-ordination of rules, with the principle of home country control, i.e. the competent authorities of the member states of origin would have the primary task of supervising, for example, financial institutions expanding activities into another member state.

The Commission called for the completion of the internal market in transport, including the phasing out of quotas on goods taken by lorry and freedom for non-resident carriers to operate transport services in another member state (cabotage), by 1988 at the latest. Sea and inland waterway transport were to be similarly liberalized but the most interesting declaration was over air transport services. The call to free these services would require changing the system of tariffs and limiting governments' right to restrict capacity or access to the market.

Finally in this section, the Commission declared its intention to abolish gradually the safeguard clauses in the Rome Treaty's articles on capital movements (Articles 73 and 108(3) and to liberalize the markets in securities and mortgages. It called for a decision by 1987 on the rules required for a Community trademark system and promised 'a rigorous policy' in regard to state aids 'so that public resources are not used to confer artificial advantages to some firms over others', though it did not explain how a rigorous policy would be implemented!

The removal of fiscal barriers

Under the fourteenth VAT directive of August 1982 the Commission pointed to the need for the collection of VAT to be shifted to inland offices. However, it urged that this in itself would not be enough to eliminate fiscal barriers to trade because different countries still had different rates of VAT and excise duty. 'It would be all too easy for traders in high rate member states to obtain supplies from low rate member states and omit them from their records. Not only would this be a loss of revenue but such practices would result in serious distortion of trade between low rate and high rate member states.' Therefore the Commission called for approximation (rather than harmonization) of VAT and excise duties within a margin of plus or minus 2½ per cent either side of whatever target rate was chosen. It justified this by asserting that retail markets are often tolerant of significant differences in retail prices as factors other than price enter into consumer choice.

Prospects of success

Such then were the main provisions of the white paper of June 1985, but would such an ambitious programme be implemented by 1992? There were reasons to hope for considerable progress but good cause for believing that full implementation would be hampered by a multitude of negative factors.

One force making for progress was that the price of failure would be great. The work of forcing through directives on the internal market would absorb the energies of many ministers and civil servants. If such work proved abortive, failure would be not merely disappointing but traumatic. The credibility of the Community would then be called into question, its future being that of a truncated, uninspiring customs union with insignificant factor market integration, partial free movement of services and ancien régime style obstacles at frontiers.

However, ministers and bureaucrats were not the only group now backing the programme. Business in general and especially the larger European multinationals changed their stance of apparent indifference to one of strong support for the internal market agenda. As merely one illustration of this, the British Institute of Directors under Walter Goldsmith in setting out its priorities for the 1984 Euro-elections particularly emphasized the need to get rid of frontier delays and to liberalize services and capital movements.

One early hopeful sign was that by the end of 1986 a considerable number of measures had been forced through. The Single Administrative Document had already been mooted by the Directorate General for the Internal Market (DG3) in December 1984, and in 1986 live trials of the document took place at Newhaven and other selected locations in the Community. SAD was soon to replace the seventy forms currently obligatory for cross-border Community trade with a seven-part carbonless set. A code that could be understood in all countries was used, thus obviating language difficulties. The SAD halved the amount of information required and pruned the duplication caused by the same information being required on several different documents. The target date for its introduction, 1 January 1988, was achieved.

In 1986 as a whole sixty-nine directives or regulations relating to the internal market were approved. The increased momentum raised hopes that the backlog would be contained, especially as the measures passed were not minor ones. Though the British failed in two areas closest to their national priorities – insurance and air fares – they did see through significant decisions on shipping, telecommunications equipment, direct satellite broadcasting standards and public purchasing. The shipping policy agreed was comprehensive; it applied the Community rules of competition to shipping and laid down measures to be taken against predatory pricing or cargo reservation indulged in by shipping companies from third countries. The only area where agreement was not reached was coastal shipping.

On the other hand, the road to further success bristled with difficulties. The programme was a very ambitious one, requiring the implementation of over 300 directives, even though the number was later pruned down to 280.

Second, the coming into force of the Single European Act, signed in February 1986, initially put a sharp brake on decisions taken by the Council of Ministers. The Act gave enhanced powers of consultation to the European Parliament and in particular was liable to impose a 3-month delay on the approval of all the decisions of the Council that were subject to the Parliament's right to be consulted. Therefore several decisions that would have been taken under the Belgian aegis in the first half of 1987 were not formally adopted until the second half of 1987 under the Danish presidency.

On the other hand, the extension of majority voting in the Council speeded up decision-making as it made it impossible for one or two states to hold up progress indefinitely against the wishes of the majority. Certainly this move towards majority decision-making was a healthy step in the right direction, and stemmed from the December 1985 meeting of Community heads of state. However, at that summit it was also agreed that ministers could still use the veto when their governments believed national interests were at risk. Such safeguards have been written into the Single European Act itself. Article 15 of the SEA required the Commission, when making proposals to achieve the internal market, to take into account the different stages of the national economies and empowered it to propose appropriate provisions, including for the first time derogations. This allowed a 'variable geometry' in progress towards completion of the internal market.

Similarly, on harmonization measures, member states could apply national provisions 'on grounds of major needs', e.g. relating to protection of the environment, and this could nullify the new co-operation procedure whereby harmonized measures could be agreed by a qualified majority. It was easy to envisage protection-minded states driving a coach and horses through such loopholes. Indeed, as Pelkmans has stressed, the heightened exposure to Community-wide competition was liable to induce member states to engage in additional interventionism as a substitute for lost autonomy.

A further institutional factor blocking potential progress was the weak political legitimacy of the Commission when it opposed national protectionist measures. Although it had ultimate recourse to the Court of Justice, it had no carrot in the form of less distortive aid or significant Community procurement. Its authority was not enhanced by the present group of Commissioners. In a stinging article Jonathan Todd of *The Sunday Times* condemned 'the blatant chauvinism of its members'. Instead of acting as guardians of Community interests (as laid down in Article 10 of the merger treaty), members acted on behalf of their own countries. Delors, the president, with the support of his fellow French commissioner Claude Cheysson, managed to postpone a Commission decision to condemn illegal subsidies by the French government to the French textile group Boussac. Other commissioners followed the president's lead, especially Carlo Ripa di Meana, who blocked an enquiry into a £70 million package of Italian government aid to Fiat.

Such a Commission seemed unlikely to relish the head-on clashes necessary to force through unpopular decisions against the wishes of member states. In addition, it still did not have the resources to play its full role. Its staff numbered 10,000 in 1984 when the British civil services totalled 648,900. Coming from different countries, with different political backgrounds. Commissioners often had little in common and found themselves jockeying for position against each other rather than co-operating for a common cause. The Commission had little wish to take risks, as it had no natural supporters (unlike governments or political parties) and was invariably the scapegoat when things went wrong. As a consequence of such factors, Christopher Tugendhat described his time as a Commissioner between 1977 and 1985 as 'the labours of Sisyphus – endlessly pushing a stone up a hill only to have it crash back to the bottom as soon as it gets within reach of the top'.

Certain specific problems would clearly be fiendishly difficult to solve. As already stated, the white paper had little to say on how it would tackle public aid to industry. In addition, technical harmonization would remain a problem despite the mutual recognition idea, which in Pelkmans' view 'grossly under-estimates the technical and economic difficulties'. It was indeed easy to see practical stumbling blocks arising over this issue. For example, when an appeal was made against an unsafe product, should it be taken off the market, pending the Commission decision? If the complaint was a justifiable one, to leave it on the market would be irresponsible but if it were to prove unfounded, the competitor (who might well have brought the complaint) could gain a breathing space in which to improve his share of the market.

With plans to cover building materials, textiles and protective clothing, among other products, the target of removing technical barriers to trade by 1992 was ambitious and soon ran into difficulties. The first of the new style harmonization directives (on pressure vessels, e.g. air brake cylinders) was tabled by the Commission in March 1986 but took much longer to be picked over by a working group of national officials than had been originally envisaged. The Dutch and the British presidencies both took the view that the national officials concerned 'had not emancipated themselves from the working philosophy of the old style detailed standardisation directives, many of which were hundreds of pages long instead of the mere eight pages of the present draft'. In October 1986 the British summoned the members of the working party to Brussels to discuss the approach with Commission experts with a view to speeding it up, but it was clear that the new harmonization procedures would be hampered by the old philosophy.

Further difficulties were to arise over fiscal harmonization, because in many states where marginal income taxes were already high indirect taxes remained the only variable tax instrument available. Harmonization of VAT could affect some countries' tax revenues drastically, e.g. Ireland with its standard rate of 23 per cent. The application of excise and VAT duty to certain sensitive areas, e.g. books and children's clothes in the UK and wine in Italy, were to provoke further storms.

The transition to the abolition of fiscal inner frontiers was littered with hurdles. The clearest difficulty was the adoption of the fourteenth VAT directive, aiming to defer VAT clearance from the frontier to inland tax offices, as Benelux had done for 17 years. Five member states opposed it at that time for the temporary loss of revenue caused by the change in system but also for the reduction in the power of customs officers.

An immense amount of work was needed to implement a common transport policy. It was significant that the British presidency saw progress over shipping but no firm agreement over air fares. The Commission initiated discussion with nine out of ten of the major European airlines in 1986 on abuses of Community competition rules they were suspected of committing. By March of 1987 the Competition Commissioner Peter Sutherland had lost patience with the airlines, seven of which were operating a price-fixing cartel, and he wanted the Commission to open up legal proceedings against these airlines. But such procedures were slow (See Chapter 5).

Discriminatory public procurement was also likely to prove an onerous obstacle. The Commission encountered national opposition in its attempt to extend competition to the former excluded areas of water supply, energy, transport and communications, as was soon highlighted by a row over the contracts for the Sizewell nuclear power station in Britain. The Commission protested at the low percentage (7 per cent) of component contracts being awarded to foreign suppliers. The Central Electricity Generating Board bluntly replied, 'We support British industry and we have never tried to conceal that'. It was hardly likely that similar 'buy national' attitudes would diminish in other member states.

Further reading

Chapatte, P P, 'Freedom to Provide Insurance Services in the EC' *European Law Review*, February 1984.

Hine, R C, *The Political Economy of European Trade*, Wheatsheaf, Sussex, 1985.

Owen, N, *Economics of Scale, Competitiveness and Trade Patterns within the European Community*, Clarendon Press, Oxford, 1983.

Owen, R and Dynes, M, *The Times Guide to 1992*, Times Books (Second Edition), London, 1990.

Pelkmans, J and Winters, L A, *Europe's Domestic Market*, Routledge, London, 1988.

Swann, D, *The Economics of the Common Market*, Penguin (Seventh Edition), Harmondsworth, 1992.

Questions

1 Why did the founding fathers of the EC set such store on the creation of a true internal market?
2 What do you understand by the term 'the four freedoms'?
3 What progress was made towards achieving a single market in the EC by 1985?
4 Explain why the EC failed to implement a single market before 1985.
5 Critically analyse the chief objectives of the 1985 single market programme.

4
The impact of the single market programme

Less a roar, more of a whimper

It was a pity that 1 January 1993, the formal date for the opening of the single market programme, coincided with a recession in the European economy. As Martin Wolf commented, 'Far from heralding renewed economic dynamism, January 1993 coincides with rising unemployment, currency turbulence and popular dissatisfaction. The European Community witnesses not a burst of confidence and creativity but a return to the gloom that occasioned the Single Market Programme'. The OECD's forecast in that same month suggested a mere 1.2 per cent growth in the EC's GDP in 1993, and later forecasts reduced the figure still further.

Such gloom seemed far removed from the optimistic report published in 1988 under the aegis of a senior Commission official, Paolo Cecchini. The report had forecast that single market legislation would increase the EC's GDP by 4.5 per cent over the medium term, reduce inflation, lower the EC's external trade deficits and create 1.8 million new jobs over the longer term. To be fair to the contributors to this report, anticipation of the changes that would ensue from the single market programme (SMP) undoubtedly speeded up trade and investment during the second half of the 1980s. Growth was also accelerated by a boom in Germany between 1989 and 1991, caused first by the collapse of the Berlin Wall and then by unification.

By 1993 some Commission experts believed that 30 per cent of the forecast effect of the SMP had already worked its way through the European economy. The fillip to European economic growth in the late 1980s certainly helped acceptance of many of the controversial proposals by member states. The economic expansion revived West European confidence and made the EC a source of hope for East European countries. Unfortunately the recession of the early 1990s forced a scaling down of expectations and proved that the single market by itself was not a panacea for all European problems. In

1993 the SMP was in any case far from completion, as many directives had yet to be implemented by member states. As the legal
adviser to BEUC (the European Consumer Bureau), Monique
Guyens suggested, 'The target of January 1st was misleading.
Creating a genuine single market will require a long hard slog and
we may get somewhere close by the end of the century'.

Nevertheless the Commission trumpeted its assertion in 1993 that
the SMP was for all practical purposes complete. After 8 years of
striving, 264 out of 282 proposals had been accepted by the Council
of Ministers, and, of the remaining eighteen proposals, five were not
given high priority by the member states. However, a high level
group headed by a former commissioner Peter Sutherland had, since
March 1992, been analysing the problems in the implementation of
the programme and felt compelled to make thirty-eight detailed
recommendations in October 1992. It stressed the need to explain
the new laws to consumers and businesses and warned of a danger
of trade barriers being recreated. Member states would need to work
more closely with the Commission in implementing the spirit as well
as the letter of the new rules.

The warnings of the Sutherland Report were only too relevant. By
the end of 1992 member states were supposed to have implemented
194 out of the 264 measures adopted by the Council of Ministers.
The state with consistently the best record in implementing single
market proposals, Denmark, still headed the field with 165 measures
implemented but Belgium just succeeded in beating Italy and
Luxembourg to the wooden spoon with only 129 measures implemented. Clearly the practical completion of the programme lay some
years in the future, and the SMP was a patchwork or mosaic of real
advances and relative failures. Even so, the efforts to advance the
programme amounted to an unprecedented legislative achievement.
In comparison with previous Community initiatives, progress had
been exceptionally rapid, despite some remaining difficulties over
such issues as trademarks, road cabotage and company law.

The major legislation of the single market programme

The amount of legislation under the SMP was daunting. Below is a
necessarily brief summary of the chief areas affected.

Public procurement

The opening of Community public procurement procedures was one
of the main priorities of the SMP. Public purchasing by central,
regional and local government, and other public bodies such as

nationalized industries represented over 1.5 per cent of the EC's GDP. As explained in the previous chapter, public bodies had traditionally favoured domestic suppliers of goods and services, a practice deemed incompatible with the principle of a single European market.

It was obviously impossible to open all public contracts to competition across the EC, as many would be too small, too specific or too sensitive. However, the Commission estimated in 1992 that about half the EC's public contracts (worth between 240 billion ECUs and 340 billion ECUs) could be opened up to cross-frontier competition. By comparison the actual trade in this sector within the EC in 1986 was worth only 500 million ECUs, so Commission aspirations could well be too optimistic. A real revolution in attitudes by public authorities would be required, a revolution made even more unlikely by high unemployment by 1991, which would lead public authorities to favour domestic suppliers even more rather than suppliers from other Community states.

The 1988 directive on public supply contracts tightened an earlier 1977 measure with effect from 1989. Public authorities are now required to publish in advance all planned contracts exceeding 750,000 ECUs. Changes to a 1971 directive on public works were implemented in July 1990. The amended directive requires purchasers to give advance notice of construction projects over 5 million ECUs.

What gave the new directives some hope of having an impact was a back-up directive of July 1989 establishing procedures for the award of public supply and public works contracts. This was implemented in 1991, and requires member states to set up systems to ensure that purchasing decisions are rapidly reviewed if a potential supplier feels unfairly treated, and to correct any unlawful purchasing decisions.

Certain sensitive or excluded sectors (water, energy, transport and telecommunications) were dealt with in a separate 1990 directive. Such sectors had traditionally been dominated by state agencies, but from 1993, with derogations for Spain until 1996 and Greece and Portugal until 1998, public procurement was opened up throughout the EC. The directive covered supply contracts over 200,000 ECUs and works contracts over 5 million ECUs. The Commission also made a recommendation, not binding on member states, urging them to use standard forms for tenders to help simplify procedures and eliminate errors. As with other sectors, an appeals and conciliation procedure was to be set up to extend the right of redress against discriminatory procurement to suppliers of goods and works in the excluded sectors.

In June 1992 agreement was reached on a directive aimed at opening up for tender contracts for most services that may be offered across Community borders. All such contracts must be advertised for tender in the official journal if the value of the bid is over 200,000 ECUs or 5 million ECUs for construction contracts for which architect firms are bidding. This group of services, called priority services, included maintenance and repair, insurance, data processing, accounting, market research, advertising, architecture, street cleaning and refuse collection.

Frontier controls

The Commission claimed that significant progress had been made in this area as decisions were adopted to abolish controls on transport vehicles, to abolish the frontier transit note, to abolish veterinary checks at frontiers and to abolish the transit system between states. A notable step was the introduction of the Single Administrative Document (SAD) in 1988 to replace the formerly complex sets of national documents needed for the transit of goods across internal borders. Even the SAD was abolished for intra-Community trade in 1993, except for certain products until 1995. A regulation was agreed on the elimination of controls on hand baggage and on baggage of passengers travelling by air or sea across the Community.

Controls relating to drug-trafficking, terrorism or clandestine immigration were deemed to fall outside the remit of the SMP. Security checks would therefore continue. For states that had signed the Schengen Agreement, which abolished border controls, such checks would be carried out through co-operation between national authorities. Other member states, especially Britain, would continue to maintain considerably greater frontier controls for security reasons.

Harmonization of technical standards

As explained in the previous chapter, the large number of technical standards imposed on goods by national authorities were justified on the grounds of protecting the consumer and the environment, but in practice had been used as a protectionist device. The Cassis de Dijon ruling was the basis of the 'New Approach' to technical harmonization. The ruling was that any product permitted for sale in a member state could be sold in any other except on the grounds allowed under Article 36 of the Rome Treaty, i.e. where public morality, public security, national treasures or industrial and commercial property were affected. The New Approach developed this position by establishing directives setting out common criteria relating to safety, public health and the protection of the environment. As long as products conformed with these directives and the national laws of their state of origin, they should be accepted in all member states.

The European standards bodies CEN (the European Standards Committee) and CENELEC (the European Electrotechnical Standards Committee) were charged with developing the details of European standards to support the essential requirements of the general directives. Products conforming to European standards now carry the stylized CE symbol. Much of the work foreseen by the 1985 White Paper was completed by the end of 1992, with New Approach directives adopted on simple pressure vessels, safety of toys, electromagnetic compatibility, machine safety, personal protective equipment, active implantable medical devices, non-automatic weighing instruments and gas appliances.

In addition, the Council had adopted by the end of 1992 forty-four technical measures on motor vehicles that allowed for complete Community-type approval. This approval was introduced in January 1993 as optional but will become compulsory for all motor cars registered in the EC from 1 January 1996. Further technical harmonization measures included safety requirements for tractors and other agricultural machinery and a battery of measures on food such as food additives, and labelling and methods of analysis. Harmonization requirements were agreed for plants, animals and products derived from them in the areas of animal health, animal feeding stuffs, meat and meat products such as eggs. Comprehensive technical legislation was applied to the fields of pharmaceuticals, high technology medicines and chemicals.

Capital movements and financial services

Financial services represent an important part of the economies of all member states, accounting for 7 per cent of Community GDP. Therefore liberalization of operating conditions in this sector was an essential part of the SMP, since its efficient operation was vital if the EC were to maintain its share of trade in the world market and customers to be given access to the best services.

In November 1992 the Commission claimed that the single market in financial services was complete, with the removal of national regulatory barriers that had previously limited the freedom to offer services in other member states. Detailed measures had been adopted in the four separate areas of banking, insurance, securities and capital movements.

In banking the major piece of legislation was the 1989 Second Banking Directive. This gave banks the opportunity to operate in any member state on the basis of authorization in one state, and they could open branches and provide banking services throughout the

EC without requiring local licences. The directive set a list of banking activities; any bank which could carry out these activities in its home country was now permitted to do so in other EC states, irrespective of whether banks in these states could carry out such activities under national law. Banks were also free to advertise their services throughout the EC. Besides the Second Banking Directive there were closely related directives on own funds, rules on adequate solvency ratios and for banks' annual reports.

Community measures to regulate the offering of insurance services throughout the EC were in the main areas of life and non-life insurance plus a number of smaller categories. The first directive on non-life insurance in 1973 had set out to co-ordinate provisions for the offering of these services. This was followed after the adoption of the SMP by the second Non-Life Insurance Directive of 1988. This now became the main legal measure in the regulation of non-life insurance. It provided for home country control by the member state in which the insurance company had its head office. The directive distinguished between large risk (mainly industrial and commerical) and mass risk (incurred by individuals and small enterprises) business and did not cover mass risk that was subject to national regulations.

Freedom to supply non-life insurance services anywhere in the EC under home country control and a single licence was granted by the third Non-Life Insurance Directive of 1992, to come into force in 1994.

Parallel measures were adopted in the field of life insurance. The second Life Insurance Directive of 1990 set down provisions to make it easier to offer cross-border services in life insurance. It strengthened the rules of the first directive, particularly regarding the powers of the supervisory bodies and penalties for non-compliance. Insurance companies established in one member state could sell life insurance products elsewhere in the EC without being established there or having a special licence. However, there were restrictions: the initiative had to come from the customer rather than the insurer and the contract had to pass via an approved intermediary in the insured's country of residence. Such rather unsatisfactory restrictions were, however, removed by the third Life Directive of 1991, which offered full freedom to provide life insurance products in any part of the EC under home country control on the basis of a single licence.

Agreement on transactions in securities was long in coming. Efforts to contrive an agreement had started in the early 1970s, but fear of encouraging more fraudulent activity in the market for cross-border sales of securities, e.g. the infamous Investors Overseas Services, delayed progress. However, in 1990 agreement was reached on the Investment Services Directive, which the Commission hailed as 'the last major component of the single market in financial services'. It allowed credit institutions to offer investment services in any member state on the basis of a licence held in one state. It set minimum conditions for the authorization of investment firms and the conditions under which such firms would have the right to establish a branch, and the freedom to provide services in another member state without needing further authorization from the host member state. Such authorized activities included brokerage, dealing as a principal, portfolio management, investment advice, underwriting, administration of tranferable securities and financial futures and options. Like the Second Banking Directive it came into force in January 1993.

Finally, measures were put in place to liberalize capital movements. Earlier directives were replaced by a third Capital Movements Directive in 1988, and when this came into effect in 1990, the liberalization of capital movements between member states was nearly completed. Four states (Greece, Portugal, Spain and Ireland) were authorized to retain certain restrictions on long-term capital movements until the end of 1992, and Greece and Portugal were given a possible further stay of 3 years. The directive required that transfer of capital should be made on the same exchange rate conditions as those governing payments relating to currency transactions. There was a safeguard clause allowing member states to take action where 'short-term capital movements of exceptional magnitude impose severe strains on foreign exchange markets and lead to serious disturbances in the conduct of a member state's monetary and exchange rate policies'. Such action could only apply for 6 months and needed the approval of the Committee of EC Central Bank Governors. This safeguard clause was soon in use when the crisis in the Exchange Rate Mechanism in September 1992 forced Greece, Spain, Portugal and Ireland to reintroduce exchange controls.

Intellectual property

The Commission had endeavoured for many years to harmonize the various means of protecting intellectual property within the EC. It realized that the rights conferred by patents, trademarks and copyright were valuable and should receive some protection, but was also aware that such rights could be used to erect barriers to trade and restrict competition. Therefore it sought both a Community patent and a Community trademark, with measures to protect owners of other types of intellectual property.

The first directive on trademarks was adopted in 1988 and tried to harmonize the requirements of national trademark authorities.

The directive was delayed owing to disagreement over the location of the Community trademark office and the choice of languages to be used. Some specific proposals, e.g. protection of computer programmes, were adopted.

In theory agreement on Community *patents* was reached at the Luxembourg Intergovernmental Conference in December 1989, as it provided for a single patent for all member states. However, Ireland and Denmark had constitutional problems in ratifying the agreement and Spain has continued to oppose the measure. Given the lack of *copyright* harmonization measures in the SMP, progress in this field was limited.

Free movement of labour and the right of establishment

The Rome Treaty emphasized that a national of any member state had an absolute right to enter another member state for the purpose of working and doing business. Nor was it necessary to have established an office in another member state. In 1981 the Commission adopted a general programme to harmonize the rules on administrative practice in this field, and later directives included activities in agriculture and public works contracts. Under current law Community workers who establish themselves in another member state are entitled to have their immediate families admitted to that state.

The Commission admitted in 1992 that it did not expect the early or easy adoption of the 1985 white paper proposals relating to free movement and residence of workers and their families by member states. On the other hand, the European Court has repeatedly stressed that freedom of movement of EC workers is a fundamental right of the Rome Treaty, and has always supported the notion in its judgments.

Freedom to work in any member state was in the past restricted by national requirements for professionals from one state to requalify before becoming established in another EC state. A number of directives adopted since 1975 created mutual recognition of qualifications for doctors, dentists, nurses, midwives, veterinary surgeons and pharmacists so that they were able to practise throughout the EC. However, progress was slow, and to remedy the problem the EC has adopted a directive providing for a general system of mutual recognition of higher education diplomas of at least 3 years' duration. The directive came into force in 1991. A second directive, adopted in 1992, covered recognition of diplomas that required less than 3 years' study. The Commission continued to work on rules for the comparability of vocational qualifications in fields like hotel and catering trades and motor vehicle repair. Whether member states have yet entered into the spirit of such directives is open to question!

Company Law

A similar guarded judgement should be recorded on company law. The Commission hoped to foster the development of co-operation between companies enabling them to operate in an environment free from legal and tax restrictions caused by differences in the laws of member states. Some measures were adopted before 1985, e.g. the directive establishing minimum capital requirements for public limited companies. In 1985 a regulation for the creation of the European Economic Interest Grouping was agreed, and it was implemented in 1989. This was the first instrument that directly encouraged co-operation between companies across internal borders and was favourably received. More than fifty EEIGs were set up in the first 9 months alone, and by the end of 1992 350 EEIGs had been established. They operate by a contract between two or more companies, and, once registered, they are subject to the internal laws of the state of registration and may operate with unlimited liability.

Progress was less spectacular on the proposal for a European Company Statute. Like the registration for an EEIG, the statute aims to introduce a new legal form for a business. As an alternative to a company formed according to national laws, groups from different member states would be able to form a single operating unit subject to EC law. The proposal remains unadopted.

Taxation

Taxation was one of the most difficult areas for the Commission to resolve for three reasons. First, indirect taxation provided much national revenue, and control of it was therefore jealously guarded by member states. Second, differences in national systems resulted in the distortion of fair trade, as shown in the previous chapter. Finally, approximation of taxation was made a difficult task by the requirement of unanimous agreement in the Council of Ministers.

Real progress was made on corporate taxation with the adoption in 1990 of three measures that had been under consideration for 20 years! These consisted of (*a*) a mergers directive providing for the imposition of taxation on capital gains arising from a merger, hive-off, transfer of assets or an exchange of shares only when these gains have actually been realized and not at the time of the operation in question; (*b*) a parent company/subsidiary directive, which aimed at eliminating double taxation of dividends distributed by a subsidiary in one member state to its parent established in another member state; and (*c*) an arbitration procedure to ensure elimination of double taxation that might arise in the case of adjusting profits of associated companies by national taxation authorities.

The central question of the approximation of VAT rates led to a long battle. In 1987 the Commission proposed a standard rate of 14–20 per cent for most goods and services, and a reduced rate of 4–9 per cent on essentials such as food, heating and newspapers. This aroused widespread opposition from member states, and the Commission conceded that zero rating, applied on some products by the UK and Ireland, could remain. In 1991 all member states agreed that their minimum standard rate would be 15 per cent from January 1993, but without any upper limit. In addition, any member state could apply one or two reduced rates of at least 5 per cent on goods or services of a social or cultural character, and member states already applying zero rates or rates of less than 5 per cent could continue to do so for the time being.

Excise duties levied on tobacco, beers, wines, spirits and motor fuel became subject to an October 1992 directive that provided for minimum rates for different categories of product subject to excise duty. This represented a retreat by the Commission from its 1987 proposal to harmonize rates of excise duty. This proposal met heavy criticism, especially from member states whose tax revenue would have fallen as a result of the measure.

Television

In October 1991 a directive on the free provision of television broadcasts in the EC was implemented. The directive harmonized national rules on advertising and sponsorship, the right of reply and the protection of minors. It also included measures to promote the production of specifically European programmes so that European television was not completely swamped by transatlantic pro-grammes.

Transport

As explained in the previous chapter, Articles 74 to 84 of the Rome Treaty required the Community to evolve a common transport policy. Progress was slow and in 1985 the European Court criticized the Council of Ministers for failure in this area. Consequently the SMP contained a number of transport measures that have all been adopted. In sea transport, regulations were adopted on freedom to provide services between member states and third countries and within member states. Other measures applied competition rules to sea transport and on free access to cargoes on oceanic routes.

Measures adopted in air transport were to a large extent related to the compatibility of practices within the air transport sector with

EC competition rules (see Chapter 5). In June 1992 after much difficulty the Council adopted liberalization of air lines in three areas: (*a*) from January 1993 airlines were to have the freedom to set fares without government interference; (*b*) as regards market access, no member state was to limit capacity to any extent on the basis of nationality, although a member state reserved the right of appeal (this meant that airlines (after a 4-year transition period) would be able to operate on routes not requiring a stop or start in their home country); (*c*) from January 1993 airlines were required to satisfy common financial, technical and safety standards annually.

The absurdly protected road haulage sector was also tackled. Traditionally licences for road haulage were arranged bilaterally between members, but the system has been slowly liberalized. To introduce this, transitional arrangements from 1988 increased the number of Community multilateral permits allowing transport between all member states. From January 1990 15,000 permits were available, allowing hauliers registered in one member state to operate wholly within another member state. By January 1993 all community quotas, bilateral quotas and quotas for transit traffic to and from third countries were abolished, so that a fully liberalized cabotage system could be implemented.

Evaluation of the 1992 programme

Such were the main provisions of the SMP. Estimating the success of such a battery of legislation is difficult, and the judgements made in this action necessarily tentative.

Certainly there were real gains for travellers in terms of unhindered passage across most of the EC's internal borders. The Schengen Convention, signed by nine member states, set out a framework for the removal of all checks on travellers at internal land and sea borders of the Community, and this should be fully applied by 1994. In member states that refused to sign the Schengen Convention (Britain, Ireland and Denmark) some border checks remained, and seemed likely to do so for several years, especially at airports that posed complex problems caused by the need to separate EC and non-EC passengers and their luggage. Controls at airports continued throughout 1993 even in the states that had signed the Schengen Convention, and for the three non-signatory states the streaming and checking of EC and non-EC citizens seemed unlikely to disappear in the short term.

The free movement of goods was rather more assured. Generally speaking, customs and other officers were no longer in attendance at borders, and lorries and private individuals were no longer subject to border checks. Such abolition of border customs was estimated to result in the reduction of 50 to 60 million forms a year and a saving to companies of about £7 billion a year.

Consumers also gained from easier travel and more generous travel allowances. Duty-free purchases at frontiers or in cross-border transit were to be allowed to continue, with the same level of allowances until 1999, when such shopping would be abolished. For all other, i.e. duty paid, purchases, provided that the goods were carried personally by the traveller and were not for commercial use, there were virtually no quantity limits and no customs procedures laid down or further taxes levied.

The consumer also stood to gain over the long term by the increased competition that the SMP promised to engender. The car industry may be cited as an appropriate example. Firms in this sector had been rationalizing before the onset of the SMP, as a result of the second oil shock in 1979 and increased competition. From 1985 on the industry gradually experienced a new environment as the European market was opened up to other countries. The national quotas that member states had imposed on Japanese cars, extremely tight in some member states, were by an agreement of June 1990 to be gradually abolished in favour of a quota covering the entire European market. In the year 2000 the EC quota itself should also be removed.

Didier Salvadori in D G Mayes (ed.) *The European Challenge* has suggested that the SMP itself would help the car buyer in four specific ways. First, a reduction in the price of vehicles arising from a decrease in VAT to 15 per cent, by changes in manufacturers' own pricing policies as a result of intensified competition, and from a reduction in production costs caused by greater use of economies of scale in the SM and cheaper components. As the supply of cars in the European market is estimated to rise to 17 million a year in 1998, compared to 14 million in 1990, producers seem likely to face over-capacity and a price war could force down prices. Second, there is likely to be a reduction in the costs of running a car, as a result of harmonized road taxes and cheaper insurance when competition in the insurance sector intensifies. Third, the consumer will also benefit from increased choice. Fourth, after-sales service will improve, again due to increased competition. Similar pressure could well benefit the consumer in terms of consumer durables generally but also in daily purchases such as groceries, with supermarket stores such as Aldi competing across national frontiers by 1992.

On the free movement of workers the SMP promised some rather mixed progress. By 1989 a clear pattern was emerging: opportunities for working in other EC states increased in high-skill or service sectors and declined in unskilled or manual sectors. Many companies across the EC had by then begun to recruit experienced staff with special abilities to meet the demands of the single market. For example, Marks & Spencer announced in 1990 a 5-year expansion plan in Europe, and in seeking 300 graduates a year began to take stands at graduate fairs in Brussels, Amsterdam, Lyon, Toulouse and Paris. Other British firms actively recruiting in the EC included BP and KPMG Peat Marwick. But if the British were actively recruiting from other EC countries, the evidence was clear by 1993 that other EC states were recruiting a larger number of able, qualified people from the UK. In 1992 15 per cent of Cambridge University graduates chose other EC countries for their first job, reflecting the view of many talented young British people that salaries and living standards were superior in many partner states.

For workers from less rarified backgrounds the alleged free movement rights were irrelevant in a time of high unemployment, and at times a bad joke. Workers in some EC states, e.g. France and Belgium, still faced a single market of red tape rather than one of free movement, as national officials continued to impose many tedious regulations on incoming workers. At times such workers faced open hostility. In February 1993 Irish and British entrepreneurs travelled to the South of France, hoping to lay tarmac drives for local residents. Unfortunately they fell foul of French laws requiring their work to be registered and residency and tax forms to be produced. French police swooped on three teams working on the Riviera and made fourteen arrests. So much for EC free movement of workers in 1993! Nevertheless more services have begun to be operated across frontiers in the EC. For example, the French firms Sita and Cory-Onyx have won contracts to clean up streets from a number of local authorities in Britain.

One certain consequence of the SMP has been its impact on the level of foreign direct investment (FDI) in the EC. The Community is the world's largest trading bloc and the scale of the market, its political and economic stability and the prospect of continuing expansion attracted investment from around the globe. In 1991 FDI in the EC reached $65 billion, mainly from the USA and Japan (see Figure 4.1). Britain maintained its position as the largest single benefactor, gaining about one-third of the investment. Japan has almost twice as much investment in Britain as in other EC countries, while the British share of American investment in the EC amounts to more than the combined totals recorded by Germany, the Netherlands and France. The British government would claim that this was due to the UK's open free market, abolition of exchange controls and able flexible workforce. Critics point to government inducements and a cheap labour market unencumbered by laws protecting the workforce.

Such non-EC investment was not overwhelmingly concentrated in high technology but continued at a high level in traditional industries as well as in service sectors, such as banking. Whether such

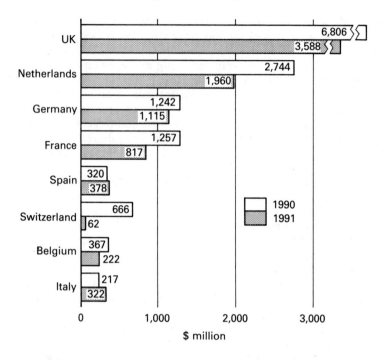

Figure 4.1   Japanese direct investment in Europe

levels of investment will be maintained in the future is open to question, as many multinationals have now made their principal investment in the EC and the European market has suffered such a recession in the early 1990s that it is less attractive for location by multinationals.

Such FDI is double-edged. In theory multinationals contribute new finance, the latest technology and more employment, while at the same time boosting the EC's exports and the quality of management techniques. At times, however, such companies avoid fair levels of taxation, retain their technology and destroy jobs by forcing competitors out of business.

The growing threat from multinationals was merely one aspect of the challenge of the SMP, which has forced through a transformation in attitudes. Many companies now think European and regard the building of mergers and joint ventures with other companies across the EC as essential for survival. The *Financial Times* in January 1993 described the 3-year-old alliance between Renault and Volvo, the French and Swedish car and truck makers, as a classic industrial response to the competitive challenges and opportunities of the single market. When the pair exhanged minority stakes in 1990, they cited as reasons the growing competition in the industry, the costs of stringent environment rules and the increase in investment needed to keep pace with technology. The purpose of their collaboration was to share these burdens by spreading the costs and ultimately working towards a full merger. The first step in 1990 was the creation of a joint car and truck research centre in France to study joint components like gearboxes. Another early step was the establishment of joint component purchasing committees, which in June 1992 evolved into formal joint ventures to represent both companies to their main suppliers. This could save both companies a lot of money, as they buy 15 per cent of their components from common suppliers. The partners also agreed to exchange some car engines, saving Renault an estimated 1 billion francs in its development costs in 3 years. On the marketing side the pair partially merged their French car and light commercial vehicle sales divisions in 1992. Finally, in September 1993 came a formal full merger.

Another example of collaboration was the creation in 1989 of GEC Alsthom, one of Europe's big three power engineering and transportation equipment groups. The company was formed from the power and transportation product businesses of the UK's GEC and France's CGE. It was recognized that Europe was the company's home market, with 60 per cent of sales in the EC. Concentration on four specialist units in steam turbines and generators to derive the benefits from joint R and D and volume manufacture has led to the development of a European product as opposed to an exclusive British or French turbine generator. The European base has been expanded by acquisitions outside the two home countries, e.g. boilermakers in East Germany and firms in the Spanish rail transport industry.

The service sector was well represented in this growing European awarness. A prime example was the 1989 acquisition of Morgan Grenfell by Deutsche Bank, Germany's largest bank. Deutsche Bank had been slow to expand outside Germany but wished to overcome its heavy dependence on the national market and become a truly European bank in the commercial and investment sectors. By acquiring an investment house like Morgan Grenfell, with its skills in equities, Deutsche Bank became overnight a major player in investment management.

Such acquisitions became a veritable mania in the late 1980s as the spur of the single market took effect. In 1987 Cadbury Schweppes, the British chocolate and soft drinks group took over Chocolat Poulain, the French chocolate manufacturer based at Blois on the Loire. The move was motivated by a desire to expand into the French confectionery market, where Cadbury had historically a small presence and where Chocolat Poulain had been established since 1848.

However, French companies were particularly active in making acquisitions in other EC states, encouraged by French banks and the French government. In 1989 alone French nationalized industries made forty European acquisitions worth £2 billion. The French government played a key role in pushing French companies into this strategy, because it hoped to increase France's industrial power in the single market by such a recourse. In 1989, for example, the French state-owned group Rhone Poulenc bought RTZ chemicals, Orphen acquired both Coates Brothers and Northernchem, and Usinor-Sacilor pounced on Howard E Perry. The French private sector followed the public sector lead. In 1990 Bernard Tapie's Donnay tennis racquet and Look ski-binding firm acquired the world's leading sports goods manufacturer, Adidas of West Germany.

One of the areas most greatly affected by the SMP was financial services. Early influences appeared to favour the increasing domination of London as the leading stockmarket in the EC. It had been helped by deregulation (Big Bang) in the 1980s to become more competitive, and by 1991 was winning business from continential stock markets such as Paris and Frankfurt. By 1991 fifty-four securities firms (of which only seven were British) decided to co-locate in London, creating a snowball effect. As Stephen Parker explains:

> 'It is almost impossible to emulate the culture, the outside services and the development that follows from this concentration. Once costs have been sunk, and the benefits of deregulation and new technology start translating into falling costs and stimulated demand, so London can expect to benefit from increasing returns to scale.'

Already London was the EC's leading fund management centre in terms of insurance and pension funds, the main location for the very institutions that were looking for new investment opportunities and the most efficient location. Naturally other European stockmarkets were determined to compete with London. From 1987 the Paris Bourse was experiencing its own Big Bang and became a much more dynamic market as activities there were liberalized and foreign companies no longer excluded. However, only British exclusion in the future from any single currency area seemed likely to pose a serious threat to London's domination (see final chapter).

If competition increased in securities, then the same was abundantly the case for other financial services, as banks, building societies and insurance companies europeanized their activities. British firms were soon active in building bases in other EC states to exploit the single market. Abbey National, which had set up in Brussels in 1979, opened up offices in Italy and Spain by 1989. These choices were conditioned by the fact that in both countries mortgage and consumer debt in relation to income were low and bank profitability high. Traditional British building societies, such as the Halifax and Woolwich, carried out a similar strategy.

British banks were also active in putting into place an infrastructure of joint ventures with European partners. Hambros, a leading London merchant bank, signed a number of joint-venture agreements with continental banks to enable it to extend its services across the EC. Between 1987 and 1991 it set up agreements in Holland, Germany, Italy and Portugal. The major commerical banks created a range of services for British businesses operating in the single market and also built links with foreign banks. Lloyds signed co-operation agreements with Crédit Agricole in France, Banco Ambrosiano Veneto in Italy, Bayerische Vereins bank in Germany and Rabobank in the Netherlands. The banks at the same time established branches in other member states; National Westminster by 1991 had branch networks in Spain, Germany and Greece, and representation in a further ten European states. Similar enterprise was shown by insurance and pensions companies, with a medium-sized company like Equitable Life establishing branches in Ireland and going hard for the German market by establishing a head office in Cologne and branch offices in Hamburg and Munich by 1992.

The extent of the single market in financial services must not be overestimated. The legal framework may be in place but genuine liberalization will take years or decades to develop. Genuine cross-border trading in insurance is still some way off. Insurers in different countries operate under different tax rules. Most continental countries allow insurers much more freedom to build up tax-free reserves than does the UK. Some life insurers must pay tax on premiums, while in some states they do not have this obligation. Penetration of some EC markets – especially in Germany, France and Italy – where retail networks are dominated by tied agents selling the products of one company rather than those of independent brokers will be difficult. Thus for some time the European insurance market will continue to be dominated by domestic companies, and so far UK companies have made little impact in it.

Barriers still remain in banking. Retail banking – providing services to individuals and small companies – is still mainly a domestic business. A range of cultural, tax and regulatory obstacles have prevented the creation of a true single market in this field. Consumers still prefer to bank with familiar institutions, and governments still act in a protectionist way. In 1992 Barclays attempted to get around a French government ban on interest-bearing current accounts by launching a new product in its French offices that combined a non-interest paying current account with an automatic sweep mechanism to shift a customer's surplus funds into a money market account. After complaints from French banks, which feared a loss of profits if they had to offer similar products, the French finance minister Michel Sapie announced in October 1992 a ban on automatic sweep mechanisms. Barclays was therefore deprived of the opportunity of marketing a product widely available in the rest of the EC, to the detriment of French consumers.

Such protectionism – practised in some form or other by all member states – threatened to undermine the effectiveness of the SMP and make the concept of a level playing field unattainable in practice. The vexed question of state subsidies remained a serious barrier in the 1990s. Some governments – particularly the French, Spanish and Italian – continued to give their ailing industries huge sums of money to enable them to exploit the wider market. Firms in countries where the governments were more free market in approach did not receive such help and had to struggle on their own. Michael Heseltine, the British President of the Board of Trade, summed up the problem in 1992 after the EC had allowed the French government to give aid of 6.6 billion francs to the French computer firm Compagnie des Machines Bull.

> 'The European competitors of Bull – including ICL – have all faced the need to respond to changes in the market place by radically restructuring their operations and carrying out significant research and development. They have funded this largely out of their own resources but now face the prospect of a major competitor being financed by its government to undertake the same tasks.'

When Leon Brittan was in charge of the EC's competition policy (see Chapter 5), state aid declined a little, but the recession of the early 1990s led to more industries falling back on state subsidies. Where state ownership exists, such help is easy to channel through grants and low cost financing. There are also other ways by which governments may covertly give aid. For example, artificially low pricing by utilities, a cornerstone of industrial policy in some EC states, serves as an indirect aid. A British company like ICI pays the market price for its electricity, while French rivals like Altochem can buy electricity from Electricité de France (EdF) at least 30–50 per cent below UK prices. Only huge subsidies from the French government enable EdF to charge such low prices.

A similar picture is revealed in the airlines industry, where state-owned airlines (see Figure 4.2) such as Air France, Sabena and Iberia have received much more direct aid than a privatized company like British Airways. Air France was able to take a controlling stake in the state-owned Czech airline CSA with the help of French state-owned banks and the European Bank for Reconstruction and Development, headed by Jacques Attali, the

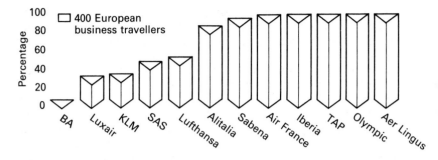

Figure 4.2 Extent of state ownership within EC

twin brother of Air France's chairman, Bernard Attali. Brotherly love is certainly alive and well in the EC!

Other examples of state aid to industry will be reviewed in Chapter 7.

The path to harmonization of technical standards was a thorny one, as publics throughout the EC were regaled with stories about the latest Commission gaffe in this area. The horror stories fell into three types. The first was where there was a fear of over-regulation by the Commission. In 1991 it was accused by Britain of trying to ban flavoured crisps, by France of trying to ban cheese made with non-pasteurized milk and by Denmark for threatening a ban on the Danes' small apples. In fact all three complaints were satisfactorily settled. Second, however, was when the Commission does *not* intervene, and it is accused of under-regulation by member states. The German government accused the Commission of dangerous liberalization in allowing inferior foreign beer to be sold in Germany. A third category of horror story is just plain misunderstanding, e.g. when in 1991 a story was circulated that Brussels was trying to standardize the size of European condoms in the interests of Aids prevention.

Such stories mask a real problem. While the Commission has worked through most of the technical harmonization measures in the SMP, every year each state produces thousands of new regulations concerning new products and technologies. If they affect the single market, they must be submitted to the Commission, as each one contains the seeds of a new barrier to trade. As one Commission official commented, 'Like buildings that need constant care, if we do not keep working on the single market, within five years it will be gone'.

Thus new national regulations will continue to block fair trade. In 1992 the Dorset MEP Bryan Cassidy pointed to the new threat posed by national enviornmental laws. In Germany 'green spot' laws, which required packaging to be recovered and recycled, favoured German companies because they were ready to meet the new rules, but non-German companies unable to meet the regulations were in danger of being excluded from the German market. Thus environmental standards, virtuous in themselves, operated as a technical barrier to trade.

Another shortcoming of the SMP lay in the failure to create a single law for companies. In 1970 the Commission proposed the European Company Statute to provide a single corporate structure for multinational companies in the EC. Instead of having to find their way round different national systems and set up a network of public limited companies around Europe, the multinationals would be able to establish a single SE (Societas Europaea) under Community law. Lawyers' fees would be cut, administrative problems banished and companies left free to pursue their business unchecked.

Unfortunately attempts since 1970 to construct a European Company Statute have foundered on the very national differences it hoped to eliminate. Even though it was added to the SMP, no agreement was in sight in 1993. Though the ECS would be voluntary, the principal obstacle has been the requirement for employee participation in the management of SEs. Britain is particularly opposed to such proposals, while Germany, which already has a strong tradition of employee participation, is in favour.

Other related directives on the harmonization of company law, such as the directive on cross-border mergers and the directive on takeover bids, also reached a position of stalemate. The whole question has perhaps ceased to be a priority for the Commission and member states, because corporate restructuring developed without the aid of a harmonized European company law as mergers and acquisitions rose threefold between 1984 and 1989. Certainly in the recession of 1991–3 the need for the ECS receded as companies became less interested in cross-frontier deals.

In conclusion, it may be asserted that the SMP for all its shortcomings has brought in direct economies by removing many of the barriers to the free movement of goods, people, services and capital. It has stimulated more competition as companies attempt to exploit the economies of scale that the wider market will permit. Industrial turbulence has increased as firms collaborate, merge, acquire or get taken over in the process of increasing the scale of their operations.

Companies that have prepared well for the single market in terms of investment in new methods and products, training of staff and the building of cross-border links benefit most. In this regard a Dunn and Bradstreet survey of 771 small and medium-sized companies in November 1992 was hardly propitious for Britain. The survey revealed that 89 per cent of companies questioned did not fear European competition, 38 per cent had sought no advice on exporting and only 13 per cent had provided external training for their export staff. As the Director General of the Institute of Export, Ian Campbell, commented, such complacency was alarming.

Further reading

Cecchini, P, *The European Challenge*, Wildwood House, Aldershot, 1988.

Colchester, N and Buchan, D, *Europe Relaunched*, Hutchinson, London, 1990.

Dudley, J W, *Strategies for the Single Market*, Kogan Page, London, 1989.

Mayes, D (ed.), *The European Challenge: Industry's Response to 1992*, Harvester Wheatsheaf, London, 1991.

Owen, R and Dynes, M, *The Times Guide to 1992*, Times Books (Second Edition), London, 1990.

Urban, S and Vendemini, S, *European Strategic Alliances*, Blackwell, Oxford, 1992.

Questions

1 Why had euphoria over the single market programme declined by 1993?
2 What, in your view, are the most important pieces of legislation in the single market programme?
3 Has the consumer gained from the single market programme?
4 What impact on company strategy has the single market programme effected?
5 Critically examine the areas of failure within the single market programme.

5
Competition policy

The origins and rationale of competition policy

The origins of Community competition policy lie in Articles 65 and 66 of the ECSC Treaty and the roughly similar Articles 85 and 86 of the Rome Treaty. The provisions in both treaties owe much to the American experience in trying to control the large trusts in the United States, as, for example, in the Sherman Act of 1890. American thinking on trusts was indeed most influential during the formative years of the Community, when the prime concern was control of a resurgent and more concentrated German heavy industry.

The Community has always demonstrated particular interest in developing a competition policy with teeth, because of the continued process of concentration among firms in Community countries. A Commission report in 1973 illustrated this growth of concentration. Between 1962 and 1970 the annual number of mergers in the Community of the Six rose from 173 to 612 – an increase of 350 per cent. Since 1965 there had been an increase in the number of mergers in Britain, a process that was accelerating. The increasing interpenetration of capital had caused the share of the 100 largest firms to rise from 26 per cent in 1953 to 50 per cent in 1973 in Britain, and from 34 per cent in 1954 to 50 per cent in 1969 in Germany. In some sectors the concentration process had gone so far that only four manufacturers were left in the Community, but in many other industries a very high degree of concentration had developed, with the four largest firms controlling 80–90 per cent of sales or production. Obviously some firms enjoying such a degree of control might be tempted to abuse their power through practices that exploited or that limited fair competition.

Competition policy in the treaties

The concept of free competition is a fundamental element in the Rome Treaty, which embodies the premise that any restriction on free competition is intrinsically reprehensible. There are in practice some exceptions but the principle itself is that of positive general condemnation of any limits on competition.

Article 85(1) of the Treaty declares:

> 'The following shall be prohibited as incompatible with the Common Market: all agreements between undertakings, decisions by associations of undertakings and concerted practices which may affect trade between member states and which had as their object or effect the prevention, restriction or distortion of competition within the Common Market.'

The Treaty then goes on to illustrate the kinds of agreements that are prohibited by Article 85: those that directly or indirectly fix purchase or selling prices, those that limit production or result in the division of markets between competitors, and those that lead to particular customers being treated differently to others. It is important to remember that the list is illustrative and not exhaustive. The principles laid down in the article apply to any arrangement that offends against those principles whether they are mentioned or not, and they also apply not only to agreements that have as their object the restriction of competition but also to those that result in the restriction of competition.

All these types of agreement prohibited by Article 85(1) are under Article 85(2) held to be automatically void, but under Article 85(3) the Commission can declare the prohibition inapplicable to particular agreements. Examples of such agreements are those that contribute to the improvement of the production or distribution of goods, on those that promote technical or economic progress and allow consumers a fair share of the resulting benefit. However, such agreements must be unlikely to eliminate competition in much of the market for the goods in question.

Article 85 deals with agreements, between two or more parties, that constitute restrictive practices. Article 86 is concerned with the abuse by individual organizations of a dominant trading position enjoyed in the Community, that is to say monoplies. Article 86 of the Rome Treaty declares: 'Any abuse by one or more undertakings of a dominant position within the Common Market or in a substantial part of it shall be prohibited'. Again, as in Article 85, an illustrative list is given of the types of abuses that will be prohibited: directly or indirectly imposing unfair purchase or selling prices or other unfair trading conditions; limiting production, markets or technical development to the prejudice of consumers; applying dissimilar conditions to equivalent transactions with different trading partners; or imposing in contracts supplementary obligations on trading partners that have no real connection with the subject of such contracts. Article 86 is concerned essentially with the abuse of a dominant position in a particular market, but there is no condemnation of a large share of the market as such. It is only when the dominant position is used against the interests of the consumer or trade generally that the Commission will be concerned. In practice the abuse of a dominant position takes one or two forms. First, the firm in question adopts policies that hinder the development of other producers or suppliers who could be competitors. Second, in the absence of other competitors, a firm may use its power to adjust the production or price of its goods to the detriment of consumers.

Over the years many cases have gone to the Court of Justice under the competition laws, and these have created precedents and led to the evolution of certain general principles. One principle is that neither in their terms nor by the interpretation put on them are the rules narrowly drawn, and in many cases the Court has adopted a wide interpretation of the intentions of the firms concerned.

The first principle is, however, constrained by a second principle: the rules only apply to trade between member states. The Community competition rules are not concerned with restrictive practices or monopolies within one state alone that do not affect inter-state trade; the national law of the state concerned will deal with such cases. On the other hand, if two or more traders within one member state make an agreement that could affect trade between member states, they will be subject to the rules. Indeed those making the agreement may be from states outside the Community entirely, e.g. the United States, but if the agreements made have an effect on trade between member states of the Community, the competition rules will apply.

Indeed this leads on to the third principle – what counts is the effect of the agreements. The Commission is only concerned with agreements that have a serious adverse effect on free trade in the Community and may allow small agreements that affect only a small part of that trade.

The fourth principle is that the rules should be vigorously applied, and the Commission has gained considerable administrative powers to fulfil this function. The principal regulation that defines the Commission's powers in this field is Regulation 17, which was first put into force in 1962. It gives the Commission wide powers of investigation, including exclusive authority to grant exemption from Article 85(1): requires the co-operation of member states in the Commission's enquiries; and gives the Commission wide powers to insist on the amendment of agreements or their cancellation. These powers are backed by a power to levy fines on firms that fail to comply with Commission instructions. As soon as the Commission has begun an enquiry, the case is taken outside the national courts

– an important custom, as it ensures that the same rules are applied consistently throughout the Common Market.

Regulation 17 is designed to make the powers of the Commission immediately effective. The Commission may prohibit the continuation of any agreement, and that agreement must cease even though the parties concerned may intend to appeal to the European Court. It is therefore difficult for defendants to play for time and gain profitable breathing spaces. It they try to be unco-operative, companies can be fined for giving false or inadequate information.

The decision-making process

The Commission can be alerted to the existence of a potential breach of the rules in a number of ways. Sometimes, as in the case of Hoffman La Roche, an individual may contact the Commission. Sometimes competitors will complain about a firm's unfair practices. Often the Commission itself from its own studies will see good reason to begin an investigation.

One practice that has developed has been that of giving publicity to any Commission decision in an attempt to influence and educate the market as a whole. Indeed, to the annoyance of a number of firms, commissioners responsible for the competition rules have often called press conferences to inform the public of decisions actually made, the state of investigations in progress and indeed those about to begin. In 1982 the commissioner in charge of Competition Policy, the Dutchman Frans Andriessen, made it abundantly clear that the Commission would investigate why cars in Britain were a third dearer than those in other Community countries.

Competition policy is handled by DGIV and the legal service, and there is an advisory committee on Restrictive Practices and Dominant Positions, which has to be consulted. Care is taken over the initial stages of investigation, and consultation also takes place, with the whole Commission itself sitting as a collegiate body, because it is not necessarily the case that all the other work of the Commission is made easier by the application of the competition rules.

When an investigation is launched, the Commission is not required to ask for the co-operation of the company concerned. It can be brusque, enter premises of the company to examine books and other business records, take copies of extracts from these documents and ask for oral explanations on the spot. This is known as 'the dawn raid'.

Sometimes the Commission will, under Article 85(3), allow certain agreements to continue, either in their existing form or after some amendments recommended by the Commission. This procedure is called 'negative clearance' and is to be distinguished from exemption. Before an agreement can receive negative clearance, it must be notified to the Commission. If an agreement is kept secret and then the Commission stumbles across it, it cannot then be given negative clearance. There is therefore no incentive for firms to gamble on never being discovered, on the assumption that if they are, they may still obtain negative clearance. The term 'negative clearance' does imply very limited approval, and if circumstances change, the Commission may review the situation and revoke that approval.

There are a number of agreements that may secure exemption from the competition rules. These include small agreements that have little or no effect on trade generally, and sole agency agreements where the effect of such agreements is little different from the supplier having his own branch in the member state concerned. However, it should be noted that in 1985 the Competition Directorate (DGIV) brought in a new approach to complaints and notifications. This is reflected in the new form A/B for notification of agreements, which will require all parties to provide the Commission with considerably more information when notifying agreements than previously. The onus of providing background information on the notification in the new form A/B will shift from the Commission to the notifying business. Businesses wishing to complain must give additional information on the new form A/B on how in their opinion the notified agreement infringes competition rules, and businesses must specify those clauses they consider are restrictive of competition. The form also requires a description of the relevant market and an indication of the size and market share of the participating undertakings.

That Community competition policy has teeth has been demonstrated by its ability to take on some of the world's biggest companies in long-running battles, e.g. its joust with International Business Machinery (IBM). The Competition Directorate began an investigation of the marketing practices of IBM in 1974 after receiving complaints from five of IBM's competitors. One of the chief complaints was the IBM generated fear, uncertainty and doubt – known as 'fud' in industrial circles – by delaying making public the operating principles of the interface between software and computer hardware on its new 360 and 370 type computer systems. The Commission determined through its investigation that IBM, which controlled about two-thirds of Europe's market for mainframe computers, had abused its dominant position in a number of ways, including its failure to supply other manufacturers in sufficient time with the technical information needed to permit competitive products to be developed and used with System 370.

In August 1984 settlement of the case was reached, with IBM agreeing to provide within 4 months after the announcement of a new computer sufficient interface information to enable competing companies in the Community to attach both hardware and software products of their design to System 370. The agreement, due to last until at least 1990, gave the Commission new confidence in its ability to analyse and decide a complex competition issue involving firms with worldwide economic power.

The widening scope of competition policy: state aids and mergers

The Treaty of Rome refers to many aspects of competition, including patents, licensing agreements and trademarks; price descrimination and fixing; resale price maintenance; state aid; abuse of a dominant market position; dumping; quantitative restrictions on imports and exports; mergers and concentrations; and state undertakings. In practice the Commission has been most active in the four areas of restrictive practices, dominant positions, mergers and state aids.

Many aspects concerning restrictive practices and dominant positions have already been discussed. But in addition to restricting unfair competition caused by the trading practices of private firms, the Community has also developed rules that regulate state aid within the Common Market to Community-based industries, and the threat to markets posed by mergers.

State aids

State aids can result in an artificially low export price, and the consequences to industry in the country where such goods are sold are the same as those caused by dumped goods. Like products may become uncompetitive and the industry suffers injury. The 1979 Community regulation deals with state aids in a similar way to the way it deals with dumping. When a complaint is received, the Commission will investigate, and if it finds that goods have been subsidized, a countervailing duty may be imposed. Various practices are deemed to constituted indirect subsidies in a list that is illustrative, not exhaustive: currency retention schemes which give a bonus on exports, government-sponsored schemes for cheaper freight charges for exports, reduced taxes levied on exports, some export credit guarantee systems, and special low interest credit schemes sponsored by governments for exports.

In practice all countries give aid to their export industries, and the Community must be aware that it cannot succeed in stamping out such practices. All it can do is to attempt to reduce the more blatant forms of state aid. The Commission is particularly vigilant in trying to remove state aid from inter-state trade in the Common Market, because such an aim is a fundamental part of the Rome Treaty. Article 92 of the Treaty lays down that 'any aid granted by a member state or through state resources in any form whatsoever which distorts or threatens to distort competition by favouring certain undertakings or the production of certain goods shall, in so far as it affects trade between member states, be incompatible with the Common Market'.

The Commission has admitted that much direct or indirect aid of this kind has always been given by member states. In trying to control such aid it is swimming against a strong nationalist tide, because in a time of recession it is natural for member states to seek to encourage their own export industries.

Commission action is likely, then, to arouse resentment. For its part, the Commission has been prepared to pursue state aid of which it disapproved, and take the member state to the European Court if necessary.

Nevertheless the Community does tolerate state aid in a number of cases. Three types of aid are specifically deemed to be compatible with Article 92: (a) aid of a social character to individuals where no discrimination on basis of origin exists, (b) aid for national calamities and (c) aid to assist regions of the Federal Republic affected by the division of Germany. But in practice aid is also permitted to help underdeveloped regions, to promote projects with a European interest, and to develop certain regions. Massive aid in fact has been granted by states to declining industries and regions, and the Commission has found it difficult to control this area because of the level of aid and the difficulty of assessing its effect on the Community.

Mergers

The years after 1985 saw a wave of mergers in the European Community. However, such mergers could threaten the existence of competition in important markets by giving the newly merged company a dominant position. It was clear that national legislation was inadequate for the control of many of the new mergers, because they were often trans-frontier, whereas national legislation was confined to the territory of the individual member state.

The Commission had long wished to deal with the merger issue. As long ago as 1973 it had drawn up a proposal for tighter control of mergers, and in 1981 Frans Andriessen revived the proposal. However, it was only in December 1989, with Leon Brittan now in charge of competition policy that the Council of Ministers adopted a Commission proposal on the control of mergers. It came into effect in September 1990. Its purpose was to establish a clear-cut division between large mergers with a European dimension, where the Commission would have responsibility of vetting, and smaller mergers or mergers of a national character, where national authorities would still apply national controls.

The new Commission regulation applied to Community-wide mergers, which were defined by three criteria:

(a) A threshold of combined worldwide turnover for the companies concerned of at least 5 billion ECU. A turnover of this scale would reflect the financial and economic power of the participants.

(b) A threshold of Community-wide turnover of at least 250 million ECU for at least two of the firms merging. Thus only companies with a definite Community presence would be governed by the regulation.

(c) A trans-nationality criterion. If each of the parties concerned derived two-thirds of their Community business in one and the same member state, the merger would not be subject to Community control. This criterion was designed to exclude from Community control predominantly national mergers, which would be subject to national merger control.

The initial thresholds were set at rather a high level, perhaps because the Competition Directorate did not have sufficient staff to cope with a flood of merger cases. However, the Commission stated its intention of revising the thresholds downwards after 4 years, with the global threshold falling to 2 billion ECU and a corresponding fall in the Community threshold. Where the merger concerned strengthened a dominant position, this would be declared incompatible with the Common Market where it significantly impeded effective competition, whether in the Common Market as a whole or in a substantial part of it. Where no such impact on competition occurred, the merger would be deemed compatible with the Common Market and allowed to go ahead. The appraisal process took in various aspects of the merger concerned – the structure of the market, actual and potential competition inside and outside of the Community, the market position of the parties considering merger, the interests of consumers, and technical and economic advantages that might accrue from the merger.

Companies considering merging were obliged to give the Commission prior notification, after which the Commission was to operate under strict time limits. It had one month after notification in which to decide whether to initiate proceedings, so that where it saw no objection, the parties would receive the green light to go ahead promptly. If an investigation into the proposed merger was mounted, the Commission had 4 months in which either to approve or block the merger. During the investigation period the companies concerned could propose changes in the merger arrangements that would make the merger more acceptable to the Commission. Given the small numbers in the Competition Directorate's executive staff, such stringent time limits appeared to be a heavy additional burden on already overstretched officials, but longer time limits could lead to unreasonable delays for companies attempting to develop appropriate strategies for the single market or for facing strong competitors from Japan or the USA.

Where the Commission decided that the merger fell within the scope of the new merger law, then it took control. Member states were not to apply their national competition laws to such cases except for minor exceptions. Thus there would be no parallel proceedings. When Gordon Borrie, the British Director-General of the Office of Fair Trading, indicated in September 1990 that his department wished to maintain an interest in all merger proposals that might affect fair competition, Leon Brittan insisted that the Commission's new powers under the new merger regulation would override the powers of merger referral retained by member states.

Problems of competition policy

Competition policy has three established objectives. As the Commission has stated, it aims to keep the Common Market 'open and unified', i.e. to create a single market for the benefit of industry and consumers. Secondly it must 'ensure that at all stages of the Common Market's development, there exists the right amount of competition'. By ensuring some degree of commercial rivalry, the Community can help European industry to be competitive in world markets, as the competition will encourage firms to rationalize and change. The third objective is to ensure that competition is subject to 'the principles of fairness in the market place', by which the Commission means 'equality of opportunity for all operators in the Common Market'. In practice this means preventing companies from setting up restrictive agreements and cartels or from abusing a dominant position.

These principles are not always easy to accommodate together. The Commission itself has recognized that 'competition carries within it the seeds of its own destruction', because a free market may result in a concentration of economic power in the hands of those firms that have proved most efficient and have been able to put competitors out of business or take them over.

Competition policy also seems to clash with other Community policies. One objective of industrial policy has been to establish cartels to protect certain Community industries in difficulty. Other major policies, e.g. the regional and social policies, which aim at protecting weaker regions and weaker groups, seem difficult to reconcile with the objectives of competition policy.

There seem to be serious difficulties in the actual operation of competition policy. The process has been criticized as being excessively bureaucratic. Commission figures show that some cases can generate between 50 and 150 transmissions of drafts and notes. Not surprisingly an average case in the 1970s took from 3 to 4 years, and the Netherlands Cement case, which began in 1964 and was not concluded until 1972, is by no means unusual. The main reason for the length of time taken in each case is that proposals have to be passed along a lengthy chain within the Community machine several times before a decision emerges. In addition to this lengthy internal scrutiny, the Commission also has to hear the opinions of the firms concerned as well as the views of interested third parties, e.g. the national experts from the member states.

The sheer complexity of the cases imposes a formidable strain on the Commission, as the Continental Can decision demonstrated. The Continental Can Company, an American packaging firm, acquired, via its Belgian subsidiary, control of the largest German producer of packaging and metal boxes – Schmalbach-Lubeca-Werke AG of Brunswick. It later acquired a majority holding in a Dutch company, Thomassen and Drijver-Verblifa NV of Deventer, which was the leading manufacturer of packaging material in the Benelux countries. The Commission felt that these mergers produced such a dominant position for Continental Can that it constituted an abuse, a violation of Article 86. Continental Can, however, appealed against the Commission decision to the European Court. The Court delivered its decision in 1973. It agreed with the Commission's legal reasoning but found in favour of the company on the grounds that the Commission had got the facts of the case wrong.

This decision highlighted a major weakness in operating Competition Policy, since the Commission lost the case because it showed inadequate understanding of the market it wished to regulate. It may be relatively easy to identify the degree of concentration among firms in a given market but it is much harder to analyse the behaviour of those firms to decide whether they are acting in the best interests of the Community. Some industries with research and development costs may need a high degree of concentration to perform efficiently, and to deal with such cases requires expert economic judgement. It is impossible to apply a set of general rules, and some criticism has been levelled at the calibre of Commission personnel, who are accused of being too bureaucratic, of lacking a sophisticated grasp of economic realities, and even of ignoring infringements of the rules in politically sensitive areas. Perhaps the essence of the problem here is that the competition department is understaffed, with only about seventy-five executive members.

Other criticisms have been levelled at competition policy. The *Economist* in April 1981 accused the Commissioners in charge of competition policy of being too timid, and hoped that the new Commissioner, Frans Andriessen, would adopt a more aggressive approach. Certainly the fines imposed by the Commission have been until recently too small. It was only in 1979 that it first imposed a really big sum when Pioneer, a Japanese hi-fi company, was fined 4.65 million ECUs (£2.5 million). But although this was the highest fine ever imposed, it still represented only 4 per cent of the firm's sales turnover, well short of the 10 per cent maximum. As the *Economist* put it, if the fines are to make any real impact, they must make sin unprofitable. In addition, appeals to the European Court by firms are too cheap. Firms can, by appealing, often make enough from the interest on unpaid fines to finance a long case.

The Commission has even been accused of being too chauvinist. American companies have felt particularly aggrieved, alleging that when Directorate IV wishes to assert itself, it decides to harass a large non-European firm rather than looking at European culprits. But perhaps the explanation for this is that the culprits are often the American multinationals anyway!

A more just criticism is that the Directorate has dragged its feet in areas that are politically sensitive, at least until Peter Sutherland became Competition Commissioner in 1985. One glaring example has been the high European air fares, where attempts to offer cheaper flights in the 1980s by independent air lines such as British Caledonian and Laker were thwarted by governments that refused to grant landing licences. The Commission has also been slow in forcing governments to open up purchasing by their telecommunications monopolies. But the chief example here remains the vexed question of state aids. By the 1980s governments had become greater enemies of free competition than private companies. As unemployment has mounted, all governments have increased aid to keep tottering firms in business. The Commission has the power to forbid governments giving out aids if it thinks such action will distort Community competition, and it has successfully controlled member states' own regional policies and prevented regional aids from being applied to too large a part of each country. But in many other areas it has backed away from challenging the aids given, chiefly in the declining industries and in agriculture. All the Commission has been able to do in these cases is to negotiate the size and scope of the aids.

Competition policy in action after 1985

European Community competition policy depends for much of its effectiveness on the beliefs, political skills and determination of the

Commissioner in charge of the Competition Directorate. The Community was fortunate to possess two outstanding individuals, who after 1985 brought a new impetus to Competition Policy.

Peter Sutherland, the Irish Commissioner, superintended the Competition Directorate from 1985 to 1988. A one-time prop forward for Dublin's Lansdowne rugby club and Ireland's attorney-general, he was not afraid to tackle sensitive areas that previous competition commissioners had rather avoided, especially areas where national governments were the culprits. A classic example of this was the cartel formed by European airlines, often state-owned, which kept out competition and maintained high prices. The problem of fair competition in the airlines industry was compounded by the arrangements over state aid to the industry. Such state aid was not vetted by the more rigorous Competition Directorate but came within the portfolio of the Transport Directorate, which adopted an easier stance over state aid. When in July 1992 Air France received a cash injection of 170 million ECU from Banque Nationale de Paris, the French state bank, the transport Commissioner, Karel Van Miert, accepted the hand-out as a 'normal financial transaction' to the dismay of Air France's competitors.

Sutherland bluntly called the airlines 'the most antiquated and anti-competitive industry in Europe'. In 1987 he forced through certain limited reforms designed to start the breaking up of the airlines cartel, which had market-shared, fixed prices and barred entry to new airlines. These reforms provided for discounts of up to 45 per cent in normal economy class fares, limited the size of the market reserved for one country's airlines to 40 per cent and, most importantly, made it easier for new airlines to compete for business.

When Sutherland announced in 1987 that he would investigate the merger of British Airways and British Caledonia, Harry Goodman, Air Europe's chairman, who was lodging a complaint against the merger of his two much larger rivals, challenged Sutherland – 'I bet you don't have the guts to get involved in this one'. Goodman had mistaken his man. Sutherland intervened forcefully in the merger; while it was allowed to go ahead, British Airways had to make significant concessions, in particular the surrender of many of British Caledonia's scheduled routes from prime airports such as Gatwick. The routes freed allowed smaller companies such as Air Europe, Dan-Air and Virgin Atlantic to achieve significant market entry and provide more competition.

However, airlines that wished to provide cheaper fares still faced a problem. They had to seek approval for their fares from governments at both ends of a route. Either government could object on the grounds that the fare was unrelated to the airline's costs and was therefore uneconomic. But the power of veto was often used simply to keep out foreign competition, which might erode the profits of that government's main airline, often a nationalized airline.

To counter the problem the Commission brought in new legislation in 1990. Airlines were now allowed to set fares approved by only one government on any route. However, the new law did not eliminate extortionate fares for business travellers in Europe. In November 1991 a British Airways club class return to Brussels cost £290, seven times the price of a flight from San Francisco to Los Angeles, a slightly longer trip. The explanation for such a discrepancy was simply that in the USA effective deregulation of the airlines had occurred in 1976, creating free competition. In contrast, on many European routes the main carrier still had only one competitor, usually charging the same price.

The Commissioner in charge of competition policy from 1989 to 1992 was Leon Brittan. His career had seemed finished when he resigned as Secretary of State for Trade and Industry over the Westland Helicopters affair, a scandal related to the potential purchase of Westland by a US–Italian consortium. However, as Brittan became one of the most active and respected of the Commission team, his career enjoyed a resurgence. The basis of his political belief was a commitment to the benefits of the free-market system. As he expressed it, 'effective competition not only ensures the most efficient allocation of resources, but provides the stimulus for efficiency, innovation and, most important of all, the widest possible choice for consumers'. In his view the establishment of rules within which competition could flourish was vital if the single market was to work properly.

Brittan enjoyed his period as Competition Commissioner, possessing more power than he had as a British minister. As he said in 1990, 'I am independent now. I can't be sacked by Mrs Thatcher or for that matter by Mr Delors'. An able man, he used his experience at Westminster to good effect. He proved clever at lobbying fellow commissioners to gain support for his actions, helped by his fluency in German and French. He was not afraid to offend vested interests by engaging in vigorous battles with more interventionist commissioners, such as Jacques Delors, or governments of member states. 'If you are afraid of being unpopular', he opined, 'you can't achieve anything worthwhile.'

Like Sutherland before him, Brittan attacked illicit state aids and mergers that might affect fair competition in the European market. In so doing, he had to be seen to be absolutely even-handed, because the governments of other member states (especially Italy and France) could be easily convinced of an alleged pro-British bias on his part. In fact Brittan wished to wage war on illicit state aid in general, but the issue was complicated by the fact that Community governments varied widely in the amount of state aid they gave. In

1986 Italy gave 13.2 billion ECU of aid to its manufacturing sector, a figure almost five times the amount given by the United Kingdom, two and a half times the French figure and almost double the expenditure incurred by West Germany. Each year the Competition Directorate had about 370 new cases of state aid to consider and, hardly surprisingly, a number of the cases related to Italy. In 1989, for example, Brittan ordered the Italian government to recover 615 billion lire given in 1985 to Finmeccanica, which then owned the loss-making car company Alfa-Romeo. The Italian government was charged 'with keeping Alfa-Romeo artificially alive in a period of over-production without any serious restructuring so that competition in the Community was seriously distorted'.

In a number of other cases Brittan showed real determination. The capacity of the Commission to fine heavily was amply demonstrated in the Tetra-Pak case. In July 1991 this Swiss-based packaging company was fined 75 million ECUs for abusing its dominant position in breach of Article 86. Following a complaint from Elepak, one of Tetra-Pak's main competitors, the Commission concluded that Tetra-Pak had carried out a deliberate policy of eliminating actual or potential competitors in the aseptic and non-aseptic markets in machinery and cartons. Tetra-Pak's restrictive use of contracts enabled it to segment the European market and therefore charge prices that differed between member states by up to about 300 per cent for machines and up to about 50 per cent for cartons. Evidence gathered during the Commission's enquiry also showed that, at least in Italy and the United Kingdom, Tetra-Pak sold its 'Rex' non-aseptic products at a loss for a long time in order to eliminate competitors.

The chemicals industry has long been steeped in a cartel culture, a tradition that reaches back to the interwar period. At that time the British company ICI, the German company I G Farben and the American Dupont agreed to a market-sharing arrangement by which I G Farben would not face competition from its cartel partners in Europe, Dupont would monopolize the North American market and ICI would monopolize the British Empire. In the postwar years giant chemical companies such as ICI and Solvay operated cartels in a number of areas of business – in soda-ash (a raw material used for making glass), in polypropylene, in PVC (polyvinylchloride) and in plastic film. Since the 1960s the Commission had sought to take action against such cartels by launching a series of dawn raids on the premises of Europe's giant chemicals companies. During the 1980s evidence of well organized price-fixing cartels was found, and these clearly distorted competition. In 1990 ICI was fined a total of 23 million ECU for participating in the soda-ash, PVC and polypropylene cartels. In the case of the soda-ash cartel Solvay and Chemische Fabrik Kalk (CFK) were also found guilty, but ICI's partners in other cartels have included Shell and the German companies BASF and Hirscht.

A contentious example of state aid was provided by Renault. In 1988 the French government wished to write off 12 billion francs of debt owed by Renault, the state-owned car company. This decision was challenged by Peter Sutherland as an unfair subsidy. The argument rumbled on until Leon Brittan became Competition Commissioner, and in May 1990 he ordered Renault to pay back 6 billion of the illicit aid to the French government. Two-thirds of this amount was to be paid immediately to the French Treasury.

The dispute was a sensitive one, partly because of Renault's historic importance as an industrial leader during France's postwar economic recovery and also because it had led the way in wage and social policies, being the scene of some of France's most heated industrial disputes since the war. The case led to a campaign against Brittan in the French press, typical articles carrying headlines such as 'Brittan: le mangeur de grenouilles' (eater of frogs) or 'the free-market ayatollah'.

The Renault judgment aroused such animosity that it behoved the Competition Directorate to be equally tough when a similar case was examined in June 1990 – the British Aerospace purchase of the Rover car group. In 1988 the British government sold the ailing Rover group to British Aerospace for £150 million, and was alleged to have sewn up the deal with secret 'sweeteners' or inducements. These included a tax-advantageous delay in paying the purchase price and a £9.5 million subsidy towards the cost of buying out Rover's remaining shareholders. Rover's debts of £800 million were also to be written off.

In 1988 Peter Sutherland forced the British government to make a cut of £331 million in the debt write-off on the grounds that this constituted a disguised and unfair subsidy. When Leon Brittan took over as Competition Commissioner, he decided in June 1990 that the other 'sweeteners' in the purchase constituted illicit state aid to the value of £44.4 million, and ordered the British government to recover this amount. British Aerospace decided to appeal to the European Court against the judgment and in January 1992 the Court ruled that the company should not repay the £44.4 million. It did not disagree with the reasoning behind the Competition Directorate's decision but stated that the Directorate had not followed the correct procedures. Accordingly, in March 1992, the Competition Directorate decided to pursue its demand for the repayment by British Aerospace, on this occasion using the correct procedure.

It was during Brittan's period as Competition Commissioner that the 1990 merger law came into operation. The new law was soon tested in the de Havilland affair. In September 1991 the French company Aerospatiale and the Italian company Alenia attempted to acquire the Canadian aircraft manufacturer de Havilland. The deal would have given the merged organisation a 69 per cent share of the European market in the manufacture of small jet aircraft, a situation the Commission considered as affecting competition. Therefore Brittan, with the backing of Jacques Delors, blocked the proposed merged after gathering information from the three companies taking part in the merger, their competitors, such as British Aerospace and Fokker, their customers and experts.

The decision led to a chorus of protest from French and Italian politicians, including the French prime minister, Edith Cresson. It was strongly hinted that a British Commissioner was favouring British industry by allowing British Aerospace an opportunity to buy de Havilland, though in fact British Aerospace, a company with real problems in 1991–2, had neither the intention nor the capability of buying it. It was also affirmed that Brittan was damaging European interests by his doctrinaire vision of competition, which was preventing the formation of large strong European companies capable of withstanding global competition.

The row highlighted several issues. In addition to the ever-present question of a Commissioner's neutrality or national bias, it was argued by governments and pressure groups that an unelected body such as the Commission should not have the power to decide crucial industrial matters against the wishes of the national governments of member states. Furthermore the de Havilland affair raised again the debate between those who favoured an interventionist European industrial policy, such as Martin Bangemann, the Industrial Commission, and those, like Leon Brittan, who believed in a free-market approach.

Further reading

El Agraa, A M (ed.), *The Economics of the European Community*, Allan (Third Edition), London, 1990.
Harrop, P, *The Political Economy of Integration in the European Community*, Edward Elgar, London, 1989.
Steiner, J, *A Textbook of European Law*, Blackstone, London, 1990.
Swann, D, *Competition and Industrial Policy in the European Community*, Methuen, London, 1983.
Swann, D, *The Economics of the Common Market*, Penguin (Seventh Edition), Harmondsworth, 1992.

Questions

1 Why is a strong competition policy required in the EC?

2 Explain the importance of Articles 85 and 86 of the Rome Treaty.
3 Describe the powers of the Commission in dealing with contraventions of the competition rules.
4 What are the chief obstacles to an effective Community competition policy?
5 Discuss the achievements of Peter Sutherland and Leon Brittan as
  Competition Commissioners between 1985 and 1992.

6
The Common Agricultural Policy

The underlying problems of agriculture

At the time of the signing of the Rome Treaty too many people in the original Six depended on farming for their main source of income; indeed 25 per cent of the total labour force was employed in agriculture, compared to less than 5 per cent in the United Kingdom. The British did not face such problems, because farms in Britain had been restructured by the enclosures of the eighteenth century, while the repeal of the Corn Laws in 1846 had drastically exposed agriculture to the cold winds of competition and cheap food from overseas after 1873. These developments had pushed workers out of British agriculture, but at the same time the process of industrialization attracted rural workers into the factories, where they could gain higher wages.

Such factors had not operated to the same degree on the Continent, where the agricultural labour force remained worse off than most groups. Many farms were uneconomically small: about two-thirds of farms were between 1 and 10 hectares in size, compared to one-third in the United Kingdom. Those who worked on the land were subject to forces that were often beyond human control. The effects of drought, flood or livestock disease could result in smaller production than hoped for by the farmers. On the other hand, favourable conditions could result in production far in excess of that planned by farmers. When actual agricultural output deviated from planned output, fluctuations in agricultural prices resulted, with the individual farmer liable to lose out either way. Excess output reduced the prices the farmer could obtain, but though a shortage in output increased prices, the individual farmer would often not have much to sell. Thus a sort of Catch 22 situation arose.

Other factors militated against acceptable living standards in farming. In advanced economies, as his income rose, the consumer tended to spend a smaller proportion of it on agricultural products.

In economist's jargon, the income elasticity of demand for food was low. Therefore in Western Europe there was a historical tendency for a relative fall in demand for farm products, with farming incomes lagging behind the incomes of groups engaged in non-farming occupations. In addition, as agriculture became more efficient, the supply of food increased, but this tended to keep agricultural prices down, especially when the competition from outside Europe, e.g. cheap American grain, became fierce from the 1870s on.

It was partly for these reasons that the founding fathers of the Community felt it necessary to introduce agricultural stabilization policies. It was believed that farm prices should be stabilized and farm incomes raised to the national average on grounds of equity, especially as increases in agricultural productivity were not normally as great as in manufacturing. Strategic considerations also affected the statemen's thinking in the 1950s; it was believed that reliance on supplies of foreign food in an uncertain world was unwise. Finally, practical political interests helped to bring about the adoption of important safeguards for agriculture in the Rome Treaty. The French government, influenced by its powerful farming lobby, agreed to free trade in industrial goods, which would help West German industrial exports to France, only if French farmers could be materially assisted to boost their agricultural exports to West Germany. Therefore in 1957 it was agreed under Article 38 of the Treaty that the development of a common market for agricultural goods should be accompanied by the establishment of a Common Agricultural Policy.

The aims of the CAP

Articles 38 to 45 of the Treaty of Rome were designed to ensure that a common market could extend to agriculture and agricultural products. Article 39 set out the aims of the CAP: (*a*) to increase agricultural productivity by developing technical progress and by ensuring the rational development of agricultural production and the optimum utilization of the factors of production, particularly labour; (*b*) to ensure, thereby, a fair standard of living for the agricultural population, particularly by the increasing of the individual earnings of persons engaged in agriculture; (*c*) to stabilize markets; (*d*) to guarantee regular supplies; and (*e*) to ensure reasonable prices in supplies to consumers.

It can be seen that these objectives are mutually contradictory as El Agraa has pointed out:

> 'Any policy which aims at providing adequate environmental conditions, secure food supplies and agricultural incomes equal to the national average interferes with the economy's natural develop-

ment ... the provision of stable farm incomes, let alone rising farm incomes, is not compatible with the promise of stable agricultural prices'.

Perhaps sensibly the Treaty of Rome left unresolved the detailed methods by which these incompatible goals were to be achieved, but Articles 40 to 47 pointed to the need for common competition rules, market organization and price policy; the setting up of the European Agricultural Guarantee and Guidance Fund (EAGGF, often known by its French initials FEOGA); joint research; consumption and promotion measures; and the granting of aid.

It was left to the Commission to put flesh on the skeleton. This took from July 1958 to December 1960, when the Council adopted the fundamental principles of CAP. The main components are, first, a single market, implying common prices, harmonization of relevant legislation and free movement of produce, and, second, Community preference, implying protection of the single market from world fluctuations through a levy system. When world market prices are lower than those of the Community, a variable charge or levy brings the price of produce imported from third countries up to the level of common prices. This makes possible free access to the Community market without disturbing European farmers. When Community prices are below the world market, the system can go into reverse so as to protect European consumers by discouraging exports. In times of shortage the Community also protects consumers by lifting import levies temporarily. The third component was common funding of the CAP by the EAGGF.

The operation of CAP really falls into two areas: price policy and policies to improve the structure of Community agriculture.

The price policy and the green currencies

The price policy is concerned with fixing internal prices for EC farmers. Separate price levels or regimes are established for most major products, and they are decided annually by the Council of Ministers. For each product covered by CAP, a common market organization has been introduced, and it aims at fixing a common price for each commodity throughout the Community. In the absence of a common European currency, common prices were expressed in agricultural units of account (UA), because the EC did not wish to make any particular country's currency seem to be more important than any other. It was not an actual currency but a common measure of value of agricultural products. The initial value of the UA was equivalent to one United States dollar or 0.888670888 grams of fine gold.

A target price level representing a desired market price is set for most products annually. Should the market price fall, a 'floor' price (or intervention price) for selected major products becomes operative in the domestic market. In the event of surplus production, commodities may be bought by intervention agencies to maintain a minimum wholesale market price level.

A common barrier operates in the form of minimum import prices (threshold prices) set annually for goods from third countries. Variable import levies compensate for the difference between fixed Community prices and fluctuating world prices. This protects the Community market from price fluctuations and from competition from low-priced imports. In the event of an EC surplus in a particular commodity the relevant management committee may authorize subsidies on exports of that commodity to third countries. This export subsidy allows Community-produced goods to be competitive in world markets even though EC domestic agriculture prices are usually above world prices.

The negotiation of prices is subject to an established procedure. The Director-General for Agriculture in the Commission works out a draft proposal with the help of experts from national governments. The draft is submitted for discussion to farmers' representatives, e.g. COPA (Comité des organisations professionelles agricoles de pays de la Communauté economique européenne), which is the federation of all farmers' unions and the representative of the farming lobby. The Economic and Social Committee and the Agricultural Committee of the European Parliament are also consulted. The proposal, which may be amended at any stage, is finally submitted to the Council of Ministers for decision before implementation by the Commission and member governments. The annual price review as a regulation is legally binding on all members states.

From 1962 responsibility for financing common measures was vested in the European Agricultural Guarantee and Guidance Fund (EAGGF). The Guarantee section has to finance price support measures and the Guidance section is concerned with structural reform. Up to 1971 the fund operated by reimbursing expenditure already incurred by member governments. Now estimates of future expenditure are submitted and member governments are awarded the necessary finance in advance. Expenditure on market support measures keeps increasing and far exceeds the revenue generated by CAP's duties and import levies. It is the major reason why by the 1980s the Community was finding it difficult to balance its budget.

During the 1960s it was possible to envisage the successful operation of the pricing policy in a period of stable exchange rates. However, in September 1968, in the 'French Revolution', the French franc was devalued, and in October 1968 the Deutsche Mark was revalued. When a country devalues, its farm prices in terms of national currencies rise (in 1968, for example, one UA became equivalent to more French francs). In addition, the price of imports rises and the price of its exports falls. In the case of a revaluation the opposite occurs. To prevent her enjoying the unfair competitive advantage of lower prices of her agricultural exports, France had to levy duties on those exports. To protect the French consumer from the higher price of agricultural imports, a subsidy called a Monetary Compensation Amount (MCA) was paid.

Revaluation reduced farm prices and incomes in Germany in terms of deutsche marks because one UA became worth fewer Deutsche Marks. The price of German food exports was increased and the price of food imports reduced, thus making German farmers vulnerable to competition from French farmers benefiting from the devalued franc. Border taxes were therefore levied on agricultural imports into Germany, while German agricultural exports received subsidies. This system of border taxes and subsidies (MCAs) became a regular feature of the CAP in the 1970s, owing to further charges in exchange rates by member countries.

This was the origin of the green currencies, which are the working currencies in the farm sector, and now each member has its own 'green' currency, e.g. the 'green' pound. Farm prices for producers are fixed in ECUs and then converted into national currencies at the 'green' currency rate. A 'green' pound therefore is used for buying farm products from EC countries or selling farm products to them. The 'green' currency or representative rate is fixed annually by the Council of Ministers, the decision requiring unanimous support, so that if a country does not want to change its green rate, it does not have to. For a time British governments refused to devalue the 'green' pound in line with the fall in sterling, so that the gap between the rate for the 'green' pound and the sterling market rate widened to more than 40 per cent by 1976. By using the 'green' pound Britain operated a dual exchange rate – the market rate for the great bulk of her purchases and the overvalued representative rate for her farm products. This meant that prices for British farmers were kept down while the British consumer benefited – at least until 1979.

The use of MCAs expanded in the 1970s in an effort to maintain unity of markets after all European currencies 'floated' in 1971 and were no longer tied by a fixed exchange rate to the US dollar. The UA itself remained tied to the US dollar until 1973; it was then re-valued, using an average of several European currencies (those of Germany, Denmark, Belgium, Luxembourg, the Netherlands and originally France – the 'Joint Float' currencies).

MCAs have allowed Community trade to continue in the absence of common pricing, but they have permitted the real level of prices to vary among member countries. They have allowed growing distor-tion of production as farmers in countries with strong currencies are paid more than farmers in countries with weak currencies. In addition, MCAs have taken an increasing share of the EC budget, about one quarter of the total expenditure of CAP. Nevertheless some elements of pricing unity remain. Changes in UA prices (now ECU prices) apply to all countries, and the Community can still give preference to its own producers as against third country suppliers. Attempts to end MCAs started in 1984 but were blocked.

The annual price-fixing exercise has posed major problems for the Community, and negotiations have often been most acrimonious, for several reasons. The exercise is itself difficult because it requires estimates of future production and markets. The tendency has been to fix prices that lead to overproduction rather than underproduction, so as to guarantee adequate supplies and give the small farmers a high enough level of prices. But the policy means transfer of income between member states, and those who gain from the policy, e.g. France, are anxious to resist charge, and those who lose, e.g. UK, demand reform. The individual governments are also influenced by the strength of the farm lobbies in their countries. Thus in 1981 the French government with an election in the offing held out for a substantial average 9.5 per cent increase in farm prices (higher than the average inflation rate expected among the Ten). The French farmers had made their feelings clear by demonstrations in Brussels and throwing rotten eggs at the conference building itself.

Another problem of the price-fixing exercise is the bias in the way the Guarantee section spends its money. Most of it has been spent on commodities produced in the northern sector of the Community, e.g. beef, cereals and milk products, whereas products from the Mediterranean zone have received relatively little support. Yet the southern region contains most of the poor farmers. The issue became more difficult in the 1980s when Greece, Spain and Portugal joined the Community.

Structural improvements in agriculture

In 1960 there were many small marginal farms in the Community. About half the 6 million farms were under 5 hectares, i.e. just over 12 acres, although many of the farmers were part-timers. In 1960 the average size was just under 11 hectares (just over 27 acres). During the 1960s the agricultural working population decreased by about one-third (c. 4 million people), but the agricultural sector did not streamline its structure in terms of size of farms.

In 1960 the Community set up a Guidance section in the agricultural fund to finance individual farm projects submitted by each member state and find solutions to specific problems in an individual state or on a Community level. The projects had to further the basic objectives of the CAP.

However, the agricultural structure showed little improvement by the late 1960s, and in 1968 Dr Sicco Mansholt, who was the Agricultural Commissioner at the time, brought out a memorandum on agricultural reform known as the Mansholt Plan. He emphasized that market supports by themselves would not solve the agricultural problem. His plan aimed (*a*) to reduce the number of people engaged in agriculture by offering older people early retirement benefits and offering younger people training and education so that they could opt for alternative jobs, and (*b*) at merging the larger number of uneconomic small farms to create larger farm units and also to reduce the area of cultivated land.

The plan encountered shocked criticism, and only in 1972 did the Council adopt a much watered-down version in the so-called Reform Directives. These directives were aimed at promoting farm modernizations, encouragement to specific farmers to leave farming and to allocate their land for the improvement of remaining holdings, and guidance and training for farmers.

These directives were, however, 'blanket' measures and were likely to create problems in poorer farming areas, e.g. rural depopulation. Therefore in 1975 a further directive was adopted on hill-farming to compensate farmers for the natural handicaps with which they have to contend. The aim was to persuade farmers to continue farming in these regions, but carry out modernization, keep the population at acceptable levels and conserve the countryside.

In 1978 certain measures were adopted to correct the bias in favour of northern products. These measures were called the Mediterranean 'package'. They included the provision of more finance in the Mediterranean regions for promoting better market structures, help for irrigation works in the Mezzogiorno, improvement of public amenities in certain rural areas, and the faster restructuring of vineyards in some Mediterranean regions of France. These measures demonstrated that one objective of CAP was now social. In 1985 Integrated Mediterranean Programmes (IMPs) were started to develop not only agriculture but also rural industry and infrastructure in Italy, Greece, Spain, Portugal and parts of France. Over 6 years a sum of 4.5 billion ECUs was available.

An evaluation of the CAP

The CAP is not without its defenders and successes. As Dennis Swann has pointed out, its original creation was an outstanding political achievement, and without such a developed common policy the EC would have become a less integrated institution. Its very existence gave the EC a forum for collective international policy-making.

In addition, the policy has allowed the various agricultural support systems that existed in EC countries before the formation of the Community to be replaced by a common, though complicated, system. To a certain extent intra-EC free trade in agricultural products has been achieved through the removal of intra-EC trade restrictions.

The EC has become more and more self-sufficient in many basic farm products, even though the Community depends a great deal on imported agricultural raw materials such as fertilisers and animal feed, i.e. the aim of secure food supplies has been achieved. By the late 1970s the EC enjoyed virtually complete self-sufficiency in pork, beef, veal and sugar, and complete self-sufficiency in wheat and butter production.

Some progress has been made in reducing the size of the agricultural population and in increasing the size of farm buildings. The proportion of the population engaged in agriculture in 1955 was 26.1 per cent; by 1976 the proportion for the enlarged Community was 8.4 per cent, with the number of persons engaged in agriculture falling from nearly 18 million (for the Six) to 8.3 million (in the Nine).

If it is argued that this is still too large an agricultural sector, then one may counter by saying that agriculture should not be seen merely in economic terms but in terms of political and social considerations. It provides employment and can help to retain a pleasant environment; this justifies protection, especially when most eminent competitors like Japan and the United States protect their agricultural sectors. Therefore the Community should continue to help the small farmers of France, Germany and Italy. Southern Italy, for example, has been called the Third World of European agriculture; farmers there are often desperately poor and excluded from the cash economy. There is no alternative employment nearby when towns like Naples suffer unemployment rates of 20 per cent. It can be argued therefore that it is better to keep such farmers going to offset urban overcrowding and prevent rural depopulation. Directives dealing with mountain and hill farming in disadvantaged areas mean that special provision can be made for poor farmers.

Finally, in this survey of the advantages of the CAP, some comments of a former commissioner for the internal market, Karl-Heinz Narjes, may be relevant. In October 1981 he pointed out that by the end of the 1990s there would be twice as many people in the world as in 1957. Developing countries by then would have a grain deficit of 100 million tonnes and would need to raise their agricultural production by 4 per cent per year merely to meet their most pressing needs. As their current rate of increase of agricultural production is only 2.9 per cent, a world food crisis seems imminent.

In the view of Narjes such considerations justified a protected European agriculture that guaranteed security of supplies.

In this connection the CAP has been successful in that its protection has spurred a dramatic growth in agricultural productivity. European farmers have had the confidence to make use of improvement grants and technical aid to become competitive with continents blessed with more sun and land. By 1984 the average Euro-cow yielded twice as much milk as it did in 1957. Quality had also improved as the organization of product markets was now virtually complete. This had enormous consequences for harmonization in the food-processing industry. For example, common standards now existed for conditions under which animals were slaughtered as well as for the grading of grains and eggs.

Against the alleged advantages can be ranged a formidable array of problems and failures. The CAP has failed to achieve real progress on structural aspects. For example, even though the drift from the country to the town is a natural one, it is hard to see how the CAP has encouraged farmers to seek alternative occupations. Many farmers on low incomes have indeed preferred to stay in farming because they are remote from alternative employment and because they have some status and property in their own community. And though their income may be poor, their land has appreciated, at least until the 1980s, making them relatively rich in terms of capital. Many farmers are old and find it harder to retrain or adjust to urban life, and there are still too many marginal farms, especially in the south of the EC.

Though the CAP has helped to raise the general level of farm incomes, there are some very unsatisfactory features. The CAP is a policy of high prices, and therefore those who produce most gain the most benefit from the policy. However, farmers in poor areas produce little and derive little benefit from the policy. Thus the CAP makes rich farmers richer and increases regional income disparities.

The CAP has also given greater support to products produced in the north than in the south. Livestock and cereals have received more support than fruit, vegetables and wine. In terms of fairness this is unfortunate, because many of the farmers in the south (the Midi in France, the Mezzogiorno in Italy) have very low incomes and depend heavily on products that receive the least support.

In global terms the CAP can be seen as undermining the interests of the Third World. By disposing of surpluses to countries behind the Iron Curtain, the EC deprived the developing countries of potential export earnings. And by protecting its own agriculture, the EC has competed unfairly against the imports from these countries. In this context it should be remembered what a massive exporter of food the Community has now become. It has been the world's chief exporter of dairy produce and sugar, the world's second largest exporter of beef behind Australia, and the world's largest exporter of poultry. Europe's subsidies have so undermined the price on international markets that the world sugar industry has suffered its worst slump since the 1930s in recent years.

The CAP has failed to provide reasonable stable prices for the consumer. Indeed the initial prices were set at the high German level of farm prices. The consumer who is hit worst by this high food price policy is the poor consumer, because he has to spend a higher proportion of his income on food than has a wealthy consumer. A policy that increases the price of food therefore represents a higher proportional tax on the expenditure of the poor, even though the total amount of tax collected per head will be higher from a rich family than from a poor family. By the 1990s, according to the OECD, the CAP's high food prices added £18 a week to the living costs of the average EC family.

It is the 'mountains' and 'lakes' which raise the guaranteed support prices for farmers that remain a major criticism of the CAP. Surpluses have long been embarrassingly large, particularly in respect of dairy products, wine, oil-seed and cereals. By 1992 there were in storage across the EC 25 million tonnes of cereals, 800,000 tonnes of beef and 900,000 tonnes of dairy products. The explanation was simple; farmers invested in new methods and machinery and were increasing production by 2 per cent a year while consumption rose by only 0.5 per cent a year. As the EC had to pay for the storage and ultimate disposal of such surpluses, costs spiralled out of control. Consequently the CAP consumed a huge proportion of the EC budget. In 1980 it was responsible for 75 per cent of all Community expenditure, starving other areas of EC activity of necessary funding. Even after the reforms of 1984, 1988 and 1992 (see later), it is predicted that the CAP will still consume 45 per cent of the EC budget by the end of the century.

The CAP is indeed a very expensive policy to operate. In 1981 it required financing to the tune of 13 billion ECU. By 1992 the figure had reached over 38 billion ECU, and is set to rise to well over 40 billion ECU by the end of the century. On top of that, national governments have also subsidized their own farming sector. The Rome Treaty forbids such national subsidies but they have become more common.

Only 10 per cent of CAP expenditure has been devoted to the Guidance section of the EAGGF, and 90 per cent or more has usually been spent each year on the Guarantee section. Much of this money has gone on export refunds, which enable traders to sell high-cost Community food on low-price world markets. To this should be added storage charges. As a result the cost of disposing of surpluses now accounts for over half of all expenditure on the CAP. The chief beneficiaries of these subsidized sales have been Eastern Europe and the Middle East.

With such amounts of money available it is not surprising that fraud has been endemic. A BBC programme, '*Panorama*', put the cost of such fraud at about 3 billion ECU in 1988. A typical case was the great Italian tomato scandal in 1980.

In 1978 the Community had decided to help tomato canning in Southern Italy. Tomato processors falsified the certificates that stated how many tonnes of tomatoes had been bought for canning, in some cases merely by adding an extra zero to their figures. The processors were already buying the tomatoes at below Community minimum prices. The Commission's motives were no doubt laudable; tomato production in the region had been very high and the farmers were dependent on the canneries to buy up their tomato crops. But 100 people were arrested for fraud in a case that cost the Community at least 130 million ECU. In 1983 news broke that the Mafia was involved in an olive oil fraud that was costing the Community 200 million ECU a year.

Canny farmers have also profited from the green money system by smuggling. When Britain had a negative MCA, Irish farmers could load their cereals into trucks, drive into Northern Ireland and collect an import subsidy. They would then drive out along a road without border controls, pick up new papers and drive through again (with the same load of cereals) to collect another MCA. The swing in recent years to a positive MCA has simply meant that the smuggling has had to be in the opposite direction.

Such devices are of course not confined to the Irish. Belgian farmers have walked their cattle or pigs into Holland at dead of night to have them slaughtered there so as to disguise the livestock's origin. They have then imported the meat back into Belgium. The reason for resorting to this practice is that Holland had a positive MCA of 5.4 per cent (equivalent to an export subsidy) while Belgium had a negative MCA of 3.1 per cent (equivalent to an import subsidy). As a result Belgian farmers picked up a total 8.5 per cent subsidy (the sum of the Dutch and Belgian MCAs). Recently more fraud has been made possible through the introduction of the set-aside scheme (see p. 114).

The CAP damaged trade relations with the United States. European farm exports into America's traditional markets, helped by export subsidies worth $2.2 billion, had by 1982 helped to intensify the worst income crisis American farmers had suffered since the 1930s. Community exports had soared to a point where they were violating an agreement made with the Americans in the GATT Tokyo Round. Similar issues poisoned US–EC relations during the Uruguay Round of the GATT after 1986 (see Chapter 11).

The CAP has not only damaged the Community's relations with the rest of the world, it has ensured constant internal friction between the member states. It has always been the fundamental cause of Britain's excessive contributions to the Community budget. Because Britain's farm sector is small, the British taxpayer pays far more into the Community farm fund than is paid back to British farmers. There is also a substantial transfer of funds from Britain to the chief Community food-exporting countries, like France, because Britain has to import food at high Community prices rather than at lower world prices. Small wonder then that British governments have tried to reduce British budgetary contributions by pushing for the reform of the CAP. Yet is is these very efforts that have contributed to British unpopularity in the Community, notably in France. In March 1982, for example, the then French farm minister, Edith Cresson, accused the British government of terrorist tactics when it attempted to hold down farm price increases. Anglo–French relations seem doomed to remain clouded by the issue, because French governments, regardless of their political complexion, wish to protect the wellbeing of French farmers.

However, the CAP has created bad relations between several member states and not merely between Britain and France. In the 1980s the French were at loggerheads with the British over lamb and turkeys, with Italy over the issue of Italian wine imported into France, with Spain over the interruption of Spanish fruit exports to France, and with the Commission over the French government's illegal subsidies to French farmers. In John Marsh's view, the French government has tolerated such gross interference with the flow of Italian, British and Spanish food into France and has given such support to its own farmers that in practice 'the major part of the cost of any resulting additional output in France is being borne by other members of the Community'.

The CAP has worrying implications for the environment. As farmers were paid more the more they produced, they invested in more intensive farming methods. These methods called for the use of more chemicals, which have damaged the soil and leeched into river systems. To achieve economies of scale, farmers have created larger fields by the destruction of trees, hedgerows and ditches, with a disastrous impact on the flora and fauna of their region. The raising of animals in intensive batteries, described by animal rights groups as no better than concentration camps, is another major concern.

Finally the most damning indictment of the CAP must be that it has failed to protect farmers themselves. Farm incomes were maintained in the 1960s and 1970s but fell both absolutely and in relation to other groups in the 1980s for a number of reasons. As explained earlier, much of the spending on the CAP never reaches the farmer; it is absorbed by the costs of administration, export subsidies to traders and storage. Disposal of surpluses cost 12 billion ECU in 1990. At the same time farmers who have borrowed heavily to invest in farming faced heavy repayment charges as interest rates rose sharply in the 1980s.

However, higher interest rates were merely one element in a fundamental contradiction within the CAP. As John Marsh has shown, price increases for farm products under the CAP only lead to an addition to farm incomes in the short run. With high guaranteed prices, farmers demand more capital to buy more land, more labour, more agricultural machinery and more chemicals. Such increased demand causes the cost of agricultural inputs to rise sharply, especially land, the main input, the supply of which cannot be readily increased. Thus the main beneficiaries are not the farmers, whose costs rise, but landowners renting out land and the suppliers of chemicals, machinery, buildings and credit. If farm incomes are to be restored, a further price increase is needed. Marsh says:

> However, as expansion occurs the price of inputs is likely to rise and less efficient inputs to be drawn into production, so the margin between total revenue and total cost per unit of output tends to narrow as expansion occurs. If this occurs, a given addition to short-run income will imply that the amount by which prices have to rise will need to increase at a growing rate. However, if incomes do increase, the cycle of further cost increases will recur. Thus the price manipulation is a self-defeating instrument to raise incomes in the long term in an industry as competitive as farming.

The system therefore worked uneasily even when price increases for farm products ran ahead of inflation. When the Council of Ministers began to put a brake on such prices after 1983, farmers across the Community, locked as they were in a high cost system, began to experience real privation. See Table 6.1.

The reform of the CAP

By 1970 it was clear to Sicco Mansholt, the Agricultural Commissioner, that he was now in charge of a monster, but the acid reception of his plan to reform agricultural structures by the Council of Ministers (he was dubbed the peasant killer) showed that reform of the CAP would meet strong opposition from vested interests. In addition to the farming community proper, groups opposing change included politicians in rural constituencies, suppliers of machinery and services to the farming industry, officials and the powerful European farmers' union (COPA). Often national farm ministers were farmers themselves, facing a conflict of interest that would have excited comment if textile magnates became trade ministers or if armament manufacturers became defence ministers. In 1986, for example, the farm ministers of France, Britain and West Germany were all farmers!

Table 6.1   Average annual rates of change in agricultural support prices, 1975/76–1990/1 (%)

Marketing year	Commission proposal (ECU)	Council decision (ECU)	Council decision (in national currencies)
1975–6	9.2	9.6	10.1
1976–7	7.5	7.5	8.1
1977–8	3.0	3.9	5.9
1978–9	2.0	2.1	7.6
1979–80	–	1.5	6.4
1980–1	2.5	4.8	5.7
1981–2	7.8	9.2	10.9
1982–3	8.4	10.4	12.2
1983–4	4.2	4.2	6.9
1984–5	0.4	0.4	4.1
1985–6	–0.3	1.8	1.8
1986–7	–0.3	–0.3	2.2
1087–8	–0.2	–0.2	2.6
1988–9	–	–	1.6
1989–90	–	–	1.6
1990–1	–	–1.0*	–0.3
1991–2	–	–	0.5

*Accounts for the effect of applying stabilizers.
Source: EC Commission.

Nevertheless the absurdities and waste of the CAP led to a growing chorus of protest from many other pressure groups, including environmentalists, who condemned the damage inflicted on the countryside by the intensive farming methods the CAP encouraged. There was, too, by the 1980s formidable academic criticism of the CAP by economists who had analysed the impact of the CAP on the EC and the rest of the world. Josling and Marsh proposed price reductions to help consumers and discourage farmers from overproduction. John Marsh, who objected to the open-ended nature of the CAP, i.e. that farmers were guaranteed high prices however much food was actually needed, also suggested the use of quotas, with overproduction penalized by a cut in price. Consumer groups concentrated on the inflationary impact of the CAP, stressing that high food prices led to higher wage claims, which in turn worsened the competitive position of the European economy and led to increased unemployment. Furthermore the CAP attracted additional resources into agriculture that could have been invested in more productive sectors of the economy.

In the 1970s the Commission merely tinkered with the problem, the only notable advance being the co-responsibility levy applied to the milk sector. The levy in effect made the milk producers partly responsible for disposing of milk surpluses.

The first real measure of reform occurred in 1984, also in the milk sector, where surpluses had been particularly costly. As the cost of the CAP grew, the Community budget was running out of resources, and it was clear that remedies were needed. However, the British government made it clear that it would not agree to a larger Community budget unless the CAP was reformed as well as a permanent solution being agreed on the budget problem. Consequently at the Fontainebleau Summit of June 1984 it was agreed that the CAP should in future consume a smaller proportion of the budget, and that quotas should be imposed on Community milk output for 5 years. The Community total would be shared out between the member states, which would in turn allocate quotas to their producers. To discourage production in excess of the quota, a punitive levy of between 75 per cent and 100 per cent of the target price was to be imposed on the excess. Thus the Commission indicated that it would pay the guaranteed price only on an agreed quantity, with the excess production harshly penalized. What really was needed was a low quota, but the 1984 milk quota was still rather generous for the EC. In December 1986, however, it was agreed to cut this by 9.5 per cent by 1989. The combination of the quota with 'in effect' a price cut on excess production became known as the 'stabilizer'.

A second attack on the expense of the CAP came from annual price increases in farm products lower than the rate of inflation. In 1985, for example, the Council of Ministers agreed a rise in agricultural prices for the next year of only 1.8 per cent when inflation was running at 5.8 per cent. Such a practice meant a fall in the real price of farm produce. In 1986 the co-responsibility principle was extended to cereals, and Community restrictions on the buying up of surplus beef led to a large reduction in its price.

However, the open-ended nature of the CAP still persisted. Farmers had only to produce food, a task at which they annually became more efficient at fulfilling. It was the Commission that had to pick up the bill for buying up, for storage or sale abroad of surplus products. Almost inevitably by 1986 the Community budget was again running out of funds and required additional finance. On this occasion the British government was joined by the Netherlands in demanding more measures to control the CAP.

The negotiations that followed were extremely acrimonious, with disagreements over what methods should be used to control output. Germany favoured set-aside measures, Britain preferred the extension of the stabilizer approach. The British also wanted low quotas on the products most acutely in surplus, such as cereals, a view fiercely opposed by Germany and France. Finally, at the Brussels Summit of February 1988 a hard-fought compromise was reached in which, first, a set-aside scheme was introduced – compulsory for member states but voluntary for individual farmers. In order to qualify for aid a farmer had to take out of production for a minimum of 5 years at least 20 per cent of the arable land used for cereals or other crops subject to Common Market supervision. The land was to be left fallow, and aid, at member states' discretion, could vary between 200 ECU and 600 ECU per hectare. The scheme had as its clear objective the reduction in cereal surpluses, and the Commission estimated that it could reduce cereal output by 3.5 million tonnes, a wildly optimistic conclusion as events were to show. It was accepted without enthusiasm by some governments, notably the French, who feared that it could lead to the 'desertification' of some marginal areas. It was significant that the highest rate of take-up for the scheme took place in poor farming areas with a large amount of marginal land, with adverse effects on the environment and the survival of rural communities.

The second scheme was an extension of the stabilizer approach to cereals from 1988 to 1992. If output exceeded 160 million tonnes, price cuts of 3 per cent would apply each season that it occurred, i.e. the price cuts would cumulate. A similar arrangement was agreed for oil-seeds. On the insistence of the British and Dutch governments further extension of the stabilizer system would be considered in the future for additional food products. Nevertheless the agreement represented a defeat for Mrs Thatcher, who had wanted a cereal threshold of 155 million tonnes.

For 2 years the reforms appeared to be effective in curbing the cost of the CAP as surpluses fell, but in fact the improvement was illusory. It coincided with certain external factors that aided EC finances. There was a drought in the USA during the summer of 1988. American output of cereals fell and a sharp rise occurred in world cereal prices because the USA was a dominant producer for the world market. The world price moved closer to the high EC price and so reduced the cost of the EC's export refunds. In addition, it was easier for EC traders to sell on the world market and the storage costs related to surpluses were also contained.

However, when world production, especially that in the United States, returned to normal levels in 1990, CAP expenditure rose again by 1991, with rising surpluses in a number of products inflating the costs of storage and export subsidies. Cereals stocks rose to 18.5 million tonnes, while the beef sector faced particular difficulties because more beef could now enter the Community from East Germany, and in Britain demand for beef fell owing to the BSE 'mad cow' disease scare. Both factors meant that beef producers had more beef to be bought up by the CAP intervention system.

The problem was compounded by the increasing international opprobrium the CAP now attracted. In 1987 the EC had subsidized wheat exports by 140 ECUs per tonne or twice the prevailing world price. Such subsidies caused problems not only for the other major world exporter of food, the USA, but also for smaller agricultural exporting nations, which could not afford to subsidize exports to the same extent as the EC. Their only recourse was to slash the price to unprofitable levels. Their common problems led to the formation of the Cairns group of four small developed states – Australia, New Zealand, Canada and Hungary – and ten developing countries. From 1986 the group pressed for world-wide reductions in agricultural protection and was joined by the USA and the World Bank in a campaign for the liberalisation of agricultural trade under the new Uruguay Round of the GATT. In 1989 the USA and the Cairns group proposed that over 10 years domestic support and border protection be reduced by 75 per cent and export subsidies by 90 per cent. All that the Community was able to offer was a cut in domestic support of between 10 per cent and 30 per cent over 10 years, but with no commitment on either border protection (the variable levies) or the export subsidies. An acrimonious row had begun, one that was only partly resolved in 1992 (see Chapter 11).

The combination of internal and external pressure did, however, prompt the able and determined Agricultural Commissioner, Ray McSharry, into further attempts to solve the CAP problem. In July 1991 the Commission introduced proposals to take effect from 1993 and be fully operational by 1996. The main features were:

(*a*) Over 3 years price reductions of 35 per cent for cereals, 10 per cent for milk, 15 per cent for butter and beef, and 5 per cent for skim milk, and price reductions in pigmeat, poultry meat, eggs and processed agricultural products.
(*b*) Supply control measures, including an extension of set-aside in cereals and tighter quotas for milk and tobacco.
(*c*) Compensation for farmers affected by the above changes, according to the tonnage produced. To qualify for compensation, farmers on relatively large farms (over 125 acres) would have to set aside 15 per cent of their land without any set-aside payment. Thus this direct income support would be targeted at farmers on small or medium-sized farms.
(*d*) Programmes to encourage afforestation of agricultural land.
(*e*) New measures to facilitate early retirement for the 50 per cent of Community farmers who were over 55 years of age.

The McSharry proposals, had they been accepted in full by the Council of Ministers, would probably have had a real impact on surpluses and export subsidies, with CAP costs contained. However, the measures were hotly debated in the Council over 10 months and it was only in May 1992 that agreement was reached. The original proposals by then had been significantly weakened. Milk prices were to stay unchanged and the butter price was to fall by only 5 per cent. The existing milk quota was to remain until 2000. The key agreement was for a 29 per cent cut in cereal prices by 1995–6, with all farmers regardless of their size being required to set aside 15 per cent of their arable land to qualify for compensation, which was to rise to £208 per hectare by 1995–6. The price cuts and direct income support were to replace the complex co-responsibility levies and stabilizers.

The 1992 package represented the most radical reform of the CAP so far achieved, but Richard Howarth represents the general view of economists when he describes them as only 'a temporary palliative' for the maladies of the CAP. Politically they went as far as was possible at the time, as the angry reactions of French and German farmers demonstrated. In the long run, however, the cereal surpluses and the cost of the CAP to the EC budget seemed certain to rise. On top of the general and inexorable rise in farm productivity, the full impact of the 1986 enlargement was being felt by 1993. Spain, the member state with the second biggest agricultural workforce after Italy, had tremendous agricultural potential and left the Community with an unenviable choice – either to let the surpluses rise or attempt to finance the modernisation of agricultural structures in Italy and Spain. Either way the budgetary costs would be opposed by other Community states.

Most of the reform measures so far attempted have suffered from severe weaknesses either because they were totally misconceived or applied in a patently feeble way. First, the EC has not made sufficiently deep cuts in prices. Price reform has consisted of a gradual lowering of price in the hope that farmers would respond by producing less, thus yielding savings to the EC budget. What occurred was the reverse, as the example of cereals has proved. Between the early 1970s and 1989 the real price of cereals virtually halved and the area of cereals planted fell by 5 per cent. Despite this, cereal production rose by 33 per cent as farmers sought to protect their income by raising production. The need was for *deep* cuts across a range of products of up to 40 per cent within 3 years, so that prices were reduced to a level where the best way for farmers to protect their profits was to cut input costs rather than to raise yields. Such cost-cutting would mean using fewer chemicals, which would in turn mean smaller crops. European prices would then move closer to world market prices and reverse the rush into high input, high output farming, which has glutted world markets and damaged the environment. Such price cuts would also increase consumption at home and facilitate overseas sales without threatening trade wars, because the subsidy would be reduced. Storage costs would be reduced, given the greater consumption, and as an added bonus the price-cutting mechanism is easy to administer.

In contrast, the second area of reform – payment to farmers to grow nothing on part of their land, or the set-aside method – is fundamentally flawed. The notion of paying farmers to do nothing is politically unpopular, especially as it is well known that the experiment failed in the USA over many years. In 1985 a US government report called the method 'costly and inefficient'. It is clear that farmers will set aside the poorest land, use EC compensation to concentrate on their best land and therefore *increase*, rather than decrease, yields. Moreover the potential environmental impact of such a policy is unfortunate, because it encourages farmers to farm more intensively, as has occurred in the USA. Finally, what was perhaps insufficiently perceived was that set-aside would be difficult to monitor and thus open the floodgates to more fraud within the CAP. A *Sunday Times* article of December 1991 exposed how badly the scheme was operating in Britain, with rich members of the aristocracy receiving sums of up to £50,000 a year under the set-aside rules. Where the scheme was run legally, it was invariably the poorest land that was left fallow. More disturbingly, reporters from the newspaper were able to make bogus claims undetected, and inspectors making an audit found set-aside money being claimed for streams, footpaths, carparks and lakes along with other property never used for farming.

The third main area of reform – quotas – is more popular with farmers and can restrain production, thus reducing the costs of the CAP budget. However, production levels need to be lower than those so far agreed, and the quota system has serious disadvantages. It is politically difficult to gain agreement in the Council of Ministers on the level of production and, like set-aside, the quota system is a complex one to administer. High prices to consumer remain and efficient farmers who could produce more than the quota they receive are penalized.

Most agricultural economists prefer a fourth approach – direct income support – because this targets the individual rather than the product. The Commission has been moving in this direction, as it showed in its 1985 green paper, *Perspectives for the CAP*. Direct income support is flexible enough to be a kind of social security, which could take several forms. It could be a payment to raise the income of a poor farming family to an agreed base income or as a means of compensation for farmers whose income fell sharply in a given season. It could be used to help farmers retire at 55, and when they reached 65 normal pension schemes would take over.

The advantage of such direct income support is that it would only go to farmers who really needed it, and would therefore be cheaper than the open-ended, high guaranteed price system. Its one disadvantage is that farmers resent the social security aspect, even though they have no objection to handouts from other sources. The 1992 package at least represents a step in the right direction of direct income support, e.g. the help to farmers over 55, though it needs to go further in targeting those in real need. For example, 40 per cent of EC farmers are part-time. Compensation for this group, should be phased out allowing more resources for the full-time professional farmers.

What is certain is that farmers now face a much more uncertain future. In Britain there is little public sympathy for the farming profession, which is regarded as rich and over-cushioned by the CAP. But farming has always been a hard and risky occupation, as the high suicide rate among British farmers in recent years has shown. Unfortunately the tendency to regard rural life as idyllic has been increased in Britain by books (and TV series) such as Peter Mayle's *A Year in Provence*, which depicts jolly bucolic peasants in the Luberon valley enjoying wonderful cuisine and a tranquil sense of community far removed from the frenetic character of urban existence. The reality is very different: farmers in Provence in common with their counterparts across the EC have faced a battery of problems. Especially worrying has been the flight of young people from the land and such low prices from agricultural produce that despite much hard work in harsh conditions the farmers face real economic hardship.

The pressure on the farming sector has implications for business generally; manufacturers of agricultural machinery, chemicals firms supplying fertilisers and pesticides, pharmaceutical companies offering medical services, food-processing firms and rural communities in general will all be affected by the squeeze on real farm incomes.

Further reading

Body, R, *Agriculture: The Triumph and the Shame*, Temple Smith, London, 1982.

El Agraa, A M (ed.), *The Economics of the European Community*, Allan (Third Edition), London, 1990.

Howarth, R in Minford, P (ed.), *The Cost of Europe*, Manchester University Press, Manchester 1992.

Marsh, J, *Europe's Agriculture: Reform of the CAP*, International Affairs, Volume 53, 1977.

Ritson, C and Harvey, D R, *The Common Agricultural Policy and the World Economy*, CAB International, Wallingford, 1991.

Tangermann, S, *Reforming the CAP?* IEA Enquiry No. 28, Institute of Economic Affairs, London, 1992.

Questions

1 Why should the European farming sector receive any special assistance?
2 In what ways are the main aims of the CAP contradictory?
3 Why has the CAP been described as the Community's 'prodigal son'?
4 To what extent will recent reforms solve the basic problems of the CAP?
5 In your view what are the prospects for European farming and related sectors?

7
Industrial policy

The origins of Community industrial policy

The Rome Treaty does not call for a specific common industrial policy; the founding fathers appear to have assumed that once a common market was established, industry would be stimulated to take advantage of that market and interventionist policies would therefore be unnecessary. Only in 1967 was a separate Directorate for Industrial Affairs (D-G III) established, followed shortly in 1970 by the first important Commission statement on industry in the EC. This was the Memorandum on Industrial Affairs produced by the Commissioner for Industrial Affairs, Colonna. It emphasized the need to continue the development of the single market, improve the legal framework within which companies operated, including the idea of a European company statute, and supported more transnational mergers and technological collaboration.

Implementation of these proposals was only really to begin in the 1980s, because although Colonna's ideas generated much discussion, little action was taken. At the Paris Summit of 1972 it was agreed, after much pressure from the Commission and the British government under Edward Heath, 'to seek to establish a single industrial base for the Community as a whole'. Unfortunately the action programme set up in 1972 to achieve industrial progress made little progress, because member states could not agree on how much power to cede to the Commission on industrial matters or indeed whether an interventionist or free market industrial policy was appropriate. It required the growing European industrial crisis after 1973 to concentrate minds on the need for a European Community industrial policy.

The Community's growing industrial crisis

The optimistic assumptions concerning steady, indeed spectacular, industrial growth were rudely shattered by a number of adverse factors that came to the fore from 1973 on. Certain external pressures affected European industry, chiefly the rising cost of oil and other raw materials. The Organization of Petroleum Exporting Countries (OPEC) increased oil prices fourfold within a few months in the winter of 1973–4 and later in 1979 it again increased the price of oil threefold. When inflation is taken into account, the real price of oil was four and a half times as high in 1981 as it had been in 1973.

The rise in oil prices was an important factor provoking a world recession, and as a consequence world demand for Europe's manufacturers slowed down significantly. International demand rose by only 1.5 per cent in 1981, compared to 6 per cent per annum during the 1970s and 8 per cent per annum during the 1960s. Some Community export markets continued to develop well, notably the Middle East, Africa and the developing countries of Asia. However, exports to Latin America, the Eastern Bloc, the rest of Western Europe, Japan and the United States stagnated.

The third external factor was the chill wind of increasing competition from newly industrializing countries such as Taiwan and South Korea, as well as from more established competitors such as Japan. Low wages and, in certain sectors, ultra-modern equipment enabled these countries to manufacture at prices much lower than their European counterparts. The rise of imported manufactures from Japan and East Asia, which accounted for nearly one-third of all Community imported manufactures, was particularly worrying, because it reflected a combination of cost and quality that European industries often could not match.

The Cambridge Economic Policy Group in 1981 saw these external pressures as the main cause of the crisis, creating a novel blend of high inflation and high unemployment. However, various internal pressures affected Community industries adversely. Their competitiveness declined, owing to increased wage claims, and high interest rates, which discouraged investment. Investment only increased by 0.7 per cent per year between 1973 and 1980. The development of competitive productive capacity was therefore restrained, growth dwindled and Europe lost ground to its main industrial competitors.

As a result of these external and internal pressures, the Community experienced a severe recession, which continued until the mid-1980s. Its most depressing characteristic was the dramatic rise in unemployment, itself a factor reducing home demand for Community manufactures. From 2.5 million in 1973, recorded unemployment drifted up by half a million a year to reach 6 million by 1979, and by 1982 it had increased to 10 million.

Nor did the later 1980s see a reversal of Europe's relative decline, and several leading industrialists were scathing about its lack of dynamism and fragmented, sluggish markets. Dr Wisse Dekker, chairman of Philips, the Dutch electronics company, warned that unless the European situation improved soon, multinational concerns would locate elsewhere. Not unnaturally non-Europeans also joined the criticism. One leading Japanese industrialist in 1985 wished Europe 'a happy catastrophe to make you wake up'.

There were of course many exceptions to such sweeping generalizations – Britain's Glaxo in pharmaceuticals, Heineken of the Netherlands in the drink trade, Germany's Bosch in electronics, and Italy's Olivetti in chips among the large companies, as well as in many niches carved out by small companies. Yet in three areas Europe's collective failure was striking. Its unemployment rate of 11 per cent in 1985 far exceeded the 7.5 per cent and 2.5 per cent rates in the United States and Japan respectively. The US creation of some 20 million net new jobs since 1970 was in stark contrast with a figure of only 2 million net new jobs in the Community. A second worrying feature was the preservation, often with government support, of outdated industries suffering excess capacity and inadequate economies of scale. While new firms changed large tracts of American business, Europe staked its hopes on established companies, and when these shed labour, there were few newcomers to take up the slack successfully. Finally, Europe was flagging in the high technology race. The OECD warned that on recent trends, 'Europe will increasingly tend to become a net supplier to the rest of the world of food and raw materials and low technology manufactured goods where it is likely to face fierce competition from less developed countries'. The figures spoke for themselves. Whereas Europe was responsible for one-third of world purchases of semi-conductors and computers, it supplied only one-tenth of the world's production. The United States and Japan respectively were selling the Community three and five times as much computer equipment and electrical goods as they brought from it and used between four and five times as many silicon chips per capita.

What particularly concerned academics and researchers was the growing weakness in the new technologies. Margaret Sharp has shown how widespread was the Community's failure here – in computer-aided design and manufacture, in advanced machine tools and robotics, in telecommunications, in videotex and in biotechnology. Such commentators emphasized that such technologies were the *seminal* or *generic* technologies that spilled over widely from their mainstream activities to affect many other areas of production, as opposed to specific technologies whose impact was limited to one industry. Such generic technologies attract new investment and activity in the mainstream activity but stimulate new investment and processes in other sectors, e.g. the traditional industries and man-made fibres and plastics. Thus a *secondary* round of investment and innovation occurs as new products and processes are developed.

Such concepts are very close to the ideas of the German economist Schumpeter, who in 1912 suggested that new technology acted as the locomotive for the rest of the economy. His ideas were applied to the late twentieth century by a number of economists, including Freeman, Clarke and Soete who in '*Unemployment and Technical Innovation*' claim that technological innovation tends to occur in 'clusters' or 'swarms' once profitable conditions exist:

> 'Once the swarming starts, it has powerful multiplier effects in generating additional demands on the economy for capital goods (of new and old types), for materials, components, distribution facilities, and of course for labour. This in turn induces a further wave of process and application innovations which give rise to expansionary effects in the economy as a whole'.

Unfortunately such beneficial Schumpeterian effects were not greatly in evidence in the Europe of the 1980s. By 1991 most firms in the European computer industry were in trouble. The French national champion, Groupe Bull, made a loss that year of about 1,000 million ECU and needed French government assistance of 600 million ECU. Apricot and ICL had been taken over, while Philips, Siemens and Olivetti were having to close down plants, with the loss of thousands of jobs. According to the Commission the Community trade deficit in computers was about 9 billion ECU per year.

Despite their technical advances in the 1980s, European manufacturers were still losing their share of world markets. They possessed much of the science of advanced microelectronics but had problems keeping up with the marketing and production process skills of their rivals. They faced acute problems in bringing good products to the market in time, given the ever-shortening product life cycle, seen in the example of microchips. Such chips had a life expectancy of 4 years in the early 1980s, but such products became obsolescent by the end of the decade in 2 years or less. Consequently, along with American companies, European firms lost market share dramatically in the 1980s, with even West Germany unable to cling to its market position in face of a Japanese onslaught in semi-conductor equipment markets. See Table 7.1.

The problem has not been a shortage of scientists. Europe's 580,000 scientists produce over three times as many scientific publications as Japan's 435,000 researchers. Nor was it clearly a lack of investment in R and D; Europe's level of investment at 2 per cent of GDP was not far behind Japan's (2.9 per cent) or that of the USA (2.8 per cent). Large European companies such as Siemens spend more on R and D than most of their foreign competitors. Therefore it may well be that the reasons for Europe's lag has been that American and Japanese companies are better at using the fruits of

Table 7.1 World share of semi-conductor equipment markets (%)

	1978	1988
USA	56	32
EC	22	14
Japan	18	45
West Germany	10	7
Others	4	9

scientific research because they have closer links with research institutions. 'In America science is business. In Europe it is still seen as culture', commented Carlo Rubbia, head of CERN, a multinational physics laboratory, who believes strongly in the need to bring Europe's businessmen and scientists together.

The development of the Community's industrial policy

The critical industrial problems summarized above led to much pessimism about Europe's industrial future. Yet talk about Eurosclerosis did not deflect the Community from making some vigorous initiatives in three areas: (1) the reorganization of industries in crisis, (2) encouraging the new technologies, and (3) the development of human resources.

The reorganization of industries in crisis

Since the late 1970s Community industrial policy has concentrated more and more on sectoral issues and has begun to look like a macrocosm of national industrial policies, with detailed planned approaches to different industrial sectors. The reason for this is that Community member governments have wanted to see the Commission contribute towards solving the problems of their declining industrial sectors, such as steel, shipbuilding and textiles. The Commission is the natural channel through which member states can combine to ward off foreign competition where it hurts most. As a result, the Commission has become more protectionist since 1974–5, but it has also argued that the protection should be used to carry out a reorganization of the Community's declining industrial sectors. It has cast itself in the role of independent umpire, attempting to ensure an equality of sacrifice in the necessarily painful readjustments.

The architect of the Commission's plans for industrial reorganization was Viscount Etienne Davignon, the Belgian Commissioner for Industry and Energy, who established himself as one of the most dominant personalities in the Commission in the late 1970s and early 1980s.

Steel

In no field is the Commission more committed than steel. It has powers under the Paris Treaty setting up the European Coal and Steel Community to organize the internal steel market without having to obtain specific approval from the Council of Ministers.

In 1977 Davignon brought out a plan for the Community steel industry. Its first and less controversial aim was the reduction of the heavy losses being suffered by the steel companies through protection and the raising of Community steel prices. Initially the Commission set voluntary production quotas for the major Community steel companies in the hope that these would bring overproduction and sluggish demand into better balance. When this proved inadequate, the Commission introduced guideline prices in May 1977 for a series of steel products and a compulsory minimum price for one product particularly in glut, concrete reinforcing bars used in the construction industry. The compulsory minimum price regime was extended at the end of 1977 to cover other basic steel products, and in 1978 guideline prices were raised by 15 per cent. Further price increases were called for in subsequent years, and in 1981 the Commission raised the price of crude steel by 25 per cent and special steels by 40 per cent. That such moves if successful would be inflationary did not seem to bother the Commission or the national governments too much, because many steel firms, notably the British Steel Corporation, were making such horrendous losses.

On the external front the Commission imposed minimum base prices for steel imports and imposed anti-dumping duties on steel shipments that entered the Community below these base prices. It also demanded that third countries either negotiated lower levels of steel exports to the Community or ran the risk of losing even these lower levels.

The second and much more controversial aspect of the Davignon Plan for steel concerned 'restructuring' or cutting down the industry to size. In 1977 the workforce in the Community steel industry was 730,000, and Davignon then warned that 100,000 jobs would have to go because the industry was in a position of serious excess capacity. It was producing over 200 million tonnes a year, with plans to increase the figure to 214 million tonnes, yet the Community demand for steel in 1977 was only about 130 million tonnes, with perhaps 15 million tonnes for net export. Therefore the Commission argued that there should be no modernization of steel plant without a corresponding closure in capacity. Davignon's industrial department also believed that bigger steel companies were desirable, partly for reasons of economies of scale and partly for reasons of price discipline.

By 1980 the Commission was enforcing compulsory and steadily deeper cuts in steel production. Using the last quarter of 1979 as a base, quotas were set 14 per cent lower in the last quarter of 1980, around 16 per cent lower in the first quarter of 1981, and 20 per cent lower in the second quarter of 1981. For each company the quota was fixed in relation to its best last quarter production during the years 1977 to 1979. In 1981 the Commission called for further cuts of 20 per cent in steel capacity over the next 5 years and the loss of 150,000 more jobs.

The hope of the Commission was that it would produce a leaner but fitter Community steel industry, but this hope has in part been thwarted by the continued plummeting of demand for steel and by the actions of the steel firms and national governments. Steel firms unloaded excess stocks of steel built up before quotas came into force, and they also sold these stocks at lower than official prices. The next step was therefore stronger disciplining of such firms by the Commission. Under Articles 60, 63 and 64 of the Community's steel treaty, the Commission can punish 'unfair and discriminatory pricing' with fines of up to double the value of the prices charged. In 1981 the Commission began to use its powers in this area when it fined the German steel company Klöchner 2.3 million ECU for exceeding output quotas.

Another major obstacle was the continuation of aid by several member governments to their own ailing steel industries. Ironically the worst offender (given Davignon's nationality) was found to be Belgium, which had provided large subsidies to the Walloon steel industry. Plans to reduce Belgium's crude steel capacity from 11.5 million tonnes to 8.5 million tonnes had consistently been delayed. In June 1981 therefore the Community industry ministers agreed that all member governments should phase out subsidies to their steel industries by 1985. Operational aid not directly linked to a reduction in capacity was to be withdrawn by June 1982, operational aid of any kind by the end of 1984, and financial aid by the end of 1985.

This agreement did not last long. From the end of 1985 a new code on state subsidies operated. All subsidies that merely helped firms to keep operations going or helped investment were banned. However, subsidies that contributed towards protection of the environment, to R and D and to closures were permitted under strict conditions. Gradually, from 1987 on, the EC tried to dismantle the quota system. This system was a flawed one, because it had penalized the efficient steel firm, which could produce more steel at a cheaper price. From 1987 to 1990 steel quotas were gradually abolished.

For a short period in the late 1980s the measures appeared to have worked, as companies such as British Steel returned to profitability. However, the recession of the 1990s caused a new crisis in the European steel industry, symbolized in December 1992 by the collapse of Klöchner, one of Germany's oldest steel companies. Many other companies had to cut production and shed jobs. Once again the basic cause was excess capacity in world steel production, which had led to competitive price cuts of 30 per cent since 1989. An additional problem was protection of other industries by state governments, with knock-on effects for steel producers. For example, Klöchner, like other German steel companies, had been compelled to buy high-priced local coal because the German government wished to protect the German coal industry. The extra cost of such coal was responsible for half Klöchner's losses.

Yet again a severe rationalization programme was needed, and the EC Industrial Commissioner, Martin Bangemann, announced a 1,000 million ECU aid package to help restructure the European steel industry from 1992 to 1995. The aim was to prune steel production, with much of the money to go on redundancy payments for up to 50,000 steel workers and a reduction in capacity of 25 million tonnes a year.

Clearly European steel companies still had a long way to go to return to international competitivity. They still lacked the large-scale modern production units of their chief rivals like Japan, and suffered higher wage costs and lower levels of investment.

Shipbuilding

By the mid-1970s shipbuilding in the Community was in a parlous state. Whereas in 1955 it had produced 70 per cent of the world total of ships built, by 1976 its share had fallen to 22.6 per cent. Competition had been particularly strong from the Japanese, and the future looked even bleaker with the rise of new rivals such as Brazil and South Korea. In 1977 the Commission estimated that the Community shipbuilding firms, which built 4.4 million tonnes in 1975, would only deliver 2.4 million tonnes in 1980, a drastic 46 per cent reduction. Its gloomy prognostication was that the workforce would fall from 165,000 to 75,000 by 1980.

In December 1977 therefore the Commission sent the Council of Ministers a Community action programme to help the shipbuilding sector. It required an ordered reduction in production capacity, the finding of alternative jobs for the unemployed and improved productivity in the surviving part of the industry. In 1978 the Council of

Ministers adopted the directive. However, much of the programme was still-born, because the Commission had little money available to persuade Community shipyards and governments to do its bidding. As a result, the main thrust of Commission activity has been the monitoring of state subsidies to shipbuilding and, if necessary, the forbidding of them. As with the steel industry, no state aid was to be allowed unless there was a compensating reduction in capacity. Davignon believed that such aid was doomed to failure and would only increase problems in the future. In December 1977 he said that the Commission would not allow a repetition of the large British government subsidy that had won a controversial £115 million Polish ships order for British yards. Member governments, which had been subsidizing their shipbuilding industries to the tune of 600 million UA a year, were asked to produce restructuring plans for their shipbuilding sectors.

The Commission also tried to negotiate with Community rivals, notably Japan, so that the worst competition might be mitigated. The Japanese government agreed to urge its shipbuilders to increase prices by 5 per cent, to promise to cut back working hours in their yards and exercise some restraint in taking orders from Community member states that had been particularly hard hit.

By 1980 the Commission began to modify its policy somewhat, because by 1979 there had been a 40 per cent cut in Community shipbuilding output since 1975 and a 35 per cent cut in employment. The Commission now suggested that some subsidies should be allowed but only where the aim was modernization. It still opposed aid that only aimed at the temporary bailing out of the shipbuilding sector in distress. The 1980s saw a number of directives on the subject, the latest, issued in 1987, limiting aid from 1990 to 20 per cent of the selling price of a vessel. Under the RENAVAL programme, assistance of 350 million ECU was given to regions hardest hit by the shipbuilding crisis. The money was used to help workers in the industry find alternative jobs and force the industry to concentrate on technologically advanced vessels.

Textiles

The Community textile and clothing industry has been another sector hard hit by the economic difficulties common to European industry as a whole, and between 1973 and 1981 textile production fell by 5.9 per cent and clothing by 6.3 per cent. This resulted in the closure of 15 per cent of all firms and a reduction in the workforce of 30 per cent (100,000 people). European textile companies have faced growing competition in their traditional markets both inside and outside the Community from a number of Asian, African and Latin American countries, such as Japan, Hong Kong, and Pakistan.

These countries offered similar products at much lower prices, since they often produced their own raw materials and had a ready supply of cheap labour. Between 1973 and 1980 the share of the European market taken by non-Community imports rose from 21 to 44 per cent.

The other major cause of decline was stagnation in demand, which had been adversely affected by the recession. The annual rate of increase in demand for textiles by 1981 was only 1 per cent; before 1975 it had been between 3 and 5 per cent.

The decline of the textile and clothing industry as an employer was all the more serious in that it primarily affected one category of workers, women, particularly in some of the poorest regions of the Community. Yet the industry remained important, as it still employed 9.6 per cent of the total employed in European manufacturing in 1981 (1.3 million people).

The Commission's attempts to improve the situation have revolved around the Multi-Fibre Agreement (MFA). The first MFA ran from 1974 to 1977 and was designed to liberalize the textile trade, but by the time that it expired, the Community found that textile imports had greatly increased. Therefore, in return for extending the MFA for a further 4 years, the Commission insisted on bilateral agreements with twenty-six major textile suppliers so that they restricted their textile exports to the Community, especially in a number of sensitive areas. The agree annual growth rate of textile imports ranged from 0.25 to 6 per cent.

The developing countries were taken by surprise by the Commission's moves in 1977, and were unable to co-ordinate their position before the negotiations. They complained bitterly that the protectionist clauses they were forced to accept did not stop the imports of textiles into the Community. They pointed out that the restrictions merely benefited textile producers in more advanced industrialized countries, who were able to increase their exports to the Community to a far greater extent than they could.

The developing countries had some justice on their side on this point, because American exports of MFA products to the Community had risen faster than those from the developing countries. The value of all United States exports of textile products to the Community virtually doubled between 1978 and 1980 from $537 million to $1,014 million. However, the 1977 MFA arrangements did help the Community by limiting the growth of textile imports. Between 1978 and 1980 they rose by only 23 per cent, compared with a rise of 75 per cent between 1974 and 1977. Only countries that agreed to limit their exports to the Community could qualify for a reduced customs levy.

The Community's synthetic or man-made fibre industry, which produced nearly 50 per cent of all textile fibre consumed, faced particular difficulties by the mid-1970s, and Community man-made fibre companies lost over £1,000 million between 1975 and 1978. Originally this was not due mainly to foreign competition; the problem was a purely internal one of excess capacity in the Community. Therefore in 1977 the Commission argued that, as capacity utilization in synthetic fibres was only some 68 per cent in 1976, no more state aid should be given to this sector for 2 years. It then approached the thirteen major synthetic fibre makers in the Community: Monte-fibre and three other Italian companies, Rhône Poulenc of France, Bayer and Hoechst of Germany, ICI and Courtaulds of the United Kingdom, Akzo of the Netherlands, Fabelta of Belgium and two United States multinationals, Monsanto and Dupont. With these firms Davignon was able to sign a cartel arrangement that froze market shares and cut capacity.

However, events overtook this arrangement, because the Americans, who were increasing their textile exports to the Community in all ranges between 1978 and 1980, made their biggest advance in synthetic products. Their artificially low prices for crude oil and natural gas gave their synthetic fibre products a cost advantage of between 10 and 15 per cent. Combined with the depreciation of the dollar and American productivity, this gave American synthetic textiles a definite competitive edge over European synthetic products. American exports of man-made fibres to the Community rose from 75 million square yards in 1978 to 194 million square yards in 1980.

In dealing with this delicate problem the Community had to move carefully. It did have safeguard clauses and anti-dumping procedures it could use against unfair American competition, but these could only be used with caution and in watertight cases because of the danger of American retaliation.

By 1982 the Commission wished to make changes in its textile trade policy. Given the weakness in the growth of demand within the EEC (about 1 per cent a year) and in the international markets, it felt that it could not return to a 6 per cent growth rate for textile imports, as set out in the 1977 MFA. Therefore in 1981 it proposed: (1) differentiating more than in 1977 between the different categories of low cost exporters of textiles to the Community; it wanted to stabilize imports from the most advanced textile countries and then be able to grant more favourable treatment to the poor developing countries; (2) making access of Community textile exports to the markets of the advanced textile countries and East European states a deciding factor in the sort of treatment the Community was willing to give imports from those sources; (3) a 5-year renewal period for the MFA from 1981 to 1986, which would provide a framework for the Commission to conclude new bilateral agreements with individual supplier countries with a view to restricting textile imports into the Community; and (4) urging the American government to give easier access to the American market for the textile exports of low cost producers.

After some difficulties the Council of Ministers reached a consensus on these proposals. The Germans had not wanted as protectionist a package as the British, French and Italians, but dropped their objections. In February 1982 the ministers ratified the new MFA, which had been agreed at Geneva at the end of 1981, but they stressed that the Commission should negotiate a 10 per cent cut in imports from the major producers of cheap textiles. The ministers also agreed on a ceiling of about 1 per cent for the average annual growth of imports of sensitive products such as basic yarns and cloths, and unsophisticated garments such as T-shirts and trousers.

The third MFA ran from 1981 to 1986 and operated in a very protectionist way. However, the fourth MFA, which ran from 1986 to 1991, was more relaxed, owing to the improved position of the Community textile industry. The EC also supported the phasing out of the MFA under the Uruguay Round of the GATT, but faced American opposition to this development.

Encouraging the new technologies: the pathway of collaboration

The failure of much of European industry to remain competitive led to collaboration between many European firms in the 1980s. A prime example of this is the European Airbus. This venture has drawn on work carried out at a dozen sites throughout Europe, it has been a technical and commercial success in producing jumbo aircraft such as the Airbus A300 and A310, and it is fighting hard to produce aircraft (the A330 and A340) for the longhaul market in the 1990s. Its success has meant that the European civil aerospace industry has been able to maintain its share of the world civil aviation market. The principal European companies collaborating in Airbus are Aerospatiale (France), Messerschmitt-Bëlkow-Blohm and Dornier (Germany), British Aerospace (Britain), Casa (Spain), Fokker (Netherlands) and Sonaca (Belgium).

Such collaboration by European firms makes sense for a number of reasons. First, soaring development costs are forcing manufacturers to seek ways to share the financial burden and risk. Second, in the fragmented European markets, national champions dominate their home markets but have a small share of the world market. They have been crowded out of the rest of Europe by other national champions. Collaboration could edge round this problem, because it may persuade the firms and governments concerned to open up their markets. Third, collaboration brings technology transfer, whether the company is Rolls-Royce working on a large turbo-fan engine with General Electric of America or Rover working with Japan's Honda on a new car.

Such projects are no easy way out. Cynics point to government interference, over-bureaucratization and duplication of effort, and to cost overruns and suspicion, compounded by lack of a common language. Many of the industrial marriages concluded in the 1970s had collapsed by the 1980s, e.g. the Unidata partnership between Bull, ICL, Philips and Siemens. Nevertheless such collaboration between companies is one pathway to salvation with the advent of the single market.

A second pathway to salvation has lain in more Community participation in collaborative ventures. In the past it has shown real interest in research and development. The main initial stimulus came from the Euratom Treaty, which created the Joint Research Centre (JRC), a body concerned principally with nuclear energy. In 1977 the Joint European Torus (JET) project was set up at Culham in Oxfordshire. Its objective is to find a way in which hydrogen atoms can be fused into helium atoms in a controlled way, thereby creating a virtually inexhaustible supply of energy. Progress so far has been slow in this field, but sufficient advances have been made to continue the project.

However, having recognized the need for Europe to make up for lost time, the Commission has initiated a series of new research programmes since 1983, when it was instructed by the Council of Ministers to encourage the integration of European research and development. The third of these 'framework programmes' is scheduled for 1990–4.

Among the most important are ESPRIT (European Strategic Programme in Information Technology), FAST (Forecasting and Assessment in Science and Technology), CUBE (Concertation Unit for Biotechnology in Europe), RACE (Research and Development in Advanced Communications Technologies for Europe) and BRITE (Basic Research in Industrial Technologies for Europe). Although each programme has a different focus, all are deeply interrelated. To succeed in involving European industry, one essential criterion for all the programmes is that research is 'pre-competitive', i.e. with specific commercial rewards only visible on the horizon. Participating firms must also come from at least two different member states. The Community alleviates the financial burden and obtains stronger commitment from companies through its 'shared cost' approach, by which it contributes 50 per cent with industry matching this amount.

By far the most important programme is ESPRIT. Its origins lie in the call made in 1981 by twelve leading European electronic companies for a concerted approach to the information technology challenge posed by the successful research programmes carried out in Japan and the United States. The firms concerned were Bull, CGE and Thomson (France), AEG, Nixdorf and Siemens (West Germany), GEC, ICL and Plessey (UK), Olivetti and STETT (Italy), and Philips (Netherlands). They consulted the Commission with a view to establishing a European strategy, and ESPRIT took shape during wide-ranging discussions with large and medium-sized firms, governments, universities and research institutes across the Community. By May 1982 the Commission was able to present the basic idea for a collaborative research programme. It also presented a detailed pilot scheme in the autumn of 1982, and this was adopted by the Council in December 1982. Launched at the beginning of 1983, the pilot scheme provided encouraging evidence that the ESPRIT approach could work, and in February 1984 the main phase of ESPRIT was given the go-ahead by the Council of Ministers.

The goals of ESPRIT are clear and ambitious. In the long run it is hoped that the Community will gain a 30 per cent share of the world market in information technology in order to balance imports and correct the intra-European situation, where only 40 per cent of all products sold are European. The information technology market is growing by 8 per cent a year, constituting one of the most significant manufacturing sectors. Its expansion could create a million extra jobs in Europe and another million jobs in the information technology service industries. The Commission believes that with the growth of worldwide communications, trade in information is overtaking trade in goods.

ESPRIT aims to help Europe by bringing together expertise scattered throughout the Community, establishing a critical mass and enlarging the market. It supports research on pre-competitive technology in five key areas – three 'enabling' technologies (advanced microelectronics, advanced information processing and software technology) and two 'applications' (office automation and computer-integrated manufacture). ESPRIT is open to firms that are already established in the Community and carrying out R and D in information technology. Contracts are awarded to research teams that must include at least two independent industrial partners from different countries, thus ensuring that the participation of industry and the transfer of technology cross at least one national frontier. The Commission will help to put potential partners in touch with each other if required.

By 1986 ESPRIT was proving a considerable success. 'We did not think it would work, now we are finding that it is working much better than expected', was the view of one firm. Another firm commented, 'Before ESPRIT we looked to the United States for partners; now we have discovered the technological capabilities of Europe and look to Europe'. Enthusiastic response does seem to have been the characteristic of the scheme. By the end of 1985 the total number of projects numbered 173, with 448 organizations participating throughout the Community. These organizations comprised 263 industrial firms, 106 universities and 81 research institutes. Universities and research institutes appear in 81 per cent of the projects, while small and medium-sized enterprises are active in 53 per cent of projects, the latter enabling small companies to undertake research they could otherwise not finance. The spread of organizations is even throughout the Community, and Spain and Portugal were invited to participate in 1986. By 1986 there were 1,300 researchers and back-up staff throughout the Community working on ESPRIT projects, compared to only 500 in 1984.

A primary justification for ESPRIT is the synergy between the creation of new technology and its transfer and dissemination as rapidly as possible round the Community. The researchers therefore need to be in close contact with each other. Instead of necessarily coming under one roof, they are linked by the ESPRIT information exchange system (IES), an advanced electronics network sometimes known as Eurokom. By providing the relevant information and remote access to it, the IES is the medium linking the various teams in the different countries and a means of disseminating their work. With connections to national networks, the IES is designed in the longer term to be part of a Community-wide network of value to the whole European research community.

In February 1984 the Council asked for a mid-term review of the ESPRIT programme to assess the extent to which it was achieving its original objectives and to consider the need for any changes in its future development. The ESPRIT Review Board chaired by Dr A Pallenborg, having canvassed the opinion of 369 participants submitted a report in October 1985. Of those canvassed, 97 per cent believed that ESPRIT had been highly successful in promoting trans-European co-operation between large and small organizations and between industry and the academic sector. Two out of every three projects were examples of co-operation between large companies with over 1,000 employees, yet over half the projects had at least one small or medium-sized firm (under 500 employees). The smaller firms were participating substantially because they did more than 25 per cent of the work in 60 per cent of the projects in which they were present. There was a real synergy being built up between industry and research organizations, since four out of every five projects had either a university or a research institute present. The contribution of the research organizations was substantial, since they did more than 25 per cent of the work in half of these projects.

There were critical comments. The main complaint was that administrative delays in the receipt of contracts and payments were worrying, especially for small firms and academic institutions. It was also rather ironic that the IES was considered to be in need of improvement when ESPRIT was created to improve the information technology industry. In addition, there were problems over language as only English was used.

The programme for Forecasting and Assessment in Science and Technology (FAST) differed from its sister programmes in being purely research-based, with social and humanistic orientations. The first FAST programme ran until 1984 and investigated the repercussions of information technology and biotechnology on society. It promoted co-operation between 100 Community research institutes and resulted in thirty-six projects, which were condensed into one final report 'Europe 1995'. The second FAST programme aimed to make practical proposals on how society could cope with information technology, and over 2 million ECUs have been allocated for research.

Many experts regard biotechnology as being capable of bringing about a revolution of equal importance to that engendered by the integrated circuit. Essentially an offshoot of the first FAST programme, CUBE (Concertation Unit for Biotechnology in Europe) was established in 1984 to co-ordinate European research in four key areas – human resources, management of the renewable resources system, Third World relations and healthcare/pharmaceuticals. CUBE had only a small staff, whose main function was to stimulate Europe-wide research in the key areas.

By 1983 the Commission was recognizing the importance of telecommunications, and it created RACE (Research and Development in Advanced Communications Technologies for Europe) to assess Community research and development needs in this important area. Its objective is conversion from the narrow-band ISDN (Integrated Services Digital Network) to IBC (Integrated Broadband Communications) by 1995. Ironically the Community is ahead of its rivals with ISDN and has a 2 billion ECUs surplus in telecommunications equipment, which it could lose by adopting the IBC system. Consequently the whole situation is uncertain; carriers do not know which system to choose and manufacturers which system to develop. Meanwhile Japanese and American investment is threatening, especially form Nippon Telegraph and Telephone and IBM. With ever tighter controls, there is little likelihood of any technology transfer from these countries to Europe. RACE is structured in three stages: Project Definition, which cost the Community 22 million ECUs in 1985; Phase I (1986–91), developing of the IBC technological base; and Phase II (1991–6), which it is hoped will see the actual laying of the IBC network capable of carrying voice, data and video communications.

The BRITE (Basic Research in Industrial Technologies for Europe) programme is designed to help the modernization of old-fashioned industries. It operates in a similar way to ESPRIT in encouraging firms to collaborate on pre-competitive research and development. However, while ESPRIT brought together information technology firms, BRITE has turned to older industries like textiles, which need to carry out much more research to meet the challenge from newly industrializing countries.

One important segment of the first BRITE programme was devoted to increasing the lifetime of products, especially machinery. Because moving parts are the first things to break down, research has gone into issues like wear and corrosion. Seven other crucial segments are:

1 Laser technology and powder metallurgy.
2 Joining techniques.
3 New computer-aided testing methods.
4 Computer-Aided Design and Manufacture (CAD/CAM) and mathematical modelling.
5 Polymers, composites and other new materials.
6 Membrane science and technology, e.g. the concentration of fruit juices to preserve better taste.
7 Catalysis and particle technology, e.g. to find ways of shifting from production to bulk to speciality chemicals without expensive production changes.

The second BRITE programme looked into new production technologies for products made from flexible materials such as textiles.

Through these various programmes the Commission hopes to make a quantum leap towards a European Technology Community that is in the forefront of development and equal in strength to its major competitors. Should the programmes operate effectively, the consequences would indeed be far-reaching in creating employment and increasing Europe's supply of foreign exchange to pay for imports of raw materials and energy. However, faith in them is not universal, as illustrated by the French desire to promote EUREKA, an embryonic scheme to encourage collaboration beyond pre-competitive research and with less Community participation.

The French wish is that EUREKA (European Research Co-ordinating Agency) would develop in Europe the same sorts of advanced technologies that the United States will cover under its Strategic Defence Initiative (SDI), including high energy lasers and super computers. It would prevent Europe's best scientists and engineers from being sucked into America's research programme. It would co-ordinate military and civilian projects by pooling existing European know-how, and some of the projects would lend themselves to space defence if Europe decided to work on a star-wars programme of its own. Nevertheless EUREKA is a wide-ranging programme, as it aims at strengthening Europe's position in biotechnology, healthcare and education in addition to space communications and computers.

In November 1985 ten projects ranging from research into lasers and computers to diagnostic kits for AIDS were put under EUREKA's umbrella. A new EUREKA secretariat was set up and eighteen countries agreed to participate as well as a number of important companies. The latter included GEC, Siemens, Philips and Thomson in information technology, and five aerospace companies – British Aerospace, Aerospatiale (France), Aeritalia (Italy), CASA (Spain) and Messerchmitt-Bölkow-Blohm (West Germany). The aerospace companies had already collaborated successfully in such projects as Concord, the European Airbus, the Tornado combat fighter and the Ariane launcher.

Most of the funding comes from the participating firms themselves, and national governments can contribute up to 50 per cent of the project costs in that country; no government money crosses national frontiers. The distinctive feature of EUREKA is that it supports projects closer to the market than other programmes, a distinction which raises the point that governments may be merely subsidizing industry.

The largest and most important EUREKA project has been JESSI (the Joint European Submicron Silicon Initiative). Approved in 1989 with a budget of 3.8 billion ECU over 8 years, it is Europe's main attempt to recover a share in the global market for commodity semiconductors. The hope is that the project will produce application-specific microchips, with measures to link JESSI's technology with potential users in industries such as vehicles and consumer electronics. The Community has agreed to give funding of up to 25 per cent of the early costs.

The development of human resources

Finally, in this analysis of Community action it would be fitting to comment on those initiatives devoted to human resources. In 1989 the Commission stated clearly how education and training were to play an increasingly important role in development strategy of the Community. Education and training were to be placed

'... at the forefront of its priorities to spearhead a new Community-wide commitment to invest in people, in their skills, their creativity and their versatility. This emphasis on human resources provides an essential bridge between economic and social policies and is also a key factor in promoting the free movement and exchange of ideas in addition to the four freedoms (goods, services, capital and persons) provided for in the Treaty of Rome'.

So far the money available for programmes supporting these objectives has been inadequate, but the initiatives have increased the awareness of the need to integrate education and economic life so as to meet the technological challenges of the 1990s. Commission guidelines have stressed the objective of a multicultural Europe characterized by mobility and training for all. Such a Community would be brought about by increased contact and co-operation while maintaining respect for the diversity of educational traditions in the member states.

The four principal elements of the Community's educational and training programme are (*a*) ERASMUS, the European Community Action Scheme for the Mobility of University Students, (*b*) COMETT, the Community Programme for Education and Training in Technology, (*c*) YES, the Youth Exchange Scheme for Europe, and (*d*) LINGUA, the Language and Training Programme.

ERASMUS, agreed in 1987, is a four-pronged programme to encourage student mobility across the EC. It gives funds to support universities in inter-university co-operation projects, pays mobility grants to staff in higher education for study and teaching visits to other EC states, as well as complementary grants for higher education co-operation activities. Its long-term objective is that future generations of decision-makers will be capable of co-operating with partners in other Community states to such an extent that they regard joint ventures with such partners as 'a natural and positive line of action rather than a potential source of risk and danger'. Only a small budget of 85 million ECUs was available from 1987 to 1990, but this did have a favourable impact on student mobility, so that more funds (192 million ECU) were made available for the period 1990 to 1992.

COMETT's purpose is to encourage co-operation between universities and industry at a European level but, given such a grandiose objective, only a small budget of 45 million ECU was made available for the period 1987 to 1989. The programme wished to promote a European identity through student placements in firms located in other member states, to encourage synergy between the worlds of academia and industry, and to encourage economies of scale through the joint organization of new training programmes. Response by firms and universities has been impressive, with many initiatives that would otherwise not have been undertaken being created. Consequently the budget for 1990–4 was raised to 200 million ECU, but external evaluation of the project warned that 'the Community network and the transnational co-operative spirit that have been created are both fragile'. Clearly, then, the Community would have to work hard in the 1990s to ensure that COMETT evolved into a really meaningful programme.

While COMETT and ERASMUS address the needs of students in higher education, YES is a travel and training programme open to all young people in the Community between the ages of 15 and 25. It was agreed in 1988, with an initial budget of 30 million ECU, to enable 80,000 young people to spend at least 1 week in another member state.

LINGUA is a Community action programme to promote foreign language training and skills. Approved in 1988, it was given a budget of 200 million ECU for the first 5 years of operation (1990–4). It aims to encourage language instruction and skills by providing funds for the training of foreign language teachers, increasing the knowledge of foreign languages in the workplace, and promoting exchanges of young people during their professional, vocational or technical education. In the view of the Commission, without these initiatives a lack of foreign skills would remain the Achilles heel in the Community-wide effort to make free movement of persons and ideas a practical reality.

Useful as these programmes are, it must be questioned whether they are addressing the central problem. Europe does lag behind its rivals in scientific and technical education. According to a study by the European Round Table of Industrialists, in 1988 Europe counted four technical students per 1000 people in the labour force, compared with seven in both America and Japan. But such technical backwardness can be remedied only by EC governments, and unless the Commission gains much more influence over education (which is unlikely), it cannot change the situation very much. Given this reality one has to concur with the *Economist*, which concluded in January 1993 that the EC's human resources programme was 'a step in the right direction, but only a small one'.

An evaluation of Community industrial policy

The money spent on the technology programmes by the EC is small compared to that spent by companies and national governments but supporters of such programmes claim that money does not tell the whole story. The programmes in their view are designed to magnify the bang for the bucks that they offer. Specific industrial sectors, such as information technology or telecommunications, are targeted and spending is strictly limited to civilian projects, whereas much national government expenditure on R and D is military. The programmes offer long-term funding (3 to 5 years), which encourages firms by reducing the risk, cost and uncertainty engendered by large projects. They try and remedy the traditionally weak links between universities and private industry, and encourage SMEs to do research.

A 1992 survey commissioned by the EC revealed that most participants in the EC's technology programmes believed that new products and applications would come out of their work by the mid-1990s and, small firms were particularly positive. Commission officials claim that the programmes have helped to restructure European industry, because collaboration has promoted mergers and alliances between companies in different member states.

The programmes have begun to produce new technologies. For example, the ESPRIT organizers claimed that by 1992 700 information technology prototypes, tools and standards had evolved under its auspices. ESPRIT officials use the Supernode project as a good example of one of their successful ventures. This Anglo-French project aimed to produce a European parallel processing computer, using a transputer – a 32-bit microprocessor with on-chip memory and communications linkages. On the British side were Inmos, Thorn-EMI, the Royal Signals and Radar Establishment military laboratory, and the University of Southampton. The French participants comprised two firms, Apsis and Telmat, and the University of Grenoble. The Supernode is very flexible, as processing power can be added almost indefinitely, and it has found buyers in the market place. Other examples include a microprocessor chip, which lies at the heart of Apple's Newton portable electronic notebook, and a prototype system for storage and retrieving images, on which Philips has based its interactive CD multimedia product. According to ESPRIT, Europe's big electronics firms believe that about 20 per cent of their recent products contain technology arising out of ESPRIT projects.

Arguably the importance of the programmes goes beyond this. As Margaret Sharp has explained, the programmes have a psychological impact and have changed attitudes. They have provided a valuable channel of co-operation between European companies. Such co-operation is a slow process, and the EC's programmes have introduced many firms to such collaboration for the first time. In so doing, they have widened their horizons, as the ESPRIT I Report emphasized. 'The most striking result of ESPRIT is that it has influenced several thousand scientists and engineers in information technology to think European.' More and more as time has gone on the programmes have created among industrialists a more determined optimism, a belief that Europe still had a future in the new technologies, especially when the single market is completed, an objective they have fervently supported.

Nevertheless, despite the successes, Europe's high technology firms have faced a depressing start to the 1990s, as explained earlier. The EC budget for its technology programmes is only 4 per cent of all civilian R and D in Europe, and as Table 7.2 demonstrates, is small beer in the context of total R and D spending, even though such funds will increase over time.

Some projects have been very disappointing. For example, EUREKA, audited in 1991, had brought only about ten out of 520

Table 7.2 EC expenditure on the three framework programmes (% of total)

	1 1984–7	2 1987–91	3 1990–4
Information technology and communications	25	42	39
New industrial technologies	11	16	16
Energy	50	23	14
Biotechnology	5	9	13
Environment	7	6	9
Human capital	2	4	9
Total cost (ECU billion)	3.8	5.4	5.7

projects supported to the market place, at a cost of 8.2 billion ECU. Its flagship JESSI was in particular trouble, because Philips, short of cash, pulled out of the project in 1990, and the Community's failure to give as much funding as hoped led to its near collapse in 1991. Despite such shortcomings, JESSI's managers have sought to prolong its life beyond 1996, when it is supposed to end, raising the question of whether such programmes have a tendency to be self-perpetuating, regardless of whether or not they are justified. In Margaret Sharp's phrase, the Commission must keep 'a hawk-like eye' on such projects, otherwise they will deteriorate into a mechanism for propping up dubious schemes and giving inefficient companies a barely disguised subsidy.

The EC's industrial policy in general faces formidable difficulties in achieving any coherent implementation. First, member states differ considerably on the *extent* of intervention required at Community level. It was significant that it was the French who pointed the way for more intervention in their September Memorandum of 1983. This was very much in line with French 'dirigiste' philosophies, which are difficult to reconcile with the German belief in the virtues of letting the market decide. The Germans fear that too much interference will reduce competition, and are keener to see the Commission develop the internal market (as are the British) rather than promote projects or supervise the adjustment of declining industries.

Another important difference at the political level is that progress in the development of the internal market has led to calls for it to be combined with *external* protection. Again the French are the chief champions of this approach, and again are opposed by the British and German governments. The French argued in the September Memorandum that harmonization will benefit not only Community exporters but enable third country exporters, chiefly Japan and the USA, to penetrate Community markets further. Thus, in the French mind, some temporary strengthening of external protection is required and justified along the lines of the infant industry argument, i.e. that if an infant industry which already exists in a more advanced state elsewhere is not given temporary protection in a country where it does not yet exist, then it will never get off the ground. Such infant industry arguments are hardly new, and have often been refuted by economists for a number of reasons, not least that such protection tends to become permanent, but the case for Euro-protection has the support of some European academics, notably Wolfgang Hager. In 1991 a group of large companies, including Bull, Siemens, Philips, Olivetti and Thomson, campaigned for more protection from Japanese competition on the grounds that Japanese companies enjoyed certain advantages, such as cheap finance.

A third problem is the political acceptability of some of the harsher measures required, notably the control or phasing out of state subsidies. Such measures, necessary for adjustment, will have a different impact in each member state. In countries where industries die out, with attendant regional concentration of unemployment, governments will face heavy pressure from interest groups and voters to prevent as many lay-offs as possible. Economically the short-run gains to society of letting large companies die are uncertain if no alternative employment is available. If the industry in question is an important strategic industry, the government concerned may oppose shrinkage of that sector on grounds of national security, arguing that its demise would put the country at the mercy of foreign suppliers of products and technology – and it is all too easy for member states to claim that an industry is 'essential'. Yet at the heart of this issue is a real problem over structural adjustment – how to strike the right balance between the social costs of rapid adjustment and the economic costs of long-term assistance. The row over cuts in European steel production in 1993 exemplified this problem, when steel companies rejected Commission proposals on reduction of capacity.

Another continuing problem concerning the evolution of the Community's industrial policy is that it often appears to be in conflict with other Community policies, especially competition policy. This occurred in the case of shipbuilding in 1978, where a clash of approach occurred between the Competition Commissioner (Vouel), who favoured a policy of curbing state subsidies, and the Industry Commissioner (Davignon), who sought capacity cuts, market-sharing and the erection of non-tariff barriers against third countries. The vigorous Belgian Commissioner achieved similar developments for steel after 1977, but the formation of a price-fixing steel cartel hardly accorded with the principles of Article 85.

A fundamental problem in Community industrial policy is the question of the best body to pick winners. If the Commission plays a leading role in stimulating R and D and technological developments, there is some assumption that civil servants are better able to identify opportunities than the senior managers of the relevant companies. Finance for R and D is a favourable weapon of industrial policy, and implies a failure on the part of companies to understand the importance of the research or an unwillingness of the capital market to finance it. Neither governments nor any specific firm have an *a priori* superior capacity to pick winners – there is no foolproof method of predicting which companies will be winners. Unpromising companies can suddenly blossom, while firms led by 'whizz kids' (Bloom, Sinclair and De Lorean come to mind) can collapse. In attempting to pick winners the Community will have to rely heavily on business or become truly entrepreneurial itself. Too directive an industrial policy 'from above' could have a negative effect on the actual supply of entrepreneurial talent, with all the risk of picking losers by throttling flexibility and new investment opportunities. Arguably politicians and bureaucrats are inferior to businessmen in picking winners for two reasons. Unlike entrepreneurs, they will not normally generate profits for themselves (and may therefore lack the same thrust), nor will they have the entrepreneur's specific knowledge of the industry. Buying in experts may turn them into salaried employees whose alertness to opportunities may be dulled by the loss of the profit incentive.

Joint programmes at a Community level face further problems. There is a natural tendency for member states to pursue national strategies for their own advanced industries, several of which are unduly dominated by defence issues. The running of such joint programmes is difficult to cost effectively, and as commitments are made for years ahead, overmanning, cumbersome administration and overpayment of personnel may result in the projects acquiring a life of their own and becoming out of control. Such projects may be supported for the wrong reasons – by governments seeking re-election, by pressure groups seeking contracts, and by experts seeking posts and prestige and thus willing to exaggerate the potential of a project.

All parties wish to share in much if not all of the technology, a reality that could reduce the potential for international division of labour. There is an understandable fear that in a joint plan firms in the partner country may be quicker and more efficient in implementing the possibilities opened up by joint development of enabling technologies. Thus the benefits may accrue in a highly uneven way among participating countries. 'Such fears', opine Pearce and Sutton, 'probably constitute the major practical obstacle to a purely European solution in this sphere'. The political need for sharing may result in the allocation of work to participating countries lacking the necessary expertise.

A final question is whether European collaboration is limiting. In the past European firms have often preferred to collaborate with American and Japanese firms rather than with companies from other European states. Collaboration with third country firms could presumably offer some of the same benefits of economies of scale and capacity to launch new projects as collaboration with fellow Europeans, although member states that have so indulged (the British with Honda) incur the wrath of other countries (especially the French), which see such schemes as merely aiding further third country competition. In 1991 ICL, after having been taken over by Fujitsu, was thrown off several joint programmes, though significantly IBM had been invited into the ESPRIT and JESSI programmes.

Given the battery of obstacles, it is hardly surprising that Pearce and Sutton believe that there is little prospect of the Community developing a co-ordinated industrial policy. A number of the characteristics required for its successful evolution appear to be missing, not least a consensus and commitment by the member states on some policy issues and a recognition of the need for more investment in human resources through retraining. However, some real progress has been made towards the completion of the internal market and the encouragement of the new technologies, and it is doubtful whether there is any alternative to programmes like ESPRIT. Collaboration may be the only way in which European companies can respond to the Japanese challenge, short of massive interventionist policies by the member states. It is therefore certain that the future will see even greater opportunities for all European firms engaged in the advanced technologies if they are prepared to find appropriate partners in other member states and produce realistic projects that the EC can then support through funding.

Further reading

Bangemann, M, *Meeting the Global Challenge*, Kogan Page, London, 1992.
Economist, Europe's Technology Policy, 9 January 1993.
Farrands, C *et al.*, *European Trends*, Number 3, 1990.
Morris, B *et al.*, *Business Europe*, Macmillan, London, 1992.
Rouffignac, P D and Gregg, P, *Profiting from Europe*, Computer Weekly Publications, Sutton, 1992.
Sharp, M and Shearman, C, *European Technological Co-operation*, Routledge, London, 1987.

Questions

1 Account for the Community's declining industrial competitiveness.
2 Discuss the success, or otherwise, of the EC's attempts to solve the problems of industries in crisis.
3 Critically analyse the rationale behind the Community's framework programmes to stimulate R and D in the new technologies.
4 What are the major obstacles to a successful Community industrial policy?

8
Structural funding in the European Community

In order to combat regional disparities in economic prosperity and to ensure that people in all groups in society and every geographical area share the benefits of Community membership, the European Community has developed a number of ways in which to assist the regions. This has been mainly by way of grants from three separate funds: the European Regional Development Fund (ERDF), the European Social Fund (ESF) and the Guidance Section of the European Agricultural Guarantee and Guidance Fund (EAGGF/FEOGA). In addition, assistance comes from the European Investment Bank and other financial instruments.

Such funding provides real opportunities for businesses large and small to obtain assistance for investment. Before 1988 the size of the funds was extremely modest, but by the end of the 1990s the annual amount available under the structural funds should reach 30 billion ECU.

The nature of the regional problem

It is unlikely that all regions of a national economy will ever enjoy an equal degree of success. Certain regions are always likely to be more prosperous than others, and today it is fashionable to point to the 'core periphery model' as an explanation of regional diversity. This model postulates the existence of a national economic 'centre' and a surrounding periphery, and suggests that resources will tend to move towards the centre by a kind of gravitational pull. The result is that the centre achieves high levels of growth while the periphery, especially those parts furthest away from the core, will become a backwater suffering poor levels of growth and remaining underdeveloped.

The origins of this phenomenon lie in a number of characteristics of a modern economy. First, the decline of agriculture has led to the depopulation of usually peripheral regions that are rather hostile to the development of urban life. A second feature has been the decreasing reliance of industry on natural materials such as coal. This development has harmed the prosperity of regions that relied on mining in earlier years and has left the environment in such regions unattractive. Third, the increasing importance of the tertiary sector – the service industries – has increased the tendency for populations to concentrate in the major cities, especially the capital cites. Finally, one must point to the replacement of the free markets of earlier periods by imperfect markets where prices are fixed for the whole country by government, businessmen or unions. This hits a declining region hard because when one of its industries is falling behind, it cannot solve the problem by reducing wages; its only recourse is unemployment. When the industry is heavily concentrated in a particular region, as is the case with coal, steel or shipbuilding, a depressed area is created.

In theory such uneven growth should lead to a movement of labour and capital out of the high-cost regions and into the depressed areas where resources are cheaper. In practice such developments occur too slowly, and often the best labour, the youngest or the most skilled, will leave the depressed region, causing it to fall even further behind. Such labour will move into densely populated areas, creating more problems of congestion while leaving behind relatively unused capacity in the declining region.

The creation of a form of economic integration like the European Community will tend to aggravate existing regional problems. The range of disparity between the richest and the poorest regions becomes greater, and may have political consequences, since attention is drawn to the wider disparity. More importantly, such integration may exacerbate the regional problem directly. More intense competition will result and this will tend to damage uncompetitive industries in the depressed regions. In addition, if the creation of the Community results in some equalization of wages, it will increase the incomes of those in work in the less prosperous regions but at the same time it will increase their unemployment. It follows, therefore, that integration will lead to some regions being very remote indeed from the economic centre of the Community, while some areas in fact become more central. Thus the Saar became more central after 1957 while the Mezzogiorno and Wales became even more peripheral than they had been in their national economies. This factor thus imposes on the EC a responsibility for the regions, especially underdeveloped rural areas and regions suffering industrial decline.

The evolution of the European Regional Development Fund (ERDF)

The idea of Community regional policy is implicit in the preamble to the Rome Treaty, in which the contracting parties stress their concern 'to strengthen the unity of their economies and to ensure their harmonious development by reducing the differences existing between the various regions and the backwardness of the less favoured regions'. However, there is no explicit call for a common regional policy and only in 1969 was the idea of a European regional fund even discussed. The major breakthrough came at the Paris Summit of 1972, at which the British Premier, Edward Heath, pressed strongly for the creation of a Regional Development Fund and won agreement in principle from Britain's partners. The British knew that their terms of entry to the EC were such that they would be net contributors to the EC budget, and a European Regional Development Fund would help to correct the imbalance, because the United Kingdom would be a major beneficiary of the ERDF. In the words of Denis Swann, 'the Regional Fund might do for the UK what the CAP had done for France'.

However, it took until 1975 to implement the ERDF, and then only in a flawed form. Its total funds for the next 3 years were a mere £541.67 millions, aid was distributed on a rigidly proportional basis (for example 40 per cent for Italy and 25 per cent for the United Kingdom), and national governments alone had the right to make applications and not the firms or authorities to whom the projects referred. This constrained the power of the Commission to help a member state's regional programme, and the following decades witnessed a struggle by the Commission to gain a more decisive say in how ERDF allocations should be spent.

In 1979, under new guidelines, the ERDF was divided into two parts. The largest part (95 per cent) continued to operate under a system of national quotas, but a new 'quota-free' section was created, marking a new dimension in Community regional policy, because it helped finance, jointly with national authorities, specifically Community regional development projects instead of merely providing support for national regional development measures. The aim was to help areas hit by the enlargement of the EC, e.g. the Midi; areas affected by crises in the steel and shipbuilding industries, like the North East in the United Kingdom; frontier regions, such as Northern Ireland; and regions short of energy resources, such as Southern Italy.

The Commission was still dissatisfied with the influence it could exert on the choice of projects to be funded, and in 1984 it persuaded the Council of Ministers to accept a new fund regulation. Coming into operation in 1985, it introduced several charges. First, instead of spreading ERDF money thinly over all member states, such money was now to be concentrated on areas particularly in need. Second, the quota/non quota arrangement was abolished and money was allocated to member states on a flexible system of upper and lower bands. When Spain and Portugal joined the EC in 1986, the bands were as shown in Table 8.1.

Table 8.1 ERDF band system

	Lower limit (%)	Upper limit (%)
Belgium	0.61	0.82
Denmark	0.34	0.46
West Germany	2.55	3.40
Greece	8.36	10.64
Spain	17.97	23.93
France	7.48	9.96
Ireland	3.82	4.61
Italy	21.62	28.79
Luxembourg	0.04	0.06
Netherlands	0.68	0.91
Portugal	10.66	14.20
United Kingdom	14.50	19.31

The banding arrangement had two objectives – to concentrate funds on the most disadvantaged regions and to give the Commission more discretion over the way in which regional aid was allocated. Member states were guaranteed the lower limit of the band, but only if their projects won Commission approval would they be allocated the upper limit.

The third change was a new emphasis on programmes rather than individual projects. Before 1984 only the non-quota section could be used for programmes. Now it was intended that programmes should gain 20 per cent of ERDF funding. They could be initiated either by member states or the Commission but had to be seen to be serving some general Community objectives. The first two programmes under this system were (*a*) STAR (Special Telecommunications Action for Regional Development), which ran from 1986 to 1991 with the aim of improving telecommunications in the most disadvantaged regions, and (*b*) VALOREN, which with a similar time span aimed at exploiting indigenous energy potential in disadvantaged regions.

Fourth, there were more attempts to encourage the growth of new firms from within the problem region rather than a reliance on encouraging existing firms to move in from outside the region. The main thrust here was the creation of an environment where small firms could start up and thrive with help from appropriate advisory services and investment grants.

These arrangements were short-lived because new pressures in the EC led to further changes. The enlargement of the Community to include Spain and Portugal meant that regional disparities were greatly increased, and the new members, particularly Spain, were vociferous in demanding adequate help. Furthermore the onset of the single market programme threatened all the poorer states with intensified industrial competition, and they demanded compensation for agreeing to support it. Accordingly the Single European Act embodied a commitment to cohesion and declared that:

> 'In order to promote its overall harmonious development, the Community shall develop and pursue its actions leading to the strengthening of its economic and social cohesion. In particular the Community shall aim at reducing disparities between the various regions and the backwardness of the least-favoured regions'.

The SEA authorized the Commission to submit comprehensive proposals for the reorganization of the structural funds, and this reorganization was agreed after tough bargaining at the Brussels summit in February 1988. Spending on the ERDF and the European Social Fund was to double between 1987 and 1993, and to be concentrated even more on the very poorest regions – a clear gain for Spain, Portugal, Greece and Ireland.

From 1989 five priority objectives were to be pursued and entrusted to particular funds:

Objective 1. The promotion of the least favoured EC regions to be assisted by all three structural funds (ERDF, ESF, EAGGF), with 38 billion ECU between 1989 and 1993. The definition of a least favoured region was where per capita GDP was less than 75 per cent of the Community average.

Objective 2. The transformation of regions afflicted by serious industrial decline. The ERDF and the ESF were to contribute 7.2 billion ECU to this objective between 1989 and 1993.

Objective 3. The combating of long-term unemployment was to be carried out by the ESF.

Objective 4. The occupational integration of young people would be assisted by the ESF to the tune of 7.5 billion ECU between 1989 and 1993.

Objective 5. The promotion of improvements in agriculture and forestry and the development of rural areas to take into account the reform of the CAP were to be assisted by all three structural funds, with 6.2 billion ECU between 1989 and 1993.

All in all, 60 billion ECU were made available to achieve these objectives by 1993, with most money for the regions (up to 80 per cent) being devoted to Objective 1. This represented a doubling of resources for structural action in real terms between 1987 and 1993 from 7 billion ECU a year in 1987 to 14 billion ECU a year by 1993. Moreover the impact of regional aid would be multiplied by the fact that support from the structural funds would usually be conditional upon co-financing from the national authorities, and EC spending on this area in fact reached 18 billion ECU by 1992.

While this was a significant advance, it was small in the context of the total Community budget, which itself represented only 3 per cent of total public expenditure in the Community. Furthermore only the following would qualify as Objective 1 regions:

(a) In Spain – Andalusia, Asturias, Castile-Leon, Castile-La Mancha, Ceuta and Melilla, Valencia, Estramadura, Galicia, Canary Islands and Murcia.
(b) In France – only the overseas departments and Corsica.
(c) All of Greece.
(d) All of Ireland.
(e) In Italy – Abruzzi, Basilicata, Calabria, Campania, Molise, Apulia, Sardinia and Sicily.
(f) All of Portugal.
(g) Only Northern Ireland in the United Kingdom.

Further advances were made in the wake of the Maastricht summit meeting of December 1991. The Maastricht Treaty provided for a Cohesion Fund to help transport and environmental projects in the poorest member states, and, to implement the Fund, the Commission under Jacques Delors proposed in 1992 a substantial increase in the structural funds. It was suggested that they should rise from 18 billion ECU a year (27 per cent of the total EC budget) in 1992 to 29 billion ECU a year (33 per cent of the EC budget of 87.5 billion ECU).

Subsequently, in December 1992, the member states attempted to agree an appropriate figure for the structural funds at the Edinburgh summit. The issue threatened to wreck the summit, because, while the member states that made net contributions to the EC budget wished to scale down the Commission's proposals, the poorer states, led by a vociferous Felipe Gonzales, wished to implement the Commission's proposals in full. Therefore, when John Major put forward a figure for the EC budget in 1999 of only 80.5 billion ECU, this was attacked as insufficient by the Spanish prime minister and indeed it fell far short of Delors' hopes.

Eventually a compromise was reached by a 7-year deal that froze Community resources at 1.2 per cent of Community GDP for 2 years, with phased increases to 1.27 per cent of Community GDP by 1999. The total EC budget would thus rise from 66 billion ECU in 1992 to an estimated 84 billion ECU in 1999. Total structural resources would rise from 18 billion ECU in 1992 to an estimated 30 billion ECU in 1999. The latter figure would be composed of two elements – 27.4 billion ECU for the structural funds as such, with

2.6 billion ECU in the Cohesion Fund. Cohesion Fund resources were to be spent solely on the four poorest states, to improve transport and the environment. Jacques Delors expressed his satisfaction, claiming that he had obtained 85 per cent of what he had sought. Certainly the greater level of funding, if used efficiently, was now sufficient to have some impact on regional problems, because from 1994 to 1999, including a new Financial Instrument for Fisheries Guidance (FIGG), a budget of 141 billion ECU would be available.

The problems of European regional policy

Nevertheless the Community has a mammoth task ahead of it if it wishes to reduce the regional imbalances significantly. A Commission Report in 1991, using the Community average of 100, drew up a league table of regions and noted that the region with the lowest GDP per head (Voreio Aigaio in Greece) had a GDP of 39.9 per cent, whereas the region with the highest GDP per head (Groningen in the Netherlands) had a GDP of 183.1 per cent of the Community average. The income per head of the top ten regions was more than three times that of the bottom ten regions in 1988, a disparity twice as wide as that in the USA.

The Commission had also carried out a survey of 9,000 companies in the disadvantaged regions. These companies faced severe problems, notably the high cost of loans and difficulties in obtaining them. Other problems included inadequate Community and government grants, a lack of sources of good advice, high taxation, a lack of skilled labour and poor transport facilities. Fundamental explanations of this state of affairs were disparities in education and training and in R and D in the member states. For example, three quarters of all R and D expenditure in the EC was concentrated in Germany, Britain and France, and in states with regional problems R and D was concentrated in the richest regions.

An earlier Commission report (1980) blamed the slump in Europe at that time as one factor causing the widening economic gap between different areas of the Community, and it is true that in a time of recession large firms and state enterprises do tend to close down their operations in the peripheral areas first. They wish to concentrate their efforts only on those areas that remain profitable and they abandon areas that have become unprofitable. Capital, in the words of Felix Damette, has become hypermobile, and this results in the acceleration of the pace at which industrial sites become obsolescent. Such a process usually hits the depressed regions hardest. Damette himself cites two examples of this hypermobility of capital in France – the plastics and steel industries. The firm of Ugine-Kuhlmann set up a plastics factory at Mazingarbe in the Pas de Calais, using coal by-products. But eventually the firm found that using petroleum made for better profits, and moved to the Basse-Seine area. As a result the collieries in the Pas de Calais all closed. But the irony was that Ugine-Kuhlmann could only have carried out the operation with state assistance. Indeed in the case of the French steel industry it was the state that closed down the steelworks in Lorraine and Valenciennes, and it is central to Damette's thesis that state intervention has created chaos of monumental proportions for the regions.

It is hard to see any rapid end to the recession of the early 1990s, and even when there is a recovery in economic growth, it is likely to be extremely slow in the next few years. Its impact will be insufficient to reduce the gaps between poorer and richer regions. The situation is made worse because population growth – and consequently the need for new jobs – will be greatest in the peripheral rural regions where creating new jobs is the most difficult. In addition, employment in the older industrial areas will continue to be threatened by growing competition from outside the Community as Third World countries, such as Korea, develop their own industries.

The task of diverting capital to the regions has become more difficult in the age of the multinationals, as Stuart Holland has shown. Governments would often prefer that a multinational setting up a new plant should locate it in the more backward regions of the national economy. In practice multinational companies can repudiate any pressure to do so by threatening to go abroad if not allowed permission to expand in the area of their choice. The example of the American computer giant IBM is illuminating. In 1982 IBM wanted to expand at Havant in the relatively developed and prosperous South of England. When told by the British government that the necessary industrial permission for such expansion would not be granted, the firm threatened that if one were not granted, it would locate the expansion outside Britain altogether. The government therefore granted the certificate to expand at Havant even though this ran counter to the policy of encouraging regional location of firms. As Stuart Holland suggests, 'Because they can locate multinationally, big firms can refuse to go multi-regional'.

There is in any case a powerful incentive for large firms to locate multinationally. Many firms have located new plants in countries like Taiwan, Mexico, Brazil, the Philippines and Hong Kong because labour costs there are so much lower than in the Community. Such savings in labour costs dwarf even massive regional incentives in developed countries, because foreign labour costs are often about a quarter of those in the EC. In other words, the Community would have to subsidize up to 75 per cent on wages to equalize the difference in labour costs, and in practice national and Community incentives are often insufficient for leading companies to locate in the problem regions.

The growth of the multinational companies has certainly become one influence undermining the effectiveness of the Regional Fund. It is one reason why the bulk of aid (84 per cent) from the ERDF so far has gone to infrastructure projects rather than to regionally mobile manufacturing firms. Leading companies are not sufficiently tempted by Community incentives, and locate in countries where the labour is cheaper and not unionized. 'Donning their seven league boots', as Stuart Holland phrases it, 'they bypass Europe's problem regions.' Certainly this issue will not be easily solved, as was demonstrated in 1993 by Hoover's proposal to reduce its operations in Dijon in favour of its plant in Glasgow, where costs were cheaper.

Ironically, other Community policies may have exacerbated the regional problems, and the 1980 Commission Report stressed the importance in this respect of the Common Agricultural Policy, trade agreements with other countries and the free movement of factors of production. The CAP mechanisms of intervention and price controls have increased the disparities in agricultural incomes between one region and another. As shown in Chapter 6, the guarantees farmers receive for their crops have been most extensive for products grown in the Community's more fertile, temperate areas, while many Mediterranean agricultural products enjoyed less favourable support. At the same time, the virtually open-ended commitment to provide farmers with guaranteed prices for certain crops until 1984 tended to help large farmers, who benefit from economies of scale and reap bigger rewards than their colleagues who work smaller farms. In addition, the Community's weaker regions have been handicapped by the main trade agreements, which have encouraged agricultural imports from other Mediterranean countries. Finally, the Commission's regional policy experts argue in their report that the free movement of the factors of production – one of the crucial Community objectives – has contributed to the growing disparity between regions. Labour has been the most mobile factor of production, and Community influence has accelerated the migration of labour from the peripheral regions. This last claim should perhaps be seen as the least important of the three policies in its influence on the regions, because migration within the Community has been relatively limited.

In addition to these underlying problems, there are difficulties and limitations in the operation of the Regional Fund itself. As described above, most of the grants from the Fund go to the governments of the member states. What is important is that the preamble to the Regulation setting up the Fund lays down the principle of additionality or complementarity. The essence of this principle is that aid from the Fund should not merely be a mechanism that would allow members to reduce their own regional expenditure but should add to those efforts. Giving extra assistance to projects already approved is called 'vertical complementarity', whereas if the aid is used to finance additional schemes, it is called 'horizontal complementarity'. Either way there should be a genuine addition to regional development and the Regional Fund operators do prefer aid going to provide more numerous projects rather than merely providing more generous aid to a static number of investors.

Unfortunately the principle of additionality is difficult to supervise, given the complexity of national accounting procedures, and there is a well-founded suspicion that the governments of some member states have simply pocketed aid from the Regional Fund and used it as a means of reducing their own levels of expenditure. An inspection of a member's total expenditure by the Commission would not necessarily prove misuse of Community aid, because even if that expenditure had fallen, the member state could still argue that it would have fallen further if Regional Fund aid had not been given.

What is clear in the years since 1975 is that the finance ministries in all governments have shown some reluctance to give a specific commitment to the principle of additionality, with perhaps the exception of the Irish and Italian governments. The British government has been particularly ambivalent on this issue, with continuing divisions between the ministries sponsoring regional development and the Treasury, which has opposed extra expenditure in the interests of controlling inflation.

A further operational problem is the extra bureaucracy of the ERDF since 1988. New regulations imposed a continuous dialogue between the Commission and the national, regional and local authorities. In addition, all programmes were to be monitored by committees composed of Commission, national, regional and local representatives, but in practice their effectiveness has been frustrated by the national authorities. Much horsetrading has gone on to decide the all-important allocation of funds, which regions qualified for it and which projects were worth supporting. David Combes and Nicholas Rees in L Hurwitz and C Lequesne (eds), '*The State of the European Community 1991*', described such decision-making as 'a time-consuming and administratively complex task which has fully extended Commission officials and national civil servants to their limits. Moreover the slow pace with which programmes have been initiated suggests that the member states have problems in formulating operational programmes'. However, there was another problem, which the Greek government in particular has experienced – a lack of sufficient national finance to match Community regional funding.

It may legitimately be queried whether the diversity of regional problems tends to make any European-level attempt to tackle regional development both haphazard and inefficient. The policy may redistribute finance between member states, but this does not mean that the real needs of poor regions are being addressed. Unfortunately there is strong evidence that much ERDF money has been wasted in the support of projects that were unwise, never completed or downright corrupt. In January 1993 the Court of Auditors revealed evidence of many questionable projects, such as a school for training waiters in Marbella on Spain's Costa del Sol, a winter ski resort on the Mediterranean island of Crete, and a fur centre at Kastoria in Greece, where mink and foxes bred on local farms were gassed so that their coats could be made into furs. The fur project had cost 5 million ECU and had included half the expenses of building an exhibition hall for international fur fairs. Imported pelts such as leopard were also processed, even though trade in such animals was illegal.

In Tarifa, on Spain's southern coast, nearly 2 million ECU were spent on Europe's largest wind-power station to supply electricity to Andalusia. However, when the wind was strong, the windmills, which only employed 7 people, switched off automatically. In Puglia, in Southern Italy, a million ECU were spent on upgrading luxury thermal baths at a four-star resort. Elsewhere in Italy Community-funded schemes have provided rich pickings for organized crime. In Spain 100 million ECU were spent to build the A92 motorway, which was to connect Seville, site of the World Fair, with the rest of the Spanish motorway network. Unfortunately work on the motorway stopped after construction costs soared, and the motorway ended in a wheatfield.

Naturally such evidence has provoked strong reactions, especially from monetarist politicians and economists. Patrick Minford, Professor of Applied Economics at Liverpool University and a former adviser to Margaret Thatcher, has called structural funding

> ... 'the economics of crazy redistribution. They are transferring billions to people who are basically well off. It's daylight robbery. Why are we paying out for grants to gas furry animals or for windmills in Spain? The whole thing stinks. Effectively it's a bribe to Spain, Portugal, Italy and Ireland, so the Commission has the votes of grateful nations locked up'.

While no doubt many projects under the structural funds have been properly costed and efficiently implemented, there is evidently a great need to monitor projects more rigorously.

The acute need for a social policy

A European Commission report on poverty in December 1981 proved, if ever one doubted it, the need for a Community Social

Policy. The report showed that some 11.4 per cent of families or about 30 million people had incomes sufficiently below average national earnings to bring them within a relative poverty line. The growing unemployment (12 million in 1982) was swelling the numbers, creating a category of new poor who had never before suffered poverty. Despite increased spending on welfare services by national governments in the previous thirty years, millions of people still lived in sub-standard housing; infant deaths in some countries were still twice as many among unskilled manual workers' children as in the professional classes; and between an eighth and a third of young people in different member countries were leaving school with few or no qualifications or vocational training.

The Community had already defined poverty in 1975 as 'individuals or families whose resources are so small as to exclude them from the minimum acceptable way of life of the member state in which they live'. The authors of the 1981 report found that certain groups of people were most vulnerable to relative poverty wherever they lived in the Community – immigrants, households headed by women, large families, one-parent families, the handicapped and the nomads or gypsies. Even when the breadwinner worked, he (or particularly she) was almost always badly paid. From the Commission evidence it was clear that once within the poverty bracket, disadvantage piled on disadvantage making escape very difficult.

A decade later the position of disadvantaged groups looked even bleaker. Community unemployment rose to 17 million in 1985 and by 1993 (albeit in an enlarged EC of 12 states) reached 22 million. Concern was voiced over the growing proportion of EC citizens who were of pensionable age and the consequently smaller proportion of employed who could support them. The position of immigrants in the EC deteriorated as the growing unemployment encouraged the rise of Le Pen's National Front in France and neo-Nazi groups in united Germany. In both countries and elsewhere, gastarbeiter (guest-workers) faced virulent racial discrimination and in Germany several immigrants were murdered. With the fragmentation of family life, more contractionary government economic policies and rising unemployment, it was possible to assert that a new underclass had developed in the EC. Living mainly in large cities as London and Paris was a growing number of individuals who were homeless, without any sources of public or private money and who had lost all contact with their families. It was for such rootless individuals that the much-loved French comedian Coluche, who died in 1986, bequeathed a network of homes and 'restaurants du coeur' in Paris to help them through the winter.

In some respects the Treaty of Rome is weak on social aspects because it does not contain a definite timetable for action as it does in the case for the introduction of the common market, though it does make provision for the setting up of a European Social Fund (ESF) to promote employment opportunities and worker mobility throughout the EC.

The evolution of the European Social Fund, 1958–85

Though some useful work was achieved in the retraining of redundant workers, the early history of the ESF was disappointing. Member states were reluctant to cede responsibility for such matters to the EC and the ESF itself suffered from two major weaknesses. Firstly, it could only intervene retroactively, that is to say, when the workers who had received vocational training had been productively employed for six months. Secondly, it did not have a budget limit: intervention from the Fund for a particular country depended mainly on the money available in that country for training. The ironic consequence was that the main beneficiary of the ESF was West Germany not the state with the worst social problems, Italy. Therefore in 1971 the ESF was reformed in several ways: private as well as public bodies were henceforth able to claim help and the Commission would decide in advance how to allocate the larger amount of money available.

From 1974 there began a series of Social Action Programmes designed to tackle three priority objectives – the creation of employment opportunities, the improvement of living and working conditions and the encouragement of worker participation in company activities.

In October 1983 the Council of Ministers approved new Social Fund rules. The system of giving aid up to 50 per cent of the cost of a project which received support from a public authority was to continue; for private schemes the Fund would match public authority support. However there was to be a new concentration on the training and employment of young people, with at least 75 per cent of the whole Fund financing projects for the under 25s. Other important 'target' groups were defined as the unemployed, particularly the long-term unemployed, women who wish to return to work, the handicapped who can work in the open labour market, migrant workers and their families, and people employed in small or medium-sized undertakings who require retraining in new technology or new management techniques. Help from the Fund was to be concentrated on 'absolute priority' regions – Greece, the French overseas departments, the Mezzogiorno, the Republic of Ireland and Northern Ireland. In addition, areas suffering from changes in the steel, shipbuilding, textile and fishing industries and areas of high long-term unemployment were to receive favourable consideration from the Fund.

Consequently this system benefited the United Kingdom and led to incensed complaints from France and Italy at the high British share of the Fund (about 33 per cent in 1984). The Commission was already in a difficult position because the number of applications for help from the Fund rose from 752 in 1983 to 4,785 in 1985. The calls on the slender ESF budgets in 1984 were too great and stricter selection criteria were needed.

Delors and the Social Charter

Community affairs in general enjoyed a new momentum after 1985 and social policy was no exception. To the new President of the Commission in 1985, Jacques Delors, the completion of the internal market required some complementary action in social matters. He believed that some degree of equality in social standards was desirable, otherwise in the more competitive single market those countries with lower standards of social protection would undercut those with higher standards. The term coined for this problem was 'social dumping'.

Accordingly, as explained in the previous chapter, the three structural funds were co-ordinated and given more resources after 1988. In February 1989 it was agreed that ESF resources were to be used for two main purposes: Objectives 3 and 4 of the revised arrangements.

(*a*) Objective 3 – a reduction in the number of long-term unemployment. This group was defined as having been out of work for more than a year and numbered 6 million by 1990.

(*b*) Objective 4 – help to young unemployed under 25 years of age, numbering 4.5 million by 1990.

The money available was to be spent on vocational training and in the case of young people should focus on the new technologies.

The types of scheme emphasized were those providing training and vocational guidance. In areas affected by industrial decline projects concerned with the introduction of new production or management techniques in small and medium-sized enterprises (SMEs) were also eligible for support. Subsidies were provided where new companies were likely to provide stable jobs and start-up cash was made available for the self-employed. Small amounts of cash were also made available for support measures such as technical assistance and apprentice training in the least favoured regions such as Northern Ireland.

Support from the ESF normally takes the form of part financing of agreed programmes and usually public funds should be available to supplement it. The exact amount of the ESF contribution depends on a number of factors but a maximum of 50 per cent of total costs and at least 25 per cent of public expenditure is expected except in the least favoured areas where the ESF contribution can reach a maximum of 75 per cent of total costs and at least 50 per cent of public expenditure. In exceptional circumstances preparatory studies and technical assistance measures may be financed in full.

However it was perceived that the Single Market Programme itself would add to social problems. Efficient companies from relatively prosperous regions would in a freer market more easily out-compete companies from poorer regions, adding to social and regional deprivation by causing more unemployment. Such risks were addressed at the Hanover Summit of June 1988 and the Rhodes Summit in the following December when the Commission was charged with the task of developing proposals for a Social Charter.

The Commission needed no second invitation; it went to work with a will and at the Strasbourg Summit in December 1989 the Social Charter was approved by 11 of the 12 member states. The Commission was also instructed to submit an action programme and a set of legal instruments whereby it might be implemented. Mrs Thatcher, the British Prime Minister, declined to give support to the Social Charter. She had already made her position clear at Bruges in 1988 and at the Conservative Party Conference in 1989 when she stated her opposition to 'Socialism by the back Delors'.

In exhorting acceptance of the Social Charter, Jacques Delors claimed that 'its sole object is to provide a formal reminder that the Community has no intention of sacrificing fundamental workers' rights on the altar of economic efficiency. How could anyone object to such an idea, which is to be found in all our social traditions? How could anyone dispute the political and rhetorical significance of this message for a people's Europe, for the man in the street?' In fact the British found it all too easy to object to the whole concept for at least three reasons – that it was unwarranted Commission interference into matters best left to the national authorities, that it would put up business costs and that it was a negation of the free market principle which the Conservative government vigorously espoused.

The Social Charter (or Community Charter of Fundamental Social Rights of Workers as it is sometimes called) enshrined the following rights for Community citizens.

The right to freedom of movement

This right enables citizens of the European Community to establish themselves and to exercise any occupation in any of the member states on the same terms as those applying to the nationals of the host country.

This right is thus concerned mainly with freedom of movement, freedom of establishment, equal treatment, and the working conditions and social protection guaranteed to nationals of the host country.

This right also implies that endeavours be continued to harmonize conditions of residence, especially as regards the reuniting of families and the elimination of obstacles deriving from the lack of equivalence of diplomas.

The right to employment and remuneration

This principle acknowledges that any citizen of the Community has the right to employment and to fair remuneration for that employment.

The right to remuneration also aims at the establishment of a decent basic wage, receipt of a fair wage and the guarantee of an equitable reference wage for workers who are not in full-time employment of indefinite duration, and the maintenance of adequate means of subsistence in the event of attachment of wages.

The right to improved living and working conditions

This right, which is concerned with the development of the single market and, above all, the labour market, aims at the harmonization of the working and living conditions of Community citizens while endeavours continue to improve them.

It is concerned mainly with the organization and flexibility of working time (maximum working time, part-time work, fixed-duration employment, temporary employment, weekend work, shift work, annual leave, weekly or regular rest periods, etc.) and the approximation of the various labour regulations in force in the Community (collective redundancy procedures, declaration and settlement of bankruptcies, etc.).

The right to social protection

This right aims at ensuring all citizens of the Community, whatever their status, adequate social protection by guaranteeing a minimum wage to workers and appropriate social assistance for persons excluded from the labour market and those who lack adequate means of subsistence.

The right to freedom of association and collective bargaining

This principle recognizes the right of all employers and all workers in the European Community to join professional organizations freely.

Apart from that, it also implies recognition of freedom to bargain and conclude collective agreement between the two sides of industry and, in the event of conflicts of interest, to resort to collective action such as, for example, strikes.

The right to vocational training

Every worker in the European Community has the right to continue his or her vocational training throughout their working life.

This right implies, in particular, the organization of training leave enabling Community citizens to be retrained or to acquire additional skills by taking advantage of the facilities for continuing and permanent training which the public authorities, companies and the two sides of industry are called on to set up.

The right of men and women to equal treatment

This right covers far more than equal pay for men and women performing the same work. It aims at ensuring equal treatment as regards access to an occupation, social protection, education, vocational training and career opportunities.

The right to worker information, consultation and participation

This principle covers the right of workers, especially those employed in undertakings established in several member states, to be informed and even consulted about major events affecting the life of the undertaking and likely to have an impact on working conditions and the maintenance of employment.

The right to health and safety protection at the workplace

The adoption of this principle acknowledges that every worker has the right to satisfactory health and safety conditions at his or her place of work. This implies that adequate measures must be taken to harmonize and improve the conditions pertaining in the individual member states.

The right to protection of children and adolescents

This principle sets the minimum working age at 16 and gives young people in employment the right to a fair wage, to be covered by the labour regulations which take account of their specific characteristics and also to embark, after completion of statutory schooling, upon two years of vocational training.

The rights of elderly persons

Any person who has reached retirement, or early retirement, age is entitled to receive a pension enabling him or her to maintain a decent standard of living.

This principle also grants to retired persons who are not entitled to a pension the right to a minimum income, to social protection and both social and medical assistance.

The rights of disabled persons

Every disabled person has the right to take advantage of specific measures, especially in the field of training and occupational and social integration and rehabilitation.

Soon the Commission proceeded to produce action programmes as it had been so charged by the European Council in December 1989. The Commissioner in charge of Social Affairs, Mrs Vasso Papandreou, used the enthusiasm for the Social Charter to begin pushing through a series of directives in a Social Action Programme consisting of 48 measures. Some vocational programmes were easily agreed, for example EUROFORM, a programme of training schemes to meet new needs resulting from completion of the single market, HORIZON, a programme to help the handicapped, and NOW, a programme to promote the vocational training of women.

A number of other directives met stiff resistance, mainly from employers' groups and Britain. The 1992 directive setting a maximum of a 48-hour working week with a guarantee of four weeks' paid holiday was particularly disputed by the British government and UNICE, the European employers' federation. Britain also disliked Commission proposals to protect part-time and temporary workers. Its government's opposition to both directives is understandable: Britain with Denmark was the only member state without laws governing maximum working hours and had a particularly large number of temporary and part-time workers.

The Commission's attempts to improve women's maternity leave were opposed by Britain which had the worst provision for maternity leave in the whole of the EC. On this occasion the British government won some support from Spain and Ireland and Mrs Papandreou's original proposals, made in October 1990, were rather watered down by the time that the Council of Ministers resolved the matter in December 1991. The original proposal had been 14 weeks' maternity leave on full pay for women who had paid social security contributions for one year with a guaranteed return to the job done prior to going on leave. The final decision replaced the full pay clause with maternity leave remuneration being set at the same level as sick pay.

At the Maastricht Summit, the Social Chapter of the Political Union Treaty was at British insistence removed from the treaty itself to form a separate protocol which enabled the other eleven states to proceed with the Social Charter. Where Britain feels that it cannot accept a proposal it will opt out of discussions and decisions. In such cases the remaining states can decide some social issues by qualified majority voting which will consist of 44 votes out of 66 votes, for example health and safety at work. Other areas, for example social security, will still require unanimity.

The problems of social policy

Despite an impressive array of schemes, Social Policy in the EC still suffers from serious weaknesses. One severe constraint has been the tiny proportion of the Community budget devoted to social work. In 1981 it gained only 850 million ECU, about 4.6 per cent of the budget. At a time when unemployment was reaching 11 million this figure was grossly inadequate. By 1991 the ESF share of the budget had risen to 4 billion ECU a year and is set to double again by 1999 but whether this is enough to fund sufficient worthwhile schemes that may reduce Community unemployment is open to question.

Even where the Community does influence employment issues, its action is often unwelcome to pressure groups such as employers' federations and to member states. Long delays then arise in implementing the social change proposed. A clear example of such delay is the cause of industrial democracy in the EC. As long ago as 1980, the Vredeling initiative (named after the Commissioner who drew up the directive) proposed formal employee information and consultative procedures. It met with strong opposition from member states and employers' groups, and the watered down version was unacceptable to the trades unions. Only in December 1990 was a new draft directive on informing and consulting employees drawn up. It proposed worker representation on the boards of directors in companies with more than 1,000 employees where at least 100 workers were employed in each of two EC states. A similar directive required such companies to set up a European works council where strategic matters would be discussed such as plant closures, employment contracts, new working practices and the introduction of new technology.

More fundamentally the question must be asked whether ESF measures will contribute to a solution of social pressures or actually aggravate them. Those who argue that a supranational EC approach is necessary in social policy use the social dumping argument. In their view, without such EC action, poorer Community states will hold down wages and social benefits in order to be more competitive. Richer member states will then be relatively high-cost and in effect have unemployment exported to them. Investment will also go to poorer regions where costs are low. Hence northern European states where standards of worker protection are high will have to lower them to stay competitive. Hence the absolute need for a Social Charter as Peter Curwen has explained: 'The purpose of the Social Charter is thus to protect the living standards and working conditions of employees threatened by the move towards the Single European Market'.

However in Curwen's view such assumptions may not be correct. Firms locate in a particular region for many reasons beyond wage costs. They require trained labour, high quality component suppliers and good transport facilities and will tend therefore to locate mainly in rich member states which preserve their share of investment. Poorer states which have to improve their social welfare measures may see their competitive position worsen. They are already facing fierce competition from Newly Industrializing Countries (NICs) as well as from more competitive partners in the EC. They have the highest rates of unemployment in the EC and a further addition to their costs brought about by ESF legislation could result in a vicious circle of cumulative decline. Faced with such prospects the poorer states may well fail to enforce the new social regulations with any fervour.

Whatever the precise effect of ESF measures, it is clear that companies across the EC will have to undertake careful scrutiny of the growing body of legislation to ensure that they are not infringing the new laws. Nor should private companies, educational institutions and public authorities neglect the opportunities for funding from the ESF. Nevertheless they should be warned that the procedures for making applications for such funding are often tortuous and lengthy. From time to time the Commission concentrates on the assistance of particular groups, and companies need to be sure that their proposal is 'flavour of the month'. The administrative procedures involved and the financial accounts required are extremely detailed. Risks and time lags are involved as regards both applications and claims. Often the successful applicant will not be notified until halfway through the programme so in effect the organization involved has to underwrite the risk of the Commission turning down the application. Even when an application is successful, ESF cash sometimes does not arrive until some time after the completion of the programme. Even then the claim may not be met in full. Auditors from the Commission can descend up to 7 years from the date of application and, if they are not satisfied with the way in which the programme was implemented, they can make deductions from the original amount promised. As with so many sources of EC cash, ESF funding has to be worked for by patience and attention to detail. Given a viable scheme, however, such perseverance is usually rewarded.

Other sources of Community funding

The third of the structural funds proper is the European Agricultural Guarantee and Guidance Fund (EAGGF). The Guidance section of the fund is principally concerned with the fifth of the five common objectives of Structural Funding, i.e. to reform the CAP by speeding up the adjustment of agricultural structures and the development of rural areas.

Funding is available to improve the marketing and processing of agricultural products, the diversification of agricultural production, the fostering of alternative activities for farmers and the development of the social fabric of rural areas.

Unlike the other structural funds the Guidance section of the EAGGF is subject to Council legislation. The Council of Ministers has shown in recent regulations particular concern to encourage diversification in farming through the development of tourism, crafts and manufacture. Grants have also been given to help young farmers get started and to help older farmers to retire.

In addition to the structural funds, the EC has contributed to regional development with a range of financial incentives in the form of both loans and grants. These sources of cash are not huge in the context of national government or business expenditure yet business people often find them a useful addition to their armoury in the fight to finance new plants, equipment or services. In coal and steel areas the European Coal and Steel Community (ECSC) gave loans totalling nearly 12 billion ECUs by 1984 for the modernization of the coal and steel industries and for the creation of new industries in regions where the coal and steel industries were in decline. Loans are offered at attractive rates of interest up to 50 per cent of the gross capital costs of the project and priority projects can receive an interest rebate of 30 percentage points per year for 5 years. Projects do not have to be related to the coal and steel industries but they must involve the creation or expansion of job opportunities in defined coal and steel areas. Loans can also be made to improve housing in such areas and grants are also given to supplement unemployment benefit and retraining schemes for workers made redundant.

In a separate initiative to provide help to regions in need of support, the Commission introduced in 1990 the RECHAR programme to improve the environment, promote new economic activities and develop human resources in coal-mining areas of the EC. Between 1990 and 1993 the ERDF and ESF provided 300 million ECUs to promote tourism, the conversion of disused industrial sites, vocational training and start-up assistance.

The European Investment Bank (EIB) grants loans from its own resources at market rates for productive or infrastructure investment projects, mainly in the problem regions. Of the total of 30 billion ECUs lent in the Community since 1958, 69 per cent has gone to projects in less developed or declining regions. Lending operations by the EIB have expanded steadily each year in the United Kingdom and reached a total of £660 million in 1985 bringing the total of funds lent by the bank to the United Kingdom to nearly £4,200 million since 1973.

The EIB was created in 1958 by the Rome Treaty which set up the bank to finance projects on a non-profit making basis contributing to the development of the Common Market. Its main task as set out in the Rome Treaty is to fund projects which contribute to the development of underdeveloped regions though it can also provide finance for projects that are of common interest to several member countries or benefit the Community as a whole. It is a Community institution set up to provide long-term funds for investments meeting Community priorities and it operates according to basic banking principles, raising the bulk of its funds on national and international markets. It is the largest institutional borrower after the World Bank. Its excellent credit rating enables it to raise funds at very reasonable rates of interest, passing on this benefit to its borrowers. The bank usually lends long-term at fixed interest rates but it also provides variable interest rate loans as well as loans on which capital is repaid in full at term, these being known as 'bullet loans'. EIB direct loans are from about £1.5 million upwards but smaller amounts of finance are made available to small and medium-sized ventures through its global loan schemes, obtainable through banks or other financing institutions.

The EIB has in the last decade tried harder to direct its finance at small and medium-sized enterprises (SMEs). However it is only one of a number of ways in which the Community has attempted to improve SME access to finance, given the needs of smaller firms in the enlarged European market. Schemes specifically designed to help SMEs innovate more successfully include EUROTECH, a scheme encouraging private companies to provide finance for the promoters of transnational high-technology projects and the SMEs taking part in them. In addition the Venture Consort scheme facilitates SME access to venture capital for innovative projects.

To provide general support for SMEs, the EC has developed a number of measures. A network of Business and Innovation Centres (BICs) has been created to stimulate the growth of new SMEs. These centres offer a comprehensive range of services such as training, marketing, finance, business planning and technology transfer.

A number of schemes have been initiated to facilitate cross-border co-operation and joint ventures between SMEs. The Business Co-operation Network (BC-NET) – nicknamed the Marriage Bureau – was set up by the Commission in 1973 to encourage co-operation between firms in different member states wishing to increase competitiveness and respond to the opportunities opened up by access to the Community's markets. It also provides information on relevant national company law and Community laws on co-operation. Any firm may use its services but its main function is to help small and medium-sized firms. The kind of co-operation that the BC-NET tries to instigate between different companies is in the field of research, joint buying and pooling of management knowledge and sales networks.

By 1984 over 100,000 enquiries had been received and BC-NET claimed that more than 800 'marriages' had been arranged. Recently much of its energy has been concentrated on helping companies in Spain and Portugal but it also responds to requests from EC firms wishing to forge links outside the Community, for example in EFTA states and Canada. Operating procedures are similar to a marriage bureau but only nominal fees are charged. The computerized network links some 350 business advisers.

A scheme complementing the work of BC-NET is EUROPARTENARIAT. This is designed to encourage cross-border business links between regions with development problems and other regions of the EC.

Funds are available under the SPRINT programme for measures helping the transfer of new technologies to SMEs. Starting in 1989 the programme has three main objectives.

(*a*) To strengthen transnational networks of specialized intermediaries who can help SMEs to find partners in other Community states with whom to make technology agreements.
(*b*) To develop and implement projects for the transfer of innovation across national boundaries.

(c) To improve the e
    developments and
    between member cc

In addition to these so
of funding for research a
the technological base of
ing that of education is an
ments of the member stat
funding for their own nati
13.

Further reading

European Policy Research (̖ _ ̖ι ̖ορean *Commission Funding for Business Development*, Kogan Page (Second Edition), London, 1993.

Hurwitz, L and Lequesne, C (eds), *The State of the European Community*, Longmans, London, 1991.

Rouffignac, P D and Gregg, P, *Profiting from Europe*, Computer Weekly Publications, Sutton, 1992.

Teagues, P, *The European Community: The Social Dimension*, Kogan Page, London, 1989.

Venturini, P, 1992: *The European Social Dimension*, European Commission, Luxembourg, 1989.

Questions

1 What are the major obstacles to an effective Community regional policy?

2 Justify the implementing of a Community regional policy to complement national regional policies.

3 What motives lay behind the creation of the Social Charter? What impact may it have on employment?

4 Do you agree with Professor Minford that the structural funds constitute 'daylight robbery'?

5 In addition to the structural funds what other sources of finance are available for business?

an Monetary Union and the
opean Monetary System

European Monetary Union: some considerations

Although the Treaty of Rome does not specifically state that European Monetary Union (EMU) should be established, the founding fathers foresaw the Community evolving into a fully-fledged common market with the complete monetary and economic integration of its members. Such integration was assumed to be beneficial for political and economic reasons and was supported down the years by ringing declarations such as the Werner Report in 1970.

EMU only moved to the forefront of the political agenda with the Delors Report of 1989 which advocated a move towards monetary union in Europe run by a European System of Central Banks (ESCB). The move was to be achieved in three stages. The first stage which started in 1990 had as its objective the strengthening of monetary policy co-ordination and the achievement of greater economic convergence by the member states. All currencies would need to become full members of the European Monetary System (EMS) and its chief component, the Exchange Rate Mechanism (ERM) (see p. 177). The second stage would consist of increased collective decision-making over economic objectives such as budgetary deficits and inflation. The third stage would see irrevocably fixed exchanged rates, preferably a single currency and a new European Central Bank acquiring and managing the reserves of Community member states as well as managing external exchange rates. A timetable for Stages 2 and 3 was agreed at the Maastricht Summit in December 1991 (see Chapter 15).

However such a blueprint begs two questions – what kind of monetary union is envisaged and is monetary union in itself an unalloyed blessing? Community plans envisage complete monetary union whereby the member states abolish their own currencies and replace them with a single currency that would be used throughout the EC. Thus there would be an end to national currencies such as the pound, franc or mark, these being replaced by a European currency, perhaps called the ECU.

Whether such a single currency system is necessary for complete monetary union is debated by economists. For there to be a monetary union in practice it would be sufficient for all the states concerned to operate a system of irrevocably fixed exchange rates with the different currencies fully convertible, i.e. exchangeable in any quantity and at any time for each other at the fixed exchange rate. Another possibility, supported by the British government, is to keep national currencies, fix exchange rates irrevocably, guarantee full convertibility and at the same time establish a *parallel* currency throughout the EC. Thus there would be a *common* currency but not a single currency. To some extent the ECU (see p. 181) has fulfilled this role of a common currency. The idea behind this method is that as the parallel currency becomes more widely used and accepted (a likely eventuality owing to its strength) it will gradually replace the national currencies and thus pave the way for a single currency system.

Whatever form of monetary union is pursued, it is clear that it will require a large amount of co-operation and joint economic policy-making by the member states, with implications for national economic sovereignty. To prepare for the monetary union, economic convergence (the achievement of similar policies and similar levels of inflation, interest rates and budget deficits) is essential, especially over inflation. A country suffering higher inflation than its partners, other things being equal, will find that its exports become expensive and its imports relatively cheap. This imposes a downward pressure on its exchange rate which in a free market is determined by the demand for the currency (inflows of foreign currencies in payment for its exports and capital movements into the country) and the supply of its currency (outflows of the currency to pay for its imports and capital movements out of the country). The balance of trade would also tend to go into deficit. In a free market such problems can be self-correcting: the country can allow its currency to float downwards thus making its exports cheaper and its imports dearer. Such an option would be lost in a monetary union and therefore member states of any intended monetary union must harmonize inflation levels before entering the union.

The second question to be addressed is whether monetary union is on balance beneficial. In October 1990 the Commissioner for Financial Affairs, Henning Christophersen unveiled a Commission report entitled *One Market, One Money*. Drafted with the help of economists from outside the Commission, it claimed to be the first study providing a comprehensive and thorough assessment of the potential benefits of EMU.

One argument stressed was the benefit arising from the elimination of exchange rate variability in the Community arising from the creation of a single currency. Businesses would enjoy freedom from exchange rate risks and would be more confident in trading goods and services across Community frontiers. Without such a single currency, uncertainties about exchange valuations between the currencies in the EC either necessitate expensive short-term hedging costs or deter long-term investment. The poorer member states, having weaker and more volatile currencies, suffer more from such currency uncertainties than the richer member states. In a single currency area businesses would also benefit from the greater economies of scale achieved while consumers would benefit from the intensified competition arising from the enlarged amount of trade.

A second advantage stressed was the saving associated with the elimination of transaction costs incurred when one currency is exchanged for another. The Commission estimated that the elimination of transaction costs could save as much as 13 to 19 billion ECU per annum or up to at least 0.5 per cent of the Community's GDP as a whole and up to 1 per cent in the case of the smaller member states' GDP. Such costs are not a negligible factor for tourists and the business sector, as a 1991 *Sunday Times* experiment proved. A team of the paper's journalists carried out the exercise of changing £100 into all the other eleven member states' currencies one by one and ended with only £65.44. Many other travellers have experienced much worse transaction costs which would have reduced the original sum by over half if they had carried out the same exercise as the *Sunday Times*. Naturally, were a single currency to be implemented, there would be losers – the financial institutions which gain commission from the provision of foreign currencies.

A third advantage in the view of the Commission was the potential improvement in monetary policy caused by the increased control over it by a European Central Bank. The thinking here is that central banks in individual member states are not free from political interference: they are, as in the case of the Bank of England, merely the lackeys of the government in office and have to co-operate in policies which are motivated by short-term political considerations and not by long-term economic issues. For example they have to support expansionary policies just before elections though such policies will be inflationary. An independent European Central Bank, the argument goes, would be more immune to such political pressures and more able to follow consistent long-term economic objectives. Thus inflation would be contained more easily under EMU than under a system run by national governments. Supporters of this view point to the German Bundesbank as an example of how an independent central bank can impose real monetary discipline.

A fourth alleged advantage of EMU is its effect on lowering interest rates throughout the EC. Currently high inflation economies have had to maintain the value of their currencies by high interest rates, usually 1 per cent to 2.5 per cent higher than those obtaining in the strongest economy, Germany. In a single currency area such a function for interest rates would be redundant and, given the added advantage of easier movement of capital, interest rates would fall to the level of those in Germany, assisting growth and reducing business costs.

Finally the Commission report stressed that monetary union would confer benefits to the union in items of its *external* position, i.e. in its relations with the rest of the world. The member states of the union would be less susceptible to changes and shocks in the global economy as a union than they would be acting as individual countries. With the European currency becoming a third great world currency alongside the dollar and the yen, member states would have more political and economic clout on the world scene. In addition, if the ECU became an international reserve currency rivalling the dollar and yen, European member states would be able to enjoy the advantages of seigniorage, a technical term denoting a situation where member states can allow imports to exceed exports, the balance being financed by the willingness of the rest of the world to hold the union currency. Consequently there results a transfer of resources from the rest of the world to the EC currency zone, though if the rest of the world earned interest on its ECU balances there would be a flow of resources out of the EC. According to the 1990 Commission report, international seigniorage revenues from long-term accumulation of the ECU abroad amount to some 28 billion ECU.

The Commission also affirmed that the pooling of the EC's exchange reserves would mean a saving of them because the reserves needed to be held by the union would be less than the sum of the reserves needed to be held if the states acted independently. The saving of the EC's exchange reserves was estimated to be about 160 billion ECU. At the same time the increased use of the ECU in world business would provide for a decrease in transaction costs with non-EC states of up to 0.05 per cent of the Community's GDP.

Commission euphoria on the benefits of EMU have not passed unchallenged; indeed the whole question of EMU has been hotly debated. Some critics, for example Professor Martin Feldstein, refute the assumption that monetary union is necessary for the creation of a true single market and claim that a shift to a common currency could actually diminish trade within the EC, raising unemployment and inflation rates along the way. Such critics accuse the supporters of monetary union of seeking EMU less for its economic benefits and more for political reasons. A single currency would be a step towards political union because it would symbolize a further development towards a European super-state.

In any case critics challenge the assumption that EMU would bring economic gains. No statistics have shown that currency fluctuations have actually inhibited businesses from expanding their sales to or purchases from other member states. If businesses are really worried about exchange risk, they can minimize it in a number of ways. They can hedge in the market for foreign exchange futures, the markets of which have become more efficient in recent years. Banks will quote firm rates of exchange for most world currencies up to a year ahead and exporters can enter into a forward exchange contract with a bank. This contract fixes the rate at which the bank will buy the currency of the country of settlement at an agreed future date or during a period of time when the funds are expected to be received. Exporters receive an added bonus because the forward bank buying rates are often better than the spot rate. Another method of reducing exchange risk is to trade in ECUs (see p. 184).

The same argument can be used against the claim that EMU is valuable because it would lower transaction costs. Sophisticated hedging can eliminate currency risks associated with portfolio investments and other financial transactions between European states.

A single currency may in some cases be an obstacle to expanded trade. Take the case of a British manufacturer attempting to sell in France and facing competition from an American producer. If the dollar then fell relative to the European currency, the British manufacturer would be at a disadvantage. If there were still a pound, free to fall in line with the dollar, the British manufacturer would compete on equal terms with his American rival but in a single currency zone such devaluation would not be possible and trade between European states would be diminished.

A single currency could reduce intra-European trade for another reason. A single tariff free market should encourage member states to specialize on those products in which they have a comparative advantage. But such specialization makes a country more vulnerable to fluctuations in demand caused by temporary changes in tastes or market conditions. Such fluctuations can be offset by a country which still has its own currency and economic policy, for example by allowing the currency to float down or stimulating the economy through lower interest rates. Such freedom is lost within a single currency system and product specialization becomes riskier.

Thus the alleged gains of a single currency union appear uncertain but the disadvantages are not. In particular there would be the loss of economic sovereignty by member states which, as Lintner and Mazy have shown, takes two forms. Firstly monetary union implies the loss of control over the *objectives* of economic policy. Targets may be set by the European Central Bank (on inflation, unemployment levels, interest rates etc.) which are very different to those which an individual member state would have chosen. Secondly membership of a monetary union deprives a country of control over important *tools of economic management*, above all the use of the exchange rate as a method of restoring competitiveness. Many other tools of economic control – taxation levels, government spending, interest rates – would also be sacrificed.

Nevertheless critics of EMU must allow that the loss of economic sovereignty within a single currency zone could be more apparent than real. Small member states in the EC such as the Netherlands have had constantly in recent decades to tie in their economic policies with those of the larger states, especially Germany. Even the largest EC states can no longer easily pursue independent economic policies as France found in the early 1980s. When the new Mitterand government attempted to implement expansionary policies between 1981 and 1983 when most other member states were following contractionary economic policies, France soon experienced rising inflation and increasing trade deficits. Accordingly in 1983 the French government was forced to abandon its previous stance and follow tight monetary and fiscal policies.

However for a group of independent countries to adopt a single currency is a risky move unless the economies of the individual members are very similar and labour highly mobile. If these two criteria are met, then there will be a particular monetary and fiscal policy appropriate for all members and if there are temporary differences in economic conditions, workers can move from regions suffering declining demand to regions enjoying stronger demand. Thus such differences would be self-correcting and make local economic policies unnecessary. In such a situation monetary union would confer gains from lower transaction costs and expanded financial markets. But in the EC individual countries are very *different* in the mix of products which they produce, in their dependence on imported oil and in the foreign markets to which they sell. Any greater specialization resulting from the completion of the single market can only increase these differences as would any enlargement involving EFTA or East European states in the mid or late 1990s. The task of developing one appropriate economic policy for such a motley collection of states would be impossible.

Nor has the EC a mobile labour force which would move from declining to prosperous regions within the EC. Labour mobility is rather limited within the Community. The key reasons would appear to be language and a culture which dislikes such mobility (the desire to maintain a family's roots, the wish to maintain the education of children without disruption, the maintenance of existing welfare benefits). Only from poorer to richer member states is migration at all significant and such migration may increase in the single market. Yet as Patrick Minford has stressed, even this mobility is not large 'because capital mobility within the free EC market enables workers in poor countries such as Spain, parts of the UK and Southern Italy, on the periphery of the EC to attract investment and enjoy improved wages without the cost of moving'.

Arguably the economies of the weaker member states will suffer in a single currency area. Outside such a zone they can allow their exchange rates to decline as a means of making their products more competitive. Inside a currency union exchange rates cannot be so adjusted and therefore uncompetitive countries can only remain competitive by reducing prices, particularly by squeezing down wages. This is a painful process and firms that cannot squeeze wages sufficiently will have to shed labour, thus increasing unemployment. Such unemployment will go on rising until there is sufficient downward pressure on wages to restore competitiveness. The greater the differences in inflation rates and the less flexible real wages are, the greater will be the resulting unemployment. At present there is no evidence that real wages are sufficiently flexible within the EC to avoid very large amounts of unemployment. Therefore at the very least it may be argued that EMU should be delayed until the different inflation levels between the member states have converged.

Thus the critics of EMU suggest that economic analysis and economic realities do not provide support for a single European currency. Furthermore they allege that supporters of EMU are politically rather than economically motivated. Such supporters see an independent European Central Bank (ECB) as a way of restricting national governments which pursue inflationary policies. European central bankers who currently must answer to their governments would be able to follow tight monetary and fiscal policies with less political interference.

Whether this would work in practice is questionable because under the rules laid down by the Maastricht Treaty (see Chapter 15) voting members of the ECB's governing board would be appointed by the member governments and would be eligible for subsequent political appointments by their own governments. Would then the ECB's governing body be in practice a united and virtuously anti-inflationary team?

In fact a second political motive is the wish of most member states to escape from the realities of the European Monetary System where in practice German hegemony has meant other member states following Germany's strong anti-inflationary stance, successfully so until 1992. Therefore there is here a rich irony: some advocates of a single currency and a European Central Bank want such developments as a way of escaping from the discipline of German policy imposed by the Bundesbank.

Those who most enthusiastically support EMU do so for a third reason, that it will be a step towards fuller political union. A single currency would give the peoples of Europe more of a sense that they are part of a single country of Europe even though they speak different languages and have different national histories. A single currency and a European Central Bank would transfer substantial power away from national governments to the centre as the EC moved towards becoming a single state.

We now turn to the progress so far achieved in the direction of EMU through the creation of the European Monetary System (EMS)

The background to the European Monetary System

In the early years of the Community, little interest in the idea of monetary union existed. Since 1945 the free world has successfully created a system of fixed but adjustable exchange rates, a system which rested on the international agreements reached at Bretton Woods in the United States in 1944. The International Monetary Fund (IMF) was set up to support this system, the foundation of which was the overwhelming economic importance of the United States in the post-war world.

The United States was ready at that time to accept that the dollAr should be the main reserve currency of the system with its value strictly tied to the value of gold, to assist the reconstruction of other countries through generous Marshall Aid and to make it possible for the central banks of other countries to rebuild their reserves of dollars. The United States was able to perform such a role because it had large gold reserves, few foreign debts, was much less dependent on foreign trade than its trading partners and had a strong competitive advantage in many products, especially high technology products. As the economies of other industrial countries expanded in the 1950s and 1960s they required greatly increased reserves of dollars which came increasingly to be supplied by the United States as credit.

Such domination by the almighty dollar was resented, particularly by the French. In February 1965 de Gaulle at a famous press conference eulogized the various qualities of gold, in particular the quality that it 'has no nationality'. Ironically, American economic domination was already coming to an end by 1965 as the strength of American industry declined relative to the rest of the industrialized world. Along with relative industrial decline came a weakening of the dollar as an automatically reliable currency. However the Bretton Woods system of fixed exchange rates survived until 1971. In that year President Nixon tried to inflate the American economy with a package of measures which caused international speculation against the dollar. The free market gold price rose sharply and several countries began to demand conversion of their surplus dollars into gold at the official price. The Federal Reserve Bank which held only $50 billion in other countries' currencies could not cope and was forced to suspend convertibility in August 1971. The dollar now became free to float, mainly in a downward direction.

The decline of the dollar was not the only cause of a breakdown in currency stability in this period. Towards 1968 came rising unemployment and an acceleration in inflation which started to rise from the annual rates of between 3 and 4 per cent of earlier years steadily into double figures, with wide differences from country to country. The first serious crisis came in France in the wake of the 1968 'French Revolution' and though a devaluation of the French franc was avoided in 1968, it became inevitable in 1969 along with a revaluation of the German mark.

These two developments seriously disrupted the Community and prompted the introduction of monetary compensation amounts. They also prompted much discussion in 1969 and 1970 on possible solutions to the new situation of currency instability. At The Hague summit meeting in December 1969 the Heads of State agreed in principle to the creation of an economic and monetary union and that work should begin on methods of implementing it.

Two schools of thought emerged on how to approach the issue – the monetarists (mainly comprising the French, Belgians and the Commission) and the economists (the Germans and Dutch). The monetarists wanted immediate implementation of fixed exchange rates within the Community, with strict controls over capital mobility. Co-ordination and harmonization of member states' economic policies should, in their view, be introduced later. A major French motive here was that the immediate adoption of fixed exchange rates would eliminate the new problem of MCAs.

On the 'economist' side, the leading protagonist was Dr Schiller, the West German Finance Minister, who produced a plan for Monetary, Economic and Financial Co-operation. He wanted more or less immediate introduction of the co-ordination and harmonization of economic policies to be followed quickly by complete freedom of capital mobility. Only then, in his view, should fixed exchange rates leading to a single European currency be introduced. What worried the Germans was that an early freezing of exchange rates could lead to heavy inflation in West Germany and an underpricing of her industrial commodities. They also argued that permanent fixing of exchange rates would force the weaker members to manage their economies by high interest rates and a pruning of government spending, both of which would be deflationary and result in high unemployment.

The West German methods, with hindsight, do seem more realistic. Until the economic policies of member states are co-ordinated, the introduction of fixed exchange rates will create problems. For example, if a country with higher inflation than its competitors is precluded from devaluing its currency, then it is likely to experience an adverse balance of payments for which the only remaining remedy is deflation – and rising unemployment.

Faced with this diversity of view, the Council of Ministers set up a group led by Pierre Werner, the Prime Minister of Luxembourg, to examine the problem. The Werner Report which encapsulated the group's findings was a compromise between the position of the 'monetarists' and that of the 'economists'. It proposed the achievement by 1980 of an economic and monetary union by stages but was specific only about the first stage from 1971 to 1973. It did not follow the wishes of the monetarists who wanted fixed exchange rates immediately but it proposed a compromise scheme in the shape of a reduction of the margin of fluctuation around the central parities when a Community currency was exchanged for another. Here lay the origins of what became known as 'the snake in the tunnel'.

Two crises in 1971 accelerated the adoption of the first stage of the Werner Report. In May speculation caused by expectations of a revalued German mark forced the closure of the foreign exchange markets in West Germany, the Netherlands and Belgium as speculators sought to buy marks. More seriously in August, the deteriorating American balance of payments forced President Nixon to announce a package of measures which included the suspension of convertibility of the American dollar for gold. The old order that had existed since 1945 had well and truly ended.

Some degree of stability was restored in December 1971 by the Washington (Smithsonian Institute) agreement which allowed exchange rates more room to fluctuate than they had under the Bretton Woods rules. After a new set of exchange rates was agreed, including a devaluation of the dollar, currencies were free to move within a band of 2.25 per cent on either side of their dollar parity. As a result, European currencies could move against each other by 9 per cent because if one currency was 2.25 per cent above its dollar parity and another 2.25 per cent below, the gap between the two was 4.5 per cent. If they were in reversed positions, they would open up a 4.5 per cent gap the other way.

Many European governments thought that this 9 per cent swing was too large a permitted fluctuation. Therefore at the Basle agreement of 1972, narrower limits were set for Europe's currencies. The Six, plus the three countries about to join the Community (Britain, Denmark and Ireland), agreed to allow their currencies to move against each other by a maximum of only 2.25 per cent. This band was to be maintained within the 4.5 per cent limits allowed against the dollar. From this arrangement came the phrase, the 'snake in the tunnel'.

The 1972 snake had a brief and unhappy life. Exchange market pressure forced Britain and Ireland (whose pounds were still closely tied) to withdraw within six weeks. In 1973 Italy also withdrew. France withdrew in 1974, rejoined in 1975 and left again in 1976. The snake by then had become merely a West German group with small countries like Holland fixing their currencies against the mark.

Whey did the snake fail? The Marjolin working group of 1974 pointed to three main factors – a lack of political will among member states, adverse events and an inadequate understanding of the nature of an economic and monetary union. The adverse events were the international monetary crisis that had continued since the late 1960s (especially the instability of the dollar) and the abrupt rise in oil prices in 1973. Member states had very mixed success in coping with the economic difficulties that resulted. Until 1972, at least in the Six, the disparities in inflation between European states had been kept within tolerable bounds, even though the inflation rate itself was becoming excessive. From 1973 on, the differences in inflation rates became so large as to be incompatible with exchange rate stability. In the years 1971 to 1975, for example, Britain's average inflation rate was 13 per cent compared to West Germany's 6 per cent. If a member state with a higher inflation rate than average found itself with a balance of payments problem, it would then need to devalue its currency.

The situation deteriorated further between 1976 and 1978 as both inflation and unemployment in the Community rose and exchange rates floated, often in a highly volatile way. Clearly a new initiative was needed.

Birth and evolution of the European Monetary System, 1979–92

The Commission proposed new measures in the Jenkins Report of 1977 which stressed the need for stronger co-ordination of short-term economic prices, measures to complete the common market and an overall strategy on industrial redeployment. Following the Commission's initiative, the European Council, mainly at the prompting of Helmut Schmidt and Giscard d'Estaing agreed to devise 'a scheme for the creation of closer monetary co-operation leading to a zone of monetary stability in Europe'. The principle was agreed at the Bremen summit of July 1978 and at the Brussels summit of December 1978 the European Council adopted a resolution on the introduction of a European Monetary System and related questions. Eight member states agreed to participate but Britain declined to enter the system which began operation in March 1979.

The European Monetary System (EMS) is a highly complex system composed of fixed but adjustable exchange rates, an intervention system, a new kind of money and large credit facilities. Its novel features are:

(a) The creation of a European currency unit (ECU), the value and composition of which are defined in terms of a basket of Community currencies, weighted according to each country's GNP and volume of intra-European trade. The value of the ECU was identical with that of the former European unit of account (EUA). The composition of the basket can be reviewed every five years or whenever the weight factors of one currency change by 25 per cent.

The ECU has become part of the international reserves of the European central banks. They obtain ECUs in return for depositing 20 per cent of their holdings of gold and dollars with the European Monetary Co-operation Fund (EMCF) which is sometimes known as FECOM from its French initials. Central banks also use the ECU to denominate their debts and credits with each other and each currency's central rate in the EMS is defined in ECUs. The ECU is also being used increasingly in commercial transactions. Companies that wish to minimize the risk of fluctuation in exchange rates find a currency basket like the ECU a more stable way to borrow or put a price on export contracts and hold bank deposits.

(b) A two pronged approach to stabilizing exchange rates by use of a parity grid and a divergence indicator. Participating Community currencies are assigned a central rate expressed as units of currency per ECU (see Table 9.1).

From these central rates can be derived a parity grid, showing the bilateral central rate between any pair of participating currencies. Bilateral intervention limits are calculated by applying margins of plus or minus 2.25 per cent to these central rates. When two currencies reach their maximum permitted divergence from the bilateral central rate, their central banks are required to intervene in the market for foreign exchange to prevent any further divergence. If, for example, the French franc falls to its 2.25 per cent floor against the German mark, the Bank of France sells marks while the German Bundesbank buys francs. This is the notorious Exchange Rate Mechanism (ERM).

This method of defending currencies is similar to the arrangements in the old snake. To avoid too many interventions by central banks, the ERM is equipped with an early-warning system known as the divergence indicator and nicknamed the rattlesnake. Each EMS currency has a divergence threshold set at three quarters of the maximum permitted difference between its actual ECU rate and its ECU central rate. Once a country's

Table 9.1   Central rates of the national
currencies in ECU (22 November 1992)

Currency	Value
Belgian Franc	40.6034
German Mark	1.96992
Danish Krone	7.5141
Dutch Guilder	2.21958
French Franc	6.06683
Irish Punt	0.735334
Luxembourg Franc	40.6034
Portuguese Escudo	182.194
Spanish Peseta	143.386
*UK Pound	0.805748
*Greek Drachma	254.254
*Italian Lira	1,690.76

*These are notional rates for the
currencies, based upon the market rate on
20 November 1992.

ECU rate diverges by three quarters of its permitted difference
from its central rate, the government of that country should
take remedial action. If the currency is weak, then interest rates
may have to be raised, taxes increased and government spending reduced. If the currency is strong, then the reverse of these
policies will obtain. A government which fails to apply remedial
action should explain its reasons for its non-action to other
governments and central banks.

In addition to these novel features there exist credit mechanisms
to enable central banks to defend par rates more easily. As stated
above, member states, including Britain, have pooled 20 per cent of
their gold and currency reserves in the EMCF in exchange for ECUs
which can be used for settling up to 50 per cent of debts arising from
intervention in Community currencies. If, in the hypothetical case
cited above, the Bank of France needs to borrow German marks
from the Bundesbank to finance its intervention, its debt will be
calculated in ECUs and repaid in them.

The new system has been alleged to be more realistic than the
snake in at least three ways. It allows margins of fluctuation wider
than the norm to countries which are experiencing economic difficulties, with the divergence threshold signalling the stage at which it
may be useful to take joint action before the problems become too
acute. The second major advantage of the EMS is that it in theory

imposed remedial responsibility on a country with an appreciating currency as well as on a country with a depreciating currency. Under the snake, action to restore the balance between the two currencies had been the exclusive responsibility of the country with a depreciating currency. The third improvement on the snake lies in the large increases in resources available for intervention in support of the system. With the previous system the funds available in 1974 amounted to about 3 billion dollars; the funds available for intervention under the new system were roughly ten times this amount and more in line with the scale of potential speculation. This at least was the hope.

However, the EMS was very unlucky in its date of birth. It was launched only two months before the second steep rise of oil prices in 1979, a rise that precipitated more inflation and unemployment. Therefore it was not surprising that as currencies exceeded their divergence indicators, governments had no alternative but to alter their central rates. These alterations occurred reasonably smoothly, albeit accompanied by tough bargaining among Community finance ministers. For example the German mark was upvalued by 2 per cent in September 1979, by 5.5 per cent in October 1981 and by 4.25 per cent in June 1982 against all other European currencies. In contrast, the French franc was devalued by 3 per cent in October 1981 and by 5.75 per cent in June 1982. The West Germans felt that there had been too frequent parity changes and insisted that the EMS rules were intended to impose more discipline on governments.

By mid-1983 there had been eight realignments within the EMS in 4½ years and the system was far from producing a zone of currency stability. However, the late 1980s and early 1990s saw the system settle down with only five realignments in 9½ years from May 1983 to September 1992. Supporters of the EMS could also point to the fall in the average changes in other EMS currencies against the mark. These changes were reduced by more than half after 1979 compared to the 1970s when exchange rates floated freely. By providing an orderly mechanism for realignment the EMS helped to prevent erratic fluctuations of real exchange rates (i.e. effective exchange rates adjusted for the inflation differential between the country concerned and its trade partners) and to ward off protectionist measures that might otherwise have been taken in response to fluctuations in rates of depreciation.

The EMS also contributed to a decline of inflation within the EC. Though this happened for a number of reasons the Commission contended that the monetary discipline required by the EMS made a significant contribution to the reduction in inflation achieved despite the second oil shock of 1980 and the impact of high US interest rates in the early 1980s, the latter factor making commodities priced in dollars more expensive. From 1983 to 1992 the EMS did indeed appear much more effective. In March 1983 the French President, François Mitterand decided that Keynesian reflation was not the right policy for France when the rest of the EC was bent on contractionary policies. Faced with three options – a fourth devaluation of the franc, trade controls against his Community partners or austerity, he chose austerity. That was a powerful advertisement for the EMS and its original goal of policy convergence.

The extent of that convergence should not be exaggerated but by effectively pegging their currencies to the deutsche mark within the EMS several countries, whose bent for inflation was stronger than West Germany's, in a sense handed responsibility for their monetary policies to the Bundesbank. While this was maintained their inflation and interest rates converged on West German levels.

The EMS made progress in another way too. For several practical reasons it needed a common currency for official dealings. It took over the European unit of account which had been used mainly for determining the Community budget and renamed it the European currency unit (ECU). The ECU was always intended to play a big role in the official workings of the EMS. Central banks hold 20 per cent of their official gold and dollar reserves in ECUs and settle their intervention accounts in ECUs.

What was not foreseen was the way in which the ECU would capture the heart of the private capital market. By 1986 it had become the fifth most widely used currency in international lending and the third most sought-after currency for long-term loans after the dollar and the deutsche mark. From virtually nothing in 1981, the ECU Eurobond market saw issues worth 4.9 billion ECUs in 1984 and over 6 billion ECUs in 1985. More and more banks are taking ECU deposits and making ECU loans. One large European company, Saint-Gobain, published its account in ECUs with a translation in French francs as well, a practice now followed by other companies.

Although an effective ECU clearing system already existed in which British banks like Lloyds took part, a group of eighteen banks worked with the Commission towards the establishment of a more formal clearing system. The Bank for International Settlement (BIS) expressed interest in acting as the central clearing agent for bank transactions denominated in ECUs. The French Treasury in 1985 announced plans to enable companies using the ECU in foreign trade to cover currency exposure on the forward market and in 1984 a French bank launched the first unit trust to invest in ECU bonds. Other developments in the use of the ECU included the issuing of traveller's cheques by the Société du Chèque de Voyage in ECU and a credit card in ECU. The late 1980s saw expanding use of the ECU by companies, Harrods in 1991 becoming the first big British retailer to accept ECU coins as payment even though they were not strictly legal tender.

The ECU has certainly become a useful weapon in the armoury of business people across the EC. When their currency fluctuates against the dollar or any European currency, any business persons expecting to have foreign exchange commitments may face significant losses if they hold their assets in one particular currency, whether they are importing or exporting. What they can now do is to hold cash and conduct transactions in ECUs; as the ECU is effectively an averaging of all the Community currencies, they have a hedge against violent and unpredictable fluctuations in market rates. They can hold ECUs before deciding or knowing whether to spend the proceeds in francs, marks, pounds or even the United States dollar. The ECU is a non-dollar hedge but holding ECUs would guarantee business people much less fluctuation in the value of their money than had it been in dollars.

Because the ECU is an average of individual European currencies, its movement relative to an individual currency like the pound or the deutsche mark is less sharp than that of most of the individual currencies.

Most banks offer accounts for business people who want to deal in ECUs or to hold deposits in ECUs and the accounts are very similar to their conventional equivalents or other foreign currency denominated accounts. No interest is paid on current accounts and there is no minimum balance required. The larger the holding in deposit accounts, the greater the interest will be though loans in ECUs are likely to cost three or four points more than loans in the national currency but, as with any other loan, rates will depend on the status of the borrower and the security offered.

Nor is the ECU something that needs to be reserved for large multinationals. Any small company can take advantage of its utility. Importers should therefore arrange if possible for their EC suppliers to invoice in ECUs while exporters should try to invoice their customers in ECUs. The advantage in both cases is the same – the elimination of the uncertainties of foreign exchange fluctuations which can destroy the profit of an importing company or result in exports from a company becoming uncompetitive.

The UK and the ERM crisis, 1990–3

When the EMS was formed in 1979, the then Labour government in Britain was sceptical about the long-term aims of the new system, preferring to see it as a first step towards the restoration of monetary stability rather than as a move towards economic and monetary union with the Community. It was also more concerned with reforming the CAP and solving Britain's budgetary problems before entering the EMS. The government perhaps felt that such a move anyway would not be popular in the Labour Party generally.

The Conservative government, elected in May 1979, though apparently more committed to the Community, effectively continued the same policy as Labour between 1979 and 1982. It did agree to pool 20 per cent of its gold and dollar reserves with the EMCF in return for ECUs as a gesture towards Europe but was in no hurry to link sterling to the EMS through the ERM. To the Thatcher government, already set on tight monetary policies, the EMS, with its central role as an external instrument of economic discipline, seemed irrelevant.

Certainly there were arguments for and against British entry into the EMS. Sterling had been volatile since 1977, its considerable fluctuations caused by Britain's trade performance, high British interest rates and Britain's new position as a petro-currency. Therefore to join in a system where sterling had a fixed parity would not be easy and would limit the government's freedom of manoeuvre in formulating economic policy.

Against this, Britain could make a demonstration of the genuineness of her European intentions by joining the EMS. Membership could also have advantages for British business which was displeased by the fluctuations in interest rates and exchange rates in recent years. In 1981 Douglas McWilliams, head of the CBI's industrial trends and forecasting department, commented that the number of businessmen complaining about the fluctuations of sterling was rising.

Such fluctuations created uncertainty for business people whether or not they were exporters. A fall in the pound created inflationary pressures and caught out companies that had run down their stocks of imports because they had to pay more sterling to replace them, especially if the commodities were priced in dollars at a time when the dollar was strong. In 1981 ICI lost heavily when the pound's international value fell because the firm's export sales were mainly in European currencies which changed little against the pound while its imports were chiefly in dollars which had risen 25 per cent against the pound.

Conversely there were problems when the pound appreciated: a rising pound made British exports less competitive abroad yet exporters were expected to plan ahead, win orders and hope that an appreciating pound would not wipe out their profits and markets. When the pound rose 30 per cent against the French franc between 1979 and 1981, the French market for some British exporters like British Leyland became virtually untenable.

British entry to the ERM was opposed by both the treasury and the Prime Minister, Mrs Thatcher, but the apparent growth in stability of the EMS led to pressure on the Thatcher government to take sterling into the ERM. Leading British industrialists increasingly made the case for joining the mechanism. They stressed that producers in member states in the ERM held a competitive advantage since their currencies were less volatile than sterling, making the planning of investment easier. British companies also had to spend more on insuring against exchange rate fluctuations. The industrialists derived growing support from politicians across all parties including the Chancellor of the Exchequer, Nigel Lawson, who by 'shadowing' the mark (keeping sterling at about 3 marks to the £) in the period from 1987 to 1989 had unofficially led sterling into the ERM anyway.

For a long time Mrs Thatcher held out against formal entry into the ERM. She disliked the loss of economic sovereignty involved and was being advised by a fierce opponent of the ERM, Alan Walters. Walters viewed the ERM as 'half-baked' because it could well impose on Britains economic policies designed to protect sterling's value in the ERM when the British economy might in fact require radically different policies. Nevertheless a position was reached by the 1980s whereby the British government vowed to join the ERM when the time was ripe. Thus evolved what Geoffrey Denton called 'the doctrine of the unripe time' because for Mrs Thatcher there would never be an appropriate time to join.

Eventually the Iron Lady was persuaded by key members of her government, John Major and Sir Geoffrey Howe, that ERM membership might after all be necessary though her assent to such a step was grudging and is partly explained by domestic economic developments. In 1990 inflation in the UK rose to over 10 per cent with wage settlements at about 11 per cent. For the Conservative government which claimed to have conquered inflation and set great store on low inflation as a platform for sustained economic recovery the 1990 inflation levels were deeply disturbing on economic grounds. In addition the next general election would have to be held by the early summer of 1992 at the latest and the party needed to show the electorate that inflation was under control.

By entering the mechanism at a deliberately high rate of 2.95 marks to the pound the government would force British firms to make low wage settlements because a highly valued currency makes imports relatively cheap and exports relatively expensive. Therefore to remain competitive against overseas competition in home and foreign markets firms would have to prune costs severely, especially wages. With this end in mind, the British government took Britain into the ERM in October 1990. The tactic worked: the level of wage settlements fell dramatically in 1991 and the overall inflation rate was reduced to 4 per cent below the EC average.

The early days in the ERM were also relatively tranquil. The fall in inflation at home did not rule out interest rate cuts from a draconian 15 per cent in October 1990 to 10.5 per cent a year later. Yet ERM had in fact imposed real constraints on British economic policy. The economy was heading into a slump and much faster and greater cuts in the cost of borrowing were needed. However the financial markets took any interest rate cut by Britain rather badly, fearing that the pound would not remain within its ERM band of 2.78 to 3.13 marks to the pound. Currency dealers sold sterling and the pound fell towards the bottom of the permitted range. Consequently during 1991 the Chancellor of the Exchequer, Norman Lamont, felt able to reduce base rates by only small percentage points when British business was crying out for large cuts.

In retrospect it can be seen that the first year in the ERM was a misleading experience for Britain. The German government had been forced to carry out a massive programme of reconstruction for East Germany following German reunification in 1990. Therefore in 1991 Germany's growing inflation led to the mark being relatively weak against the pound on the foreign exchanges. But worried at the growing threat of inflation, the German Bundesbank raised interest rates in December 1991. Other ERM countries followed the German example but Britain did not. Once again the pound came under heavy selling pressure and the Bank of England and other European central banks had to intervene in the currency markets, buying pounds in exchange for other currencies.

Meanwhile all the indicators (save the inflation rate) showed that the British economy was plunging further into a slump in 1992. Unemployment rose by 1,270,000 to 2.87 million from May 1990 to October 1992 and seemed clearly set to top 3 million in 1993. Statistics collected by Dun and Bradstreet showed that 47,777 companies collapsed in 1991 and 46,000 in the first 9 months of 1992. The UK's international competitiveness was also in question; despite the slump imports were increasing faster than exports, leading to Treasury estimates of an overall current account deficit of £12 billion for 1992.

Given such grim realities it seemed clear to currency experts that the pound was hopelessly overvalued in the ERM and against the dollar. Were any recovery to occur in the UK economy more imports would be sucked in, exacerbating the trade deficit and putting further pressure on the pound in the ERM. By August of 1992 currency dealers were seeing a devaluation of the pound as inevitable sooner or later and they did not believe that the British government could shore up the pound for long by raising interest rates in the middle of a slump.

The crisis came sooner rather than later in September 1992. The French President Mitterand, had called for a referendum on the Maastricht Treaty on 20 September, hoping that this would give him greater authority in pressing ahead with political and economic union in the EC. However as polling day drew nearer opinion polls showed that the French public might reject Maastricht; a French rejection combined with the earlier rejection of the treaty by Denmark would have effectively killed off hopes of achieving union.

This political uncertainty worried the foreign exchange markets; currency experts believed that a French rejection of the treaty would force a realignment of currencies within the ERM. They did not believe that European central banks could indefinitely prop up the weaker currencies such as the pound and the lira which would therefore have to be devalued against stronger currencies like the mark. Accordingly currency speculators in August sold sterling and lira and bought marks.

The British government made spirited but unavailing attempts to stop the process. The Treasury stated that the Bank of England would 'defend sterling to the hilt' and on 3 September Lamont announced plans to borrow £7 billion of foreign currency to buy sterling. On 11 September John Major ruled out devaluation of the pound against the mark 'even if every other EC member does so'.

Such actions did not convince the dealers and in any case the problems of sterling were merely part of a wider picture of general turbulence on the foreign exchange markets as currency dealers and financial institutions moved out of weaker currencies and bought stronger currencies. On 9 September the Finnish currency, the Markka, which was linked to the ECU, was devalued and the Swedish Krona also came under heavy pressure.

It was now obvious that the whole ERM might unravel; once one currency was forced to devalue, attention would turn to the perceived next weakest currency which would also be devalued after heavy selling of it by the markets and a domino effect would ensue.

In the event this is exactly what transpired. On 13 September the lira was devalued by 7 per cent and, after the Bundesbank offered only a 0.25 per cent cut in German interest rates on 14 September, the pound came under very heavy pressure on 15 September along with the krona and lira. Then came 'Black Wednesday', 16 September. Sterling was sold in massive quantities and Bank of England spending of £13 billion of foreign currency to buy back pounds to support sterling's value was futile. So were the government's attempts to impress the markets by raising UK interest rates by 2 per cent at 11 am and by a further 3 per cent at 2 pm; the pound's value on the foreign exchange markets continued to fall. By the evening it had fallen to 2.76 marks, below its ERM floor rate of 2.78 marks. A desperate British government suspended Britain's ERM membership, reduced interest rates back to 10 per cent the next day and allowed the pound to float free. By the close of 17 September it had slumped to 2.63 marks to the pound. John Major was soon to rule out any rapid return to the ERM by Britain and certainly not until, in his phrase, 'fault lines' in the mechanism had been remedied.

This debacle was merely the most spectacular event in the near collapse of the ERM. Italy also suspended its membership of the ERM on 16 September. The Spanish peseta was the next to come under pressure being realigned twice within the ERM, in September and November. In November also the Portuguese escudo was devalued and the Swedish krona, previously linked to the mark, was allowed to float and was soon devalued by 9 per cent.

Italy, Spain and Portugal had high inflation, big budget deficits or large trade deficits, giving objective reasons for believing that their currencies would be weak and likely to be devalued. However in the final days of 1992 and during 1993 member states within the ERM whose economies were in good shape found that their currencies were coming under pressure on the foreign exchange markets. In January the Irish government was forced to devalue the Irish pound by 10 per cent, the biggest devaluation by an ERM member since the EMS was created in 1979. Yet Ireland had a small budget deficit, a trade surplus and an inflation rate of 2.3 per cent compared to Germany's 4.4 per cent. Ireland's problem was its dependence on Britain which bought one third of its exports. The fall in sterling hit Irish exports to Britain and with unemployment rates of 17 per cent, in Ireland, the Irish government's ability to maintain high interest rates to support the Irish pound was clearly weakening.

The Danish krona and French franc were next in the firing line and in February the Danish government was forced to raise interest rates by 2 per cent to protect its currency while the French government, despite France having with Denmark the lowest inflation rate in the ERM, had to raise its key interest rate to 13.5 per cent. Such high interest rates threatened to deepen recession in France where the unemployment rate was already 10 per cent. Clearly the domino effect was still in force. The ERM, as James Capel the stockbroking firm commented, was 'on death row' as 'one by one the soft currencies are being picked off'. Such ERM instability undermined prospects of an early move towards European union. Under the Maastricht Treaty some member states at least would have achieved monetary union by 1 January 1999 but Commission sources increasingly believed that the timetable to achieve the union could not be achieved. At the very least the EC seemed likely to polarize and a two-speed Europe emerge. Member states with 'hard' currencies (the Benelux states, Denmark, France and Germany) would make faster progress towards monetary union than the remaining states with 'soft' currencies.

Explanations for the ERM crisis

There are a number of factors, both short-term and long-term, which explain the near collapse of the ERM. Certainly much blame can be laid at the door of the British government which entered the ERM in 1990 at far too high a rate. Since the government requested this rate, responsibility for the fiasco of Black Wednesday must to some extent be with the Conservative government, led at the time of entry by Mrs Thatcher, with John Major as Chancellor.

The government has defended itself by pointing to exceptional circumstances in Germany (the costs of reunification) which caused German interest rates to rise and consequently lead to pressure on UK interest rates and sterling. But the German situation was known in 1990 when Britain entered the ERM, and its implications for sterling should have been gauged by the government as it was so acutely by economists at the time. Writing a week after Britain's ERM entry, the economist Brian Reading stressed that Major had pegged sterling at a 'manifestly over-valued' rate, pointed to the German government's intended spending on restoring East Germany and drew the right conclusions. Germany would raise interest rates, the mark's value would soar on the foreign exchanges and pressure would grow on the weaker currencies to devalue. 'Overvalued sterling is in the running', commented Reading presciently.

Arguably, other short-term factors contributed to the crisis, notably very low American interest rates which led to a surge of money from dollars into marks. The Danish and French referenda in June and September respectively also created uncertainty over the road to EMU and, by extension, over the ERM.

But a stable system would have surmounted such pressures and the September crisis arose from more fundamental factors – what John Major termed the 'fault-lines' in the system. Firstly the EC had tried to treat the EMS as a fixed-rate system whereas its original conception was as a system of fixed but adjustable exchange rates. In other words the ERM was not used in a pragmatic but a rather inflexible way after 1987 and realignments should have taken place before September.

A second fundamental weakness was the practice that if a weak ERM currency were under pressure, remedial measures fell upon the country with the weak currency; it would have to raise interest rates, attempt to prune government expenditure and buy up its currency on the exchange markets. There was no obligation on countries with strong currencies to share the cost of defending the weak currency, for example by lowering interest rates. Thus the British in September 1992 and the Irish in January 1993 complained that the German Bundesbank behaved in a half-hearted way when its vigorous support was needed. There is a measure of truth in the complaint; though the Bundesbank supported the pound in the September crisis by buying up £18 billion, it supported the franc and the Danish krone more publicly and with more resources, including an interest rate cut.

At the heart of the crisis was a chronic failure of all the main EC governments to co-operate. Instead, they acted in what they saw as their own national interests. Anglo–German relations were particularly poisoned, especially the relations between leading British politicians and the President of the Bundesbank, Helmut Schlesinger. In the British view, Schlesinger's loose talk on several occasions about the need for an ERM realignment created pressure on the pound, especially his comment on 15 September that another realignment was needed after the devaluation of the lira. The normally equable John Major was reported to be incandescent with rage. 'The Germans have totally undermined the pound', he told a group of Conservatives, at lunchtime on 16 September. 'It is absolutely unforgivable'.

Such was the degree of mistrust between the four major EC states that communications virtually broke down in the week before Black Wednesday. In particular an offer by the Bundesbank to cut interest rates by 1 per cent in return for a devaluation together by Spain, Italy and Britain was never properly presented to the relevant governments. The French official asked to communicate the offer was Jean-Claude Trichet, the head of the EC monetary committee who was also a director of the French Treasury. It appears likely that he delayed communication of the offer because if it became public the next currency under pressure from the speculators might be the franc and Trichet along with the French government did not wish to leave the franc exposed to the markets in the week before the French referendum on the Maastricht Treaty.

Clearly then the EMS proved to be a fair weather system in 1992 and in the future would require more co-operation and flexibility than it had demonstrated in the September crisis. However there is one final factor which raises the question whether any fixed but adjustable exchange rate system is now feasible in the EC. Before 1992 Community leaders had come to believe that the ERM could be defended over quite long periods because it had won the confidence of the foreign exchange markets. Unfortunately such a belief failed to take into account crucial developments in international money markets from the middle of the 1960s. The liberalization of capital movements on a global basis meant that the potential weight of any speculative attack on a weak currency became massive. To an extent this was a consequence of improved communications: foreign exchange markets are always open somewhere in the world and the media is always eager to communicate the latest developments not to mention leaking a banker's off-the-record comment about the stability of the ERM.

But it is the sheer scale of the speculation which highlights the difficult or indeed impossible task facing European central banks (even when working in unison) when they attempt to defend a weak currency. A Bank of England survey in 1992 pointed to how huge the flows of foreign exchange had become. The daily turnover of the three major world financial centres (London, Tokyo and New York) by April 1992 was $623 billion with London still the major centre with $303 billion (£177 billion) a day in foreign exchange dealings. Thus when speculators believe an ERM currency is likely to be devalued they sell it with the intention of buying it back at a lower rate once the devaluation has taken place – and they sell in massive quantities. At the height of the speculation against the pound in the September crisis, the turnover in London money markets rose to about £300 billion in one day. Joint action by the British and German central banks in buying up £30 billion could not save the pound from falling below its floor in the ERM. As one economist at the Bank of America, Jeremy Hawkins commented at the time, 'The market is just too big for the central banks to control by intervening'.

Much resentment was aimed at the role of currency speculators in the crisis. Some indeed did make small (or large) fortunes while the British government which had spent £15 billion to £20 billion defending sterling suffered losses of nearly £3 billion as a result of sterling's 15 per cent devaluation. As the magazine 'Central Banking' commented, it was 'just as if Norman Lamont had personally thrown entire hospitals and schools into the sea all afternoon'. One speculator, George Soros, borrowed £5 billion two weeks before Black Wednesday, converted it into marks and ended up with £600 million profit by converting the marks back into pounds after the pound was devalued.

It would be very wrong to point to currency speculators as solely responsible for the pressure. Mainstream financial institutions, many of them British, also sold off weaker currencies; they included the big four high-street banks, top pension funds and large insurance companies. All were convinced that sterling and other currencies would be devalued and therefore sold the weaker currencies heavily. Many investors had invested in Britain (to the tune of £50 billion between 1985 and 1992) to enjoy the high interest rates of the late 1980s and early 1990s; they did well because they enjoyed a long period of high interest rates but were able to leave sterling by selling their pounds while the Bank of England supported the currency.

Further unravelling of the ERM was always likely and occurred in August 1993. Given the depth of the French recession, speculators believed that the French government could not for ever hold interest rates high in France to maintain the 'franc fort'. Accordingly these speculators sold francs heavily in July and by early August the franc fell below its ERM floor. Central banks spent £27 billion in trying to prop up the franc and other weak currencies but were powerless against the weight of speculative selling. Many of the speculators were French though French official sources discerned in the massive selling of francs an 'Anglo-Saxon' plot to destroy the ERM.

As in September 1992 demands were made on the Germans to cut their interest rates to relieve pressure on the franc and as in September the Germans refused, and treated with contempt a call by Jacques Delors for the mark to leave the ERM temporarily. On 2 August it was agreed that the only way to retain some semblance of the ERM was the replacing of the previous 2.25 per cent band by a 15 per cent band.

The new crisis marked the virtual collapse of the ERM and threatened to destroy any hope of achieving the timetable for the move to a single currency (see Chapter 15). The inflexibility of the Germans in refusing to cut interest rates infuriated the French. Thus the Maastricht spirit, which had been based on Franco-German accord, was well and truly extinguished.

Further reading

Barnes, I, *Crisis in the ERM*, Hidcote Press, Hull, 1993.

Britton, A and Mayes, D, *Achieving Monetary Union in Europe*, Sage, London, 1992.

The Economist, *Europe's Currency Tangle*, 30 January, 1993.

Levich, R M (ed.), *ECU*, Euromoney Publications, London, 1987.

Minford, P (ed.), *The Cost of Europe*, Manchester University Press, Manchester, 1992.

Smith, D, *From Boom to Bust*, Penguin, Harmondsworth, 1992.

Questions

1 Discuss the potential advantages and disadvantages of European Monetary Union.
2 How did the EMS improve on the earlier 'snake in the tunnel'?
3 Critically analyse the achievements and shortcomings of the EMS between 1979 and 1992.
4 For what reasons did the United Kingdom delay and then enter the ERM?
5 Human error or fault lines in the system? Which is the more convincing explanation for the crisis in the ERM in 1992 and 1993?

10
The Community budgetary policy in transition

Keeping the budget in perspective

The Community's budget has been increasingly in the public eye in recent years and yet it is a grey area not fully understood by Community citizens. It forms an extra tier on top of the local, regional and national levels of public finance which have gradually evolved in the member states. This has required new forms of financial adjustment in the handling of an ever-growing volume of funds. Such forms of adjustment, for example the precise contribution of the individual member states, are customary procedures in federal states like Germany but most EC countries are centrally constituted where such practices are unknown. As a consequence, Community finances have seemed strange and unfamiliar to many citizens.

The Community budget in 1981 was worth some 20 billion ECUs (£11 billion). Such an amount may look enormous but it is a modest sum when put into perspective. In 1981 the Community budget represented only 0.9 per cent of the member states' joint Gross Domestic Product. By contrast the national budgets of the member states accounted for 710 billion ECUs, 32 per cent of the Community's Gross Domestic Product. Thus the EC budget was equal to only 2.7 per cent of national spending. Even in 1989 the picture was not radically altered. The EC budget had risen to nearly 45 billion ECUs but this fugure represented only 3.69 per cent of the spending carried out by the 12 member states and only 1.04 per cent of the Community's Gross Domestic Product. Even if the EC budget rises to the planned expenditure of 84 billion ECUs or more by 1999, the sum still represents barely a quarter of British government expenditure alone in 1992–3.

Nevertheless Community finances have increasingly been a target for criticism, especially in the recession of the early 1990s when member states' finances are under pressure. In 1983 the author suggested that much of the criticism had little substance but since

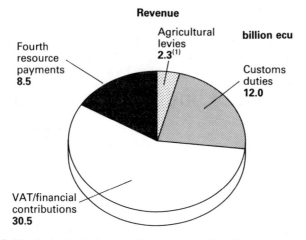

(1) Also includes levies raised on sugar and isoglucose

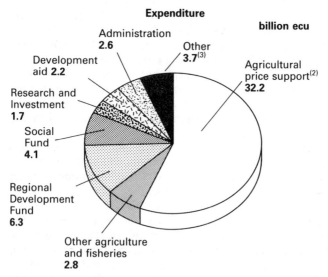

(2) Includes allowance for depreciation of produce held in storage
(3) Includes 1 billion ecu monetary reserve to allow for the effects of exchange rate fluctuations between the ecu and the US dollar

Figure 10.1   1991 Budget: revenue and expenditure by type

then the size of the EC budget has risen steadily (as Figure 10.1 demonstrates) yet some of the extra spending has been of doubtful validity.

The Community's taxing powers

The Community has no bottomless purse because its taxing powers are rather limited. Under Article 201 of the Rome Treaty, the EC was to be financed mainly by contributions from member states in a fixed agreed proportion. The Commission was, however, instructed to study the conditions under which these contributions 'may be replaced by other resources available to the Community itself, in particular by revenue accruing from the common customs tariff when finally introduced'. After long and difficult negotiations the results of the ensuing Commission study were incorporated in a decision of April 1970 which provided for the replacement of financial contributions from member states by the Community's 'own resources'. This was to be achieved by a process of gradual transition between 1971 and 1978. As Michael Shackleton has shown, the importance of this change cannot be over-emphasized. 'It meant that the EC was no longer dependent upon the member states agreeing to provide national contributions but that it could call upon these resources and consider them as collective Community property'. Other international organizations have been much less fortunate; United Nations' members, for example, often either refuse to make their full contribution or claim that they are unable to pay it at the time when payment is due. By contrast EC member states are not entitled to withhold payments under the system of 'own resources'. When Britain in 1983 delayed crediting her own resources for the month of April to the Commission's account, the issue was taken before the European Court of Justice and the Court ruled in December 1986 that Britain was not entitled to act in this way and should pay interest in respect of the delay.

As a consequence of the 1970 decision the Community's 'own resources' until 1988 consisted of three parts:

1 Customs duties are the duties levied on imports from outside the Community. They are collected by member states under the Community tariff and passed on to the Commission which refunds the cost of collection – about 10 per cent of the total collected.
2 Agricultural levies are charged on agricultural products imported from non-member countries. They are chiefly designed to offset the differences between the normally higher Community price and the price at which the products are supplied, i.e. the world price. Often included with agricultural levies are sugar levies, charged on the production of sugar and isoglucose (a sugar derived from corn starch) to pay at least part of the cost of market support of these products.

   Such 'own resources' were over time found to be unreliable and inadequate sources of revenue. The volume of customs duties has tended to dwindle as those duties have been progressively reduced through agreements with non-member countries. The Kennedy Round of the General Agreement on Tariffs and Trade (GATT) resulted in the Community reducing tariffs by 30 per cent after 1967. The Tokyo Round of GATT resulted in further tariff reductions of 33 per cent between 1980 and 1987 by which time the average EC tariff was only 4.5 per cent compared to 9 per cent in 1982. If the Uruguay Round of GATT is fully implemented then EC tariffs will be cut by a further 30 per cent.

Two other factors reduce the EC's own resources from tariffs. Over time the volume of imports is rising but in times of recession this process can be reversed as businesses and consumers in the EC purchase fewer products from the rest of the world. Secondly the EC tariff structure is like a wall with many gaps in it because the Community has given preferential trading terms to many countries in the Mediterranean and the Third World so that the bulk of their exports to the EC carry no tariff burden.

Agricultural levies reflect the difference between the Community price for a given product and its price on the world market so that import prices are brought up to the Community level. Agricultural prices, however, are not fixed at a higher level in the EC for the purpose of raising revenue. The yield from agricultural levies depends on trends in Community and world food prices. Occasionally world food prices have been higher than EC food prices (1974–5) and it therefore follows that the revenue from this source is unpredictable. As was shown in Chapter 6, Community farm prices rose much more slowly in the 1980s, thus reducing to an extent the difference between EC and world prices and consequently reducing the yield from agricultural levies.

3   Given the in-built unreliability of the first two sources of revenue, an additional source was needed and the Community agreed in 1970 to create an additional source of finance by claiming a share of Value Added Tax from member states. VAT soon became the EC's biggest source of revenue, providing 54 per cent in 1981. Under the Community's 1977 directive, VAT systems were harmonized in the member states. This does not mean that the rates charged were the same (after 1979 Britain's VAT rate was 15 per cent compared to Denmark's 22 per cent) but that the value of taxable goods and services was assessed in the same way in each country. Member states agreed to assign to the Community's own resources a rate not exceeding 1 per cent of a uniform basis of assessment of Value Added Tax. This was a ceiling which could only be exceeded, if member states agreed to amend the April 1970 decision and if the amendment was ratified by national parliaments. Such an amendment occurred in 1984 (See p. 205).

The 1 per cent ceiling was always regarded as an inadequate rate and financial pundits were soon predicting that Community spending would soar above this ceiling – they were to be proved right by 1984. In any case, VAT, though a more reliable source of income for the EC than the first two, had its limitations. It is a complicated tax, rather unsuited to a Community in which some states have stronger traditions of tax evasion than tax collection. Also, as Daniel Strasser (Director of Budgets in the Commission in the 1980s) pointed out, VAT was a rather regressive tax, i.e. it tended to penalize poorer member states because consumption in such states is a higher proportion of GNP and attracts VAT whereas other components such as investment (which is a higher proportion of GNP in richer member states) do not. Finally VAT receipts, though less volatile than the other sources of income, are affected by recessions when consumers and businesses curtail their spending.

Community expenditure

Community revenue is spent mainly on five policies.

1 Until the 1990s the CAP swallowed up two thirds of Community funds, mostly on price support for commodities where the EC's self-sufficiency is high. Until 1984 it was in milk and dairy products that the operation of the price support system was most expensive. These absorbed about one quarter of the whole budget between 1977 and 1982. For many years considerable expenditure was incurred by 'monetary compensation amounts' – payments made to offset discrepancies in the cost of agricultural products from different countries in the Community. These discrepancies arose from charges in the green rates (see Chapter 6). The remorseless improvement in agricultural technology meant that huge surpluses occurred for cereals and oilseed after 1984 and with them rose the cost of price support of such products. Expenditure on 'guidance' (i.e. structural charges in agriculture) has generally run at about 10 per cent of agricultural expenditure. Even with the reforms of 1984 and 1988 (see p. 205) the CAP consumed 60 per cent of the EC budget in 1992 and, even assuming the MacSharry reforms are effectively implemented, will still consume 45 per cent of the EC budget by the end of the century.

2 There has been significant expenditure on the European Regional Development Fund (ERDF) since its inception in 1975. In 1981 when the EC spent 2 billion ECUs under this fund on

grants and subsidized loans for industrial and infrastructure projects in Europe's depressed regions, the sum amounted to 10 per cent of total Community spending. At the same time the European Social Fund (ESF) was gaining about 4 per cent of the EC budget to spend on projects for retraining, rehousing, education and other social measures. However it is not an exaggeration to suggest that spending on these so-called 'structural funds' has been revolutionized since February 1988 when it was agreed at Brussels to double their resources in real terms by 1993 (see p. 205). At the Edinburgh Summit in December 1992 a further increase in structural funding was decided; the structural funds' resources are planned to rise from 18 billion ECUs in 1992 to 30 billion ECUs in 1999, by which time these funds will claim over 35 per cent of the proposed Community budget.

3 Given the domination of the CAP and structural funding, other EC policies receive relatively small amounts of support. Research on new industrial technologies, the environment, energy and transport developments, supporting, for example, scientific research projects like the Joint European Torus (JET) at Culham in Oxfordshire received an average of about 2 billion ECUs a year from 1987 to 1991 though the Community hopes to increase this amount by the mid-1990s.

4 Development aid to the Third World reached just over 1 billion ECUs, 5 per cent of the EC budget in 1981. Such aid was mainly directed at the African, Caribbean and Pacific (ACP) countries that have signed the Lomé Conventions. By the time that the fourth Lomé Convention was implemented in the 1990s, this sector of EC expenditure was receiving 2.2 billion ECUs a year.

5 The remaining areas of Community expenditure – administrative costs, repayments such as the UK rebate and reserves receive about 4 billion ECUs a year.

The budgetary procedure

Under pressure from the European Parliament, the budgetary procedure has been considerably revised in recent years.

Before 1 July each year the institutions draw up estimates of their expenditure in the next financial year (1 January to 31 December). The Commission then consolidates these estimates into a preliminary draft budget that it places before the Council of Ministers before 1 September if possible. The Council consults other concerned institutions whenever it intends to modify the draft budget, acting by qualified majority. Its next action is to forward the now established draft budget to the European Parliament by 5 October.

The Parliament has the right to amend the draft budget as regards non-compulsory expenditure and can propose modifications to compulsory expenditure to the Council. If within 45 days of the draft budget being placed before it, Parliament proposes changes, the draft budget, with the proposed modifications, is returned to the Council.

If within 15 days the Council accepts the changes proposed by the Parliament, the budget is finally adopted. If the Council revises the Parliament's suggested changes, the draft budget is again forwarded to the Parliament with a report on the Council's deliberations. Within 15 days the Parliament acts by a majority of its members on its response to the Council's modifications to its amendments. Normally it must vote by 19 December on whether to accept or reject the entire budget. In 1979, the Parliament rejected the budget as it tried to exert more influence on Community spending and the whole budgetary procedure became more fraught as time went on with the Parliament attempting to gain more real control over Community expenditure. Its increasingly combative mood was again seen in December 1982 when it voted against the rebate due to Britain as a way of trying to force the Council to tackle the question of permanent reform of Community finances. Such tactics were repeated in 1984, 1987 and 1988. Community activities still continued because if an EC budget remains unadopted, the EC can spend per month one twelfth of what was spent in the previous year.

The chief budgetary problems

It is clear that several problems bedevil Community budgetary issues – the amount of revenue, the excessive proportion of revenue devoted to agriculture, the question of equitability and the increasingly dubious projects funded by the Community, i.e. waste and corruption.

The size of the Community budget has been a major problem since the early 1980s when it was realized that though EC revenue was expanding by about 10 per cent a year because of inflation and economic growth, expenditure was growing even more quickly, especially spending on farming which was increasing by more than 20 per cent a year. Hence the moment would surely arise when increases in expenditure would no longer be covered by increases in its own resources and Community revenue would be exhausted. As early as 1977 the MacDougall Report warned of an impending budgetary crisis.

The relatively small size of the budget means that it has at present only a small impact on the European economy, with the exception of agriculture. Even in the agricultural sector the expenditure does not seem to result in diminishing welfare differences between the rich and poor regions of the Community, in fact the reverse situation applies. By the same token, the budget does little to stimulate economic activity in either particular member states or in the European economy as a whole and there is an urgent need for the Community to expand its spending on research, energy, industry and transport beyond the present pathetic 2 per cent of resources. This whole question has become more critical since Spain and Portugal acceded to membership in 1986.

The second major problem is the inequitable burden that the budget places on Britain and Germany. The budget is so structured at present as to make Britain a net contributor to the budget. The net contributions and net receipts of member states are calculated as the difference between their gross contributions to, and gross receipts from, those parts of budget expenditure which the Commission is able to 'allocate' between member states. A member state whose contributions to the allocated budget exceed the amounts of Community expenditure received by its residents is said to be a net contributor to the budget. A member state whose residents receive more from the budget than its contributors is said to be a net recipient.

Two member states – Britain and Germany – have consistently tended to be net contributors while the other ten tend to be net recipients. This pattern reflects the budgetary impact of the CAP which accounts for about two-thirds of allocated budget expenditure. The result is that member states whose share of Community agricultural production or surpluses exceeds their share of Community GDP or who are large producers of Mediterranean produce are likely to obtain net receipts from the budget while Germany and Britain, whose share of Community GDP exceeds their share of Community agricultural production or surpluses, are likely to make net contributions. However, whereas it is arguably not unreasonable for Germany, one of the richest members of the Community, to make such contributions, it is manifestly unreasonable for Britain to do so when she is the poorest member of the Community bar Ireland, Spain, Portugal and Greece.

Britain's partners often argue that net contributions and receipts are irrelevant concepts that have no place in the Community. The Community has, they insist, certain policies in areas such as agriculture, and these policies transfer resources from Community consumers and taxpayers to Community producers and other beneficiaries. The fact that they also transfer resources from some member states to others is incidental and unimportant.

Such arguments do not convince British people because net transfers represent flows of real money from the citizens of some countries to the citizens of others. The scale and the direction of these transfers serve to increase the differences in prosperity between the member states. Yet the Community is supposed to be committed to economic convergence between member states and the pattern of net transfers should bear some relationship to relative prosperity.

The French also produce a further argument – that the net contributions are an avoidable problem, for which the net contributor countries have only themselves to blame. If such countries would import less from non-Community countries or increase their agricultural production, so the French argue, their net budget contributions would rapidly disappear.

However this line of argument ignores the Community's commitment to open trade in Article 110 of the Rome Treaty and even if Britain were to reduce her agricultural imports from outside the Community, this would in fact not make much difference to Britain's net financial position. The idea that Britain could solve her budget problems by increasing agricultural output is neither realistic nor sensible. To eliminate the UK's budgetary losses would require an increase in agricultural production of about one third, followed by annual increases in production in line with the Community average. Even if this were possible the Community as a whole would be harmed owing to the steep rise in the cost of disposing of surplus agricultural production.

In 1984 the Fontainebleau Summit contrived what was hoped to be a permanent solution to the US problem but Britain remained a net contributor to the EC budget to the tune of £2.6 billion in 1992.

Clearly budget reform has been essential and this will be surveyed in the next section. However before moving on to this area, it is pertinent to point to one other question. If poorer member states expect more help from the Community budget this necessarily means, over time, increased net contributions from the richer member states. Such developments become politically less acceptable in times of recession but in any case richer member states will be more reluctant to see the EC budget increase if the funds are seen to be used inefficiently. In the chapters on agriculture, structural funding and enlargement the reader will unfortunately find much evidence of waste and corruption in EC spending. In 1993 the impression was gained that such waste was increasing rather than being curtailed. In April the President of the European Bank for Reconstruction and Development, Jacques Attali, was assailed by the British press and Community politicians when it was revealed that twice as much money had been spent on his bank as on projects helping Eastern Europe. Questionable spending items included £600,000 on Attali's private jet, £52,000 on a Christmas party and £750,000 for expensive Carrera marble. One of the biggest East

European projects was a 20 per cent stake in the former Czechoslovak national airline; Air France, another 20 per cent partner in the project, was run by Attali's twin brother Bernard. Small wonder that Jacques Attali was forced to resign his post of president in June 1993.

Reform of the Community budget

By the early 1980s the EC's budgetary system was reaching the exhaustion of its resources predicted by the MacDougall Report. In 1984 it ran out of its own resources completely and a budgetary crisis arose. Unlike member states, the Community had no right to cover any deficit by borrowing and in principle the budget had to balance. To meet immediate needs, the Commission asked member states to give repayable advances to cover the rising budget deficit. A similar device was contrived in 1985 except that the advances were not repayable.

The crisis did at least concentrate minds and indeed reform possibilities were already being discussed. In February 1983 the Commission produced a green paper, *The Future Financing of the Community*, in which it pointed to the need to raise the VAT rate above 1 per cent, given the expectation that EC expenditure would rise even more once Spain and Portugal joined the Community. Earlier Commission reports, especially one in 1981, had stressed that EC funding should be less concentrated on agriculture and shifted towards regional and social funding. To reduce CAP spending, the gap between Community and world food prices would have to be narrowed and surpluses reduced.

For the EC to implement much in the way of reform required some permanent solution of the UK budgetary problem. Since 1980 the British government had won annual rebates but both Britain and the European Parliament felt that a permanent mechanism was needed. The Thatcher government made it abundantly clear that it would not support any move to increase the Community's own resources unless both the thorny issues of farm spending and the UK net contribution to the EC budget were also tackled.

At the Stuttgart Summit in 1983 such an agenda was taken on board when it was agreed that there was a need for adequate budgetary resources combined with fairness for Britain and some control on agricultural spending. At last at the Fontainebleau Summit in June 1984 the first real measure of budgetary reform was achieved. The Community decided to impose quotas on milk output because the surpluses in that sector had been particularly expensive. It was also agreed to raise the ceiling on VAT contributions to 1.4 per cent from 1986. This level disappointed the Commission which had hoped for a 2 per cent ceiling. The UK problem was given a solution which it was hoped would be permanent: from 1985 the UK would receive a rebate equal to 66 per cent of the difference between its share of VAT payments to the EC and its share of expenditure from the EC. This would have the effect of roughly halving the UK's net contribution and was therefore a move towards more fairness. It was also agreed that expenditure on farming should grow at a slower rate than the growth of the Community's own resources and that therefore over time the CAP would consume a smaller proportion of the Community budget.

At the time the Fontainebleau Agreement was hailed as a panacea but such hopes were quickly shown to be illusory. The open-ended price guarantee to farmers combined with their increasing productivity meant that as early as 1986 a new budget crisis was seen as imminent. Accordingly in 1987 Jacques Delors put forward a package of proposals for Community finance but the Brussels Summit in July rejected them because, while new ways of increasing the EC's own resources were suggested, the proposals contained little or nothing on controlling the spiralling costs of the CAP and were vigorously opposed by Mrs Thatcher.

Negotiations were resumed after July 1987 to construct a new reform agreement and a deal was finally concluded, after much acrimony, at the Brussels Summit in February 1988. The UK and the Netherlands had held out for strong measures to curtail agricultural spending and gained a partial success with the introduction of a set-aside scheme and controls on the production of cereals and oil-seed as detailed in Chapter 6. The Summit also agreed that EC budgetary expenditure should not exceed 1.2 per cent of Community GNP and that the growth of agricultural spending should be no more than 74 per cent of the growth rate of Community GNP. Spending on the structural funds (the ERDF and the ESF) was to be double the 1987 level by 1993 with greater concentration on the poorest regions of Greece, Spain and Portugal.

To meet the extra spending entailed, the three main budgetary resources (food-import levies, external tariffs and the VAT) were to be retained with the VAT rate ceiling pegged at 1.4 per cent. Crucially a new 'fourth resource' was created for the EC based on each member paying a given percentage of its GNP. As with the VAT arrangement, one of the principles underlying the introduction of the new resource was a contribution based to a greater extent than with other own resources on the member states' ability to pay. Thus the difference between the other sources of revenue and the amount of Community expenditure is raised from member states in proportion to their national income. This was clearly a useful step towards basing Community financing on more progressive principles but it should be noted that this GNP-based resource has so far accounted for only about 10 per cent of total Community finance and is not forecast to grow in importance in the immediate future.

If the UK was disappointed over its failure to effect tighter controls over agriculture there was a consolation prize in the form of a renewal of its budget rebate. In 1984 the rebate had been 66 per cent of the difference between the UK's VAT-related payouts and EC spending in the UK. With the inception of the 'fourth resource', the rebates are now based on the difference between its VAT and GNP-related payments and EC spending in the UK.

The Community budget in the 1990s

It would be naive to believe that the reforms of the 1980s have solved the EC's budgetary blues. The core problems discussed earlier have not gone away and will continue to resurface at inconvenient times. Undoubtedly fraud and waste stalk the corridors of power in the Commission and urgently require tough action though whether the EC has the necessary guts to act is open to question. In March 1993, a formerly respected Commission bureaucrat, Antonio Quatraro, committed suicide (or was he pushed?) when his part in a gigantic EC fraud (bogus tobacco exports from Italy and Greece) was on the point of being investigated. His death opened the lid on corruption in Brussels and raised the spectre of the Mafia in the heart of Europe as well as on Italian politics. The other intractable consumer of Community money – the CAP – has only partly been dealt with by the 1992 MacSharry reforms (see Chapter 6).

Even without such excessive waste, the strains on the EC budget would be great because the legitimate demands on it are constantly growing – valid agricultural assistance, environmental measures, structural funding, research in the new technologies and aid to Eastern Europe and the Third World. Fertile minds in the Commission are always capable of demanding more spending by the Community; in February 1992 Jacques Delors put forward a Five Year Plan for EC spending to rise from £47.2 billion a year in 1992 to £62.3 billion in 1997 with increased spending on agriculture, structural funding, industrial research and security. But where would such extra resources come from? Delors suggested that the provision of 1.2 per cent of Community GNP would provide ample opportunity for the EC to expand its activities because its natural economic growth would provide an automatic 3.5 per cent per year in real Community resources. A second factor would also increase the scope for more Community spending – the accession in the 1990s of several rich European states (Sweden, Austria and Norway), all of which would become net contributors to the EC budget.

Such assumptions seem highly dubious. When in 1988 Delors first succeeded in increasing EC spending the economies of the member states were buoyant, and even then securing an agreement on the EC budget was a tortuous business. In the 1990s such agreements will be even more difficult because the economies of both the major net contributors have faced acute difficulties. Germany has a particular problem over the costs of reunification. Britain has been emerging slowly in 1993 from a deep recession. In addition France is now a net contributor to the EC budget to the tune of about £1 billion a year, a sum that is likely to rise sharply, while Italy will soon become a net contributor. Thus rises in EC spending are likely to be opposed by the four largest states as politically unacceptable with the poor southern states, supported by the Commission, demanding more assistance from the structural funds in return for their support for more political and economic union.

To assume a Community economic growth rate of over 3 per cent in the 1990s appears unwarranted optimism. The major economies will struggle to attain a 2 per cent growth rate with Germany and France in recession in 1993 and economic growth forecasts being revised downwards. Consequently EC resources will not grow at the rate hoped for by Jacques Delors and the Commission will be forced to search for extra sources of revenue. New taxes such as the EC tax on energy, proposed in April 1993, might be a partial solution. Another recourse would be to open up an old wound by attempting to abolish the UK rebate which by 1992 had reduced the UK's payment to the EC by £12 billion compared to 1980 and which in 1992 reduced the UK net payment by £1.9 billion to £2.6 billion. Certain members of the Commission support such an abolition and it would also gain approval from other member states, not least Germany which in 1992 paid a net contribution of £6 billion to the EC budget. If the almost inevitable increase in Community spending in the 1990s were to be combined with a partial or complete ending of the UK rebate, the British net contribution to the EC budget would rise by at least 70 per cent to £4.3 billion per year or more. UK reactions to this scenario are all too predictable!

Further reading

Lintner, V and Mazey, S, *The European Community* (Chapter 6), McGraw Hill, Maidenhead, 1991.

Shackleton, M, *Financing the European Community*, RIIS, London, 1990.

Swann, D, *The Economics of the Common Market*, Penguin, (Seventh Edition), Harmondsworth, 1992.

Questions

1 Critically examine the reasons for the existence of the Community's budgetary problems.
2 Discuss possible ways in which these problems may be solved in the 1990s.
3 Why is the United Kingdom a net contributor to the Community budget?
4 Examine the effectiveness of attempts to reform the Community budget since 1984.

11
The Community and the external world

The EC: protectionist or free trade?

Since 1957 the Community has developed some form of trade agreement with virtually every country in the world and has played a leading role in the activities of GATT (General Agreement on Tariffs and Trade), the world organization created in 1947 to open up international trade. The EC is the largest member of GATT in terms of trade; including intra-EC trade, the Community accounted for 38 per cent of world merchandise trade in 1989 and 20 per cent even when internal trade is excluded. Deepening integration between member states over the years has reduced the Community's dependence on trade with third countries from 63 per cent of its total trade in 1958 to 40 per cent in 1989 but business with the rest of the world is still an important feature of the EC economy. Trade plays a greater role in the overall economic activity of the EC than of the USA or Japan, the other two leading trading nations. The EC ratio of merchandise trade to GDP (excluding intra-EC trade) is close to 10 per cent, which is 20 per cent higher than that of the USA and 40 per cent higher than that of Japan, even though the EC has a larger internal market and its per capita income is lower.

The Community tends to run a sizeable trade deficit with the rest of the world. It enjoys a balance of trade surplus with the non-EC industrialized countries of Western Europe, with its ex-colonies and with its Mediterranean neighbours but runs deficits with the USA, with OPEC, with Latin America and South East Asia, including a large and persistent deficit with Japan. The Community's commodity pattern of trade reflects the level of its industrialization. Its largest exports are motor vehicles, aircraft, pharmaceuticals and machinery while its largest imports are petroleum products, paper, computers and motor vehicles.

The Rome Treaty required the EC to develop a Common Commercial Policy (CCP), the aim of which was to liberalize world trade. The key element of the CCP is the Common External Tariff

(CET) which all member states must apply, though the Community has a number of other instruments at its disposal by which it regulates business with its trading partners. It has been a party to many preferential trade agreements, for example those with EFTA states and Mediterranean states such as Turkey. Such agreements have always been a source of tension between the EC and GATT. In addition though GATT prohibits quantitative import restrictions, there are in practice many exceptions to the general rule and the EC has imposed variable levies on imported food and quotas on imported textiles through the MFA (Multi-Fibre Arrangement). It has also been able to take action against imports that harm other sensitive domestic industries.

The Community is fond of claiming that it has a good record in working for free trade. It points to the weighted average of EC customs duties which have been reduced from 9 per cent in 1982 to 4.5 per cent in 1993. It has stressed that despite the CAP it has become the world's largest agricultural importer. It takes about a quarter of all world food imports and, unlike the USA, has a trade deficit in agricultural produce. Many third world countries have free access to Community markets. Thus the EC with the USA has become a principal pillar of the Western political and economic system.

Such influence does however bring with it some responsibility for the functioning of the world trading system and it is debatable whether the EC's credentials as a free trade organization are valid. One measure must be the state of its relations with its major trading partners. It is in conflict with the USA over a number of issues such as steel and agriculture, in conflict with developing countries over access for their textiles into the Community market, in conflict with Japan over the latter's trade surplus with the EC and in permanent conflict with traditional agricultural exporters like New Zealand, Canada and Australia. Martin Wolf in wittily paraphrasing Oscar Wilde comments that to be involved in one dispute may be thought a misfortune, to be involved in disputes with everyone looks very much like carelessness, even if the other parties to the disputes are far from blameless.

Critics of the EC point to a sulky obstinacy in defending vested interests, especially in times of high unemployment. Besides agriculture and textiles there are about 130 other products restricted by nationally administered quotas. In some 70 cases the quotas apply to products originating from particular countries. (Japan is the largest target in 50 cases.) France and Italy maintain the bulk of these national quotas with 71 and 68 restrictions respectively. The affected product categories include consumer electronics, semi-conductors, motor vehicles, steel and machinery.

The EC has, as Phedon Nicolaides stresses, a particular liking for anti-dumping measures. Between 1980 and 1990 it initiated 421 anti-dumping investigations, mainly against state trading countries in Eastern Europe and in 306 cases there was a positive finding after which in many cases the offending party agreed to increase its price.

Another popular EC instrument is the use of VERs (Voluntary Export Restraint). EC states are not supposed to enter into special trade arrangements with third countries but in practice they still impose VERs on exporters from outside the Community with the implied threat that if no agreement is reached, tougher restrictions will soon follow. In 1989 the EC and its member states accounted for 125 known VERs, mostly affecting steel, textiles, agricultural products, footwear, cars and electronic products.

The EC and GATT

The GATT is in essence an international treaty signed by 23 industrialized and developing countries in 1947. It committed the signatories to abide by certain rules which would open up world trade and put an end to the disastrous 'beggar-my-neighbour' protectionism that has deepened the Great Depression of the 1930s. It has developed its own small organization in Geneva and it now has 108 member countries. It is not, as commonly supposed, simply 'free-trade' in philosophy; it permits some protectionism but it does promote 'fair trade', based on the fundamental principle of non-discrimination which says that countries must offer the same trading terms to all members.

GATT can claim some real successes, in particular the fall in average tariffs in industrialized countries from an average of 40 per cent in 1947 to 5 per cent at the end of the 1980s. However the economic difficulties that beset the world in the 1970s nurtured a climate of growing protectionism, a climate that threatened both GATT's credibility and the open trading system it upholds. Cars, steel, videos and semi-conductors followed textiles into 'managed trade', a euphemism for the imposition of VERs by many states on important products. The organization has failed to apply its rules to agriculture and has never covered services.

The EC has been a contributor to all GATT negotiations designed to reduce the level of tariffs, for example the Dillon Round (1961–2), the Kennedy Round (1964–7) and the Tokyo Round (1973–9). In 1985 an international conference was held at Punta del Este in Uruguay where it was agreed that a new round of negotiations should be commenced. It was generally acknowledged that this Uruguay Round, as it came to be known, could be a make or break affair for GATT's credibility because the intention was to strengthen the organization's rules in areas where they had been weak, for example intellectual property rights, services, textile quotas and agricultural subsidies. GATT wished to phase out the Multi-Fibre Arrangement which had been negotiated as a temporary agreement in 1973 but which over time had imposed rather permanent restrictions on exports not only of textiles but of fibres and clothing as well from newly industrializing and developing countries to industrialized areas such as the EC. GATT also wished to liberalize agricultural trade by improving market access and the competitive environment through the reduction of direct and indirect agricultural subsidies.

Such an agenda was always going to be difficult. The Uruguay Round was supposed to be completed by December 1990 but a precarious deal was concluded only in November 1992. Predictably the most contentious area was agriculture with the EC in the dock, under pressure from the Cairns Group, the USA and the World Bank to reduce the CAP's aid to European farmers. At an early stage a major difference of approach to the negotiations by the Community and the USA became apparent. Initially the US administration insisted on a firm commitment by all parties to a total dismantling of all agricultural subsidies by the year 2000 (the so-called 'zero option'). Such a commitment was considered unrealistic by the EC and until 1989 it refused to negotiate seriously on the issue. Eventually in April 1989 it did agree with all other parties that 'the long-term objective is to establish a fair and market-oriented agricultural trading system'. Soon afterwards the USA and the Cairns group proposed that over 10 years domestic support and border protection be reduced by 75 per cent and export subsidies by 90 per cent. The EC's counter offer was for a cut of between 10 per cent and 30 per cent over 10 years in domestic support but with no specific commitments on either border protection or export subsidies. This inadequate offer precipitated a breakdown in GATT negotiations in December 1990. In 1991 the MacSharry proposals generated a renewal of GATT discussions but it was highly displeasing to other parties that MacSharry's original proposals were watered down and only agreed in May 1992. Eventually the patience of the American government ran out and in November 1992 it threatened to impose punitive tariffs of 200 per cent on $300 million of EC exports to the USA, mainly French table wines. At the heart of the dispute was an American demand for the EC to give a definite figure on its planned reduction of oilseed production, which excluded American soya beans from the EC market. Events now took a farcical turn with MacSharry, the Commissioner for Agriculture, threatening resignation when he believed (with some justice) that Delors was not giving him adequate support in his negotiations with the Americans.

Nevertheless the American action, unwise in itself in that it risked the outbreak of a trade war, did concentrate EC minds wonderfully. Carla Hills, the formidable US trade representative commented that the threat of trade sanctions had 'a therapeutic effect' on European thinking. Certainly both sides now worked hard to reach a compromise on the vexed question of EC oilseed production, though in fact the Americans made real concessions. They did not insist on limiting production of the crop, merely demanding that over two years the land devoted to it should be cut by nearly 25 per cent. This would allow annual production of between 8.5 and 9.7 million tonnes compared to the 1992 production figure of 13 million tonnes, using present farming methods. The Americans had sought an 8 million tonnes limit. In return the EC was to cut the money on export subsidies by 36 per cent and reduce subsidized exports by 21 per cent compared to 1986–90 levels. When the MacSharry reforms of 1992 (see Chapter 6) are also borne in mind the overall package represented a severe blow to EC farming interests and in France there was fierce reaction against the deal.

The row over agriculture rather obscured useful progress on other GATT measures. Tariffs were to be cut by 30 per cent. This did not greatly affect Western industrial countries directly because their tariffs were already low but could be important for the developing and new industrializing countries where tariffs were high. China's tariffs, for example, averaged 41 per cent and those of India 80 per cent. A cut in such tariffs would help EC exports to the Third World and industrializing states and make these countries more attractive for foreign direct investment.

The Uruguay Round also brought the world's services under international trading rules. Though accounting for only 20 per cent of world trade, economists believed the liberalization of this sector could be the most important measure. In the West 70 per cent of GDP already flowed from services. With agreements from the contracting countries covering insurance, transport, tourism, consultancy and telecommunications, the way was more open for a freer pattern of global investment.

Protecting copyright was a fiercely argued matter but agreement was reached. At first sight it appeared a Western ploy to prevent entrepreneurs in South East Asia and elsewhere from plagiarizing the intellectual property of IBM and the software firms, or banning Korean 'champagne'. GATT officials insisted that copyright protection was also in the interests of developing countries. If Western firms knew that their patents, copyright and technology will not be stolen, they are more likely to set up production in the countries concerned.

Agreement was also reached over textiles. Again it was a difficult question because the world textile industry was worth $177 billion and accounted for 9 per cent of world trade. However the MFA was to be phased out though the process was expected to take 10 years.

Finally, in an effort to give GATT more teeth, a new mechanism was set up for settling disputes with deadlines for rectifying offences as well as a Multilateral Trading Organization to oversee the 10 year implementation of the agreement.

According to the OECD development centre in Paris, the deal if fully implemented would generate extra world growth of $475 billion a year and a cumulative gain by the year 2000 of $5,000 billion. In addition the negative gain should not be omitted – the gain of avoiding the costs of a trade war. In the last great period of protectionism – the 1930s – the value of world trade fell by two thirds and the national income of major industrial countries like the USA by one third.

Unfortunately uncertainty over ratification of the Uruguay round persisted in 1993 owing to entry to office of a more protectionist president in the USA and the election in March of a more protectionist right-wing government in France. Both states appeared to wish reopening of the GATT accord in the hope of gaining a better deal for their farmers. Jacques Chirac, leader of the French Gaullist party, even went so far as to suggest that GATT itself as an institution was outmoded and should be ignored in the future.

The EC, the USA and Japan

The Western economic triangle of trade between the EC, the USA and Japan has been the centrepiece of the world economy during the last two decades. The USA is the EC's biggest supplier and customer. In 1990 US exports to the EC reached £100 billion and sales from American subsidiaries in the EC amounted to $400 billion. Over time the two economies have become very interdependent with massive investment in the EC by American multinationals and with European companies reciprocating by heavy investment in the USA. In 1989 the value of the two-way trade and investment neared a record $500 billion.

At times the close economic relations were complemented by close political relations. For example after the collapse of Soviet Russia and the completion of German reunification in 1989–90 there was a precise and determined effort by the Commission and the Bush administration to co-ordinate policy on world trade, aid to developing states and Eastern Europe. Delors was able to calm American fears that the single market programme would result in a Fortress Europe with American products excluded. During his 1989 visit to Washington, Delors said, 'The completion of the internal market will increase the purchasing power of the EC, providing vast opportunities to our partners worldwide, and firstly to the United States'. By September the US trade representative, Carla Hills, was able to respond by stating that the US administration strongly supported the 1992 programme and believed that its open and non-discriminatory implementation would benefit both the EC and its major trading partners, including the USA.

This improved tenor of relations was in marked contrast to the soured character of EC–US relations during the previous Reagan administration. The 88 per cent drop in the US trade deficit with the EC in 1989 over the previous year (later to turn to a surplus) also helped ease bilateral frictions. The US trade deficit with the EC of just $1.5 billion in 1989 seemed tiny when compared to the US deficits with Japan of $49 billion and the newly industrializing countries of $31 billion.

Co-operation was made easier by the practice of much consulta-tion between EC and US officials, frequent visits to the USA by ministers and European Commissioners and close contacts between the Commission Delegation in Washington and the US Mission in Brussels.

Nevertheless such cordiality has been the exception rather than the rule since the early 1980s when relations deteriorated rapidly for polit-ical and economic reasons. Europeans were worried by the intensely anti-Communist tone of American foreign policy under President Reagan and angered by the American incursion into Grenada, by Reagan's attempts to prevent European companies supplying equip-ment to the Soviet gas pipeline and by an American policy of high interest rates with its knock-on effect on European economies. But a more jaundiced American perception of Europe was also developing. In January 1984 *The Economist* published a leading article in which it showed that an image of the 'Useless European' was taking shape in the American mind. The accusations were of European tightfistedness in defence spending, of turning a blind eye on inconvenient problems and of always asking what America could do for Europe rather than what Europe could do for America. Such a perception, *The Economist* suggested, would cause Europe to be pushed another notch downwards in America's order of priorities, below the Pacific basin, south-west Asia and Central America.

On trading issues as such both the Community and the USA have accused each other of gross protectionism. Many demands were made in the American Congress during the 1980s (which to their credit Reagan and Bush mainly resisted) for protectionist measures against imports from the rest of the world, including the EC. Such a protectionist clamour from business interest groups was only to be expected as imports penetrated the American market and the USA experienced record trade deficits. In 1988 the Omnibus Trade and Competitiveness Act went through Congress; its objective was to open up foreign markets to American goods and to provide effec-tive sanctions against those states believed to be trading unfairly.

Given this climate of opinion it was only to be expected that EC–US trading relations were clouded by disagreements on several issues, disputes that seemed destined to be aggravated by the new Clinton administration in 1993. Firstly criticism of the CAP, surveyed earlier, has been a constant theme in American comments on the Community. Secondly there have been many disputes over steel. The Americans claimed in 1980 that EC steel, bolstered by unfair state subsidies was being dumped in the USA and imposed countervailing duties. The EC steel exporters then faced the imposition of quotas in 1982 and 1984. The EC retaliated by imposing its own anti-dumping duties on American steel exports to Europe. Eventually a compromise was reached by which the EC was able to export a reduced amount of steel to the USA.

However when this quota arrangement ran out in 1992 American steel companies filed dozens of suits against foreign producers, alleging that they were dumping steel on the American market. In January 1993 the US Commerce Department imposed severe duties on steel imports worth $2.6 billion from 19 countries. On some categories of steel the duties were very heavy indeed: on carbon-steel plate from Britain, for example, the duty was 109.22 per cent. When added to duties imposed earlier on the grounds that foreign producers were receiving state subsidies, the new impositions threatened to bar many European steel companies from the American market.

The duties were to be formally imposed only after the US International Trade Commission was satisfied that dumping and subsidies had really injured American steel companies. Yet damage to EC steelmakers was immediate because the duties had to be paid in advance, in practice by the producers depositing a bond with American customs authorities. The money would only be returned in the unlikely event that the preliminary findings of the Commerce Department were to be reversed. The EC decided immediately to take the case to GATT under that organization's Anti-Dumping Code. The new Trade Commissioner, Sir Leon Brittan, stressed that the duties were not only unjustified on economic grounds but sent the wrong political signals at a time when the world needed reassurance of America's intention to stand by its commitment to free trade. EC negotiators questioned the methods used by the US to calculate subsidies made to EC producers and doubted whether EC steel exports to the US had caused injury to American producers, given that since 1989 the share of EC production in the American steel market had stagnated or dropped in almost every product sector. At the root of the quarrel was the world recession which affected steel demand globally and while the recession was acute the dispute over steel seemed set to continue indefinitely.

A third contentious issue which surfaced by 1991 concerned civil aircraft production in the EC and the USA. American aircraft producers, especially Boeing, the king of the civil aircraft industry, expressed outrage in 1991 at the allegedly unfair subsidies enjoyed by the European Airbus, Boeing's fastest rising challenger. Airbus is a four-nation consortium of French, German, Spanish and British companies which Boeing claimed in June 1991 had already received up to $26 billion in direct subsidies plus billions more through indirect military subsidies and privileged access to Community research programmes. The European response was combative, Jean Pierson, Airbus's chairman, claimed that indirect American government support for Boeing and McDonnell-Douglas totalled $23 billion between 1978 and 1987, implying at the same time that Boeing's complaints were merely sour grapes at Airbus's infringement of the near-monopoly enjoyed by American companies in the civil aircraft market.

The chief American trade negotiator, Carla Hills, demanded that government aid for Airbus be limited to 25 per cent of its product development costs and such aid be provided by loans repayable within 15 years at a real rate of interest. The European position was that they would provide a 45 per cent limit on launch aid but only if the USA disclosed the true level of support (through tax relief and government orders) enjoyed by American aircraft producers. To Europeans the American attitude seemed hypocritical and a response to Airbus's success in 1990 in capturing 36 per cent of the jetliner orders won by the three largest producers, compared to Boeing's 48 per cent share and Douglas's 16 per cent share – the first time that Airbus had pushed Boeing below 50 per cent of the market in any one year.

Eventually in April 1992 the two sides reached a compromise whereby government support for Airbus was capped at between 30 and 35 per cent of development costs but the quarrel was not so easily forgotten. When the American company, United Airlines, agreed to lease 50 of Airbus's A320 aeroplanes in July 1992 Carla Hills promised an immediate investigation of the deal in case Airbus was being offered at an artificially low price. In February 1993 the Clinton administration appeared to be threatening to renege on the April 1992 accord. The EC response was to stress that Airbus was not responsible for depressed conditions in the American aircraft industry; aircraft manufacture worldwide was experiencing a crisis as a result of a global recession and the reduction in defence spending arising from the end of the Cold War.

The advent of the Clinton administration created a climate of uncertainty for many EC firms wishing to do business in the USA. One of the first actions of the new government was a proposal for a government prohibition on the award of contracts by federal agencies to companies in some or all EC states. EC companies were already effectively barred from defence and public health contracts owing to rules under a Buy American Act. The American action was in retaliation against the EC's own public procurement policies which favoured Community companies.

The Clinton government also put forward a proposal that four-wheel-drive cars be treated as trucks. Such vehicles would then incur a 25 per cent tariff instead of the 2.5 per cent tariff on cars. The main objective of this move was to reduce imports of Japanese four-wheel-drive cars but Community vehicles such as British Aerospace's Range Rover as well as models made by Mercedes-Benz and Volkswagen would also be affected. It was also feared that the new administration would revive the idea of a tax on so called 'gas-guzzling' cars put on ice by the Bush government. This could be implemented at a level that did not affect American-built cars but would hit sales in the USA of Rolls-Royce, Jaguar, Mercedes-Benz and BMW models.

Other potential areas of discrimination threatened EC business in the USA, for example new taxes on foreign businesses in general. In the view of the Democrats, foreign companies in the USA fiddled their accounts so that they paid less in tax than American companies but the imposition of such new taxes would violate existing laws which ensure that foreign companies operating in the USA are taxed on an equal basis with domestic companies. To single out foreign businesses for special treatment would be discriminatory.

Finally, the new president's wife looked set to add to business uncertainty. As head of a taskforce for reforming America's health-care system, Hillary Clinton, more radical than her husband, wished to reduce the $90 billion (£60 million) spent on drugs each year in the USA by the imposition of price controls. Such actions were likely to harm the profits from sales previously gained by EC pharmaceutical companies operating in the American market. British companies such as Glaxo, Wellcome and Smithkline Beecham had made profits of £1.5 billion in the American market in 1992 but new price controls would also hit the profits of pharmaceutical firms from other EC states, especially German companies like Merck.

American protectionism and productivity have long concerned Europeans; Japanese commercial rivalry is of more recent development. European fear of Japanese competition was well depicted in a *Sunday Times* cartoon in 1982 which showed Japan as a Samurai warrier using heavy cannon to bombard a crumbling fortress Europe with cars and all manner of electrical goods. The Europeans were right to be apprehensive. Japanese industry had become extremely competitive through emphasis on technical innovation, penetration of well-defined target markets and a combination of value in terms of price and quality of product. Its expansion was assisted by powerful government support, particularly by the Ministry of International Trade and Development (MITI).

Three major factors have created strains in European-Japanese relations:

1 The imbalance of trade, with Community exports to Japan representing only one-third of Japanese sales to the Community.
2 The concentration of Japanese exports on the most sensitive sectors of the European market – cars, motor-cycles, machine tools and domestic electrical goods.
3 The innumerable obstacles faced by European firms wishing to export to Japan. Japanese customs duties are on average no higher than those in the Community but the real problem is the manipulation by Japanese authorities of technical barriers to trade as a device to keep out imports.

Japan is now responsible for one-tenth of world output. Despite rapid moves towards the development of a high technology service economy its unemployment rate was only 2.7 per cent in the 1980s. Its population is now 120 million and it is a healthy population; life expectancy for women is now on average eighty years and for men seventy-five years, both the longest in the world. The retirement age which used to be fifty-five, has been raised to sixty and now government advisers are urging extension to sixty-five years by the end of the century to expand employment opportunities for the growing ranks of the elderly.

Thus Japan as an export market has huge potential but this has made Japanese malpractices all the more galling for European business. When Trebor tried to sell sweets to Japanese consumers the Japanese foodstuff inspectors took exception to the colour. It was not, they said, the effect of the sweets on digestive systems so much as their effect on eyesight! As Terence Spurling, Trebor's Managing Director, scathingly remarked, it was the first case of sweets posing a risk to eyesight. Before Trebor sweets were allowed into Japan, the colour had to be modified.

Such examples of Japanese non-tariff barriers abound and threaten to distort world trade patterns. Japan's trade showed a surplus of $45.6 billion in the year ending March 1985 but in 1992 this visible trade balance reached $107.1 billion.

If the Community has suffered from this trend, the United States has suffered more. Japan's surplus with the United States grew from $21.7 billion in 1983 to $52 billion in 1987 and was still $44 billion in 1992. It increased the protectionist sentiment in Congress. In trying to force Japan to liberalize trade, the Americans have sent officials to Japan to push for concessions. In so doing they have found a set of obstacles deeply embedded in Japanese practices. For example, tight medical coteries promote certain drugs and do their best to keep competitive medicine out of the market. The system is reinforced by the Japanese practice of Amakudari, literally descent from heaven. Health ministry bureaucrats can expect to 'retire' to compatible jobs with the drug companies if their record of making matters awkward for foreign drugs firms is deemed satisfactory.

There are other complaints against Japanese trading practices. It takes nine days for imports to clear Japanese customs because goods must be inspected and then given at least eight safety and certification tests required by Japanese ministries. Goods are returned to their country of origin if there are errors, however slight, in customs documentation or if they offend absurd safety rules. Aluminium baseball bats were sent back to the United States on alleged safety grounds.

The British, along with other Europeans, feel as exasperated as the Americans. Negotiating with the Japanese is like 'shooting at a changing target. As soon as you shoot one restriction down, another is put in its place', an official at the DTI comments. One dispute has centred on aerospace products. Sales to Japan of the BAE 146 were held up in 1985 by bureaucratic wrangles over safety. This was very convenient for the Japanese firm KHI which was developing a very similar aircraft. Another area of complaint has been motor components. In 1983 Adrian Potter of Automotive Products led a mission sponsored by the Society of Motor Manufacturers and Traders (SMMT) to Tokyo and in 1984 the Japanese were invited back to Britain for talks with individual British companies. But owing to discrimination the results were disappointing: in 1984 Britain imported £157 million of components from Japan but exported only £9 million of components to Japan. Anthony Fraser, Director-General of the SMMT, felt that British components were competitive in price, quality and reliability of supply and that more political pressure was needed.

Exporting to Japan is difficult without added problems. The low value of the yen has made foreign goods expensive in Japan. Another factor is the need for exporters to use a Japanese import agent to circumnavigate the technical barriers; the agent's mark-up adds substantially to prices. In 1985 a BMW car that cost the equivalent of 2,700,000 yen in West Germany retailed at 4,950,000 yen in Japan.

In 1990 the yen fell sharply on the foreign exchange markets because the Japanese government failed to support it by the necessary rise in interest rates. Such an undervalued yen made exporting to Japan even more difficult and increased the attractiveness of the country's exports.

The size of the Japanese trade surplus with the EC has tried European patience and led to the risk of a trade war. Between 1986 and 1992 this surplus almost doubled from $18 billion to £31 billion. Consequently the EC has attempted to put pressure on the Japanese to open up their markets. Japanese promises so to do led to relatively limited action and when Japan's economy went into recession in 1992 it was even less likely that its government would embrace free trade.

Japanese inaction on the trade imbalance has led to more aggressive EC tactics. Sometimes the measures have been national in character. In 1983, for example, in retaliation against slow processing of Renault cars through the port of Yokohama, the French government decided to impede the imports of Japanese video cassette recorders by channelling them through a single inspection point at Poitiers, though the tactic was abandoned after a few months. More widespread since 1977 has been the imposition of national quotas on the imports of Japanese cars. For many years Italy had an import quota for Japanese cars of little over 2000 a year, while in France the Japanese share of the French car market was fixed at 3 per cent by an agreement between the French government and Japanese producers. This figure contrasted with the share enjoyed by the Japanese in the UK (11 per cent) and in Germany (16 per cent).

On a Community level, the EC embarked on a series of anti-dumping actions to protect sensitive industries where the Japanese success was most marked – colour television sets, CD players, and audio tapes for example. The use of VERs has been widespread and since 1983 the Japanese have been forced to limit their exports to the EC of video cassette recorders, motor-cycles, machine tools and vehicles.

Such protectionist measures have not cured the EC's trade deficit with Japan nor arguably have they helped EC firms. The Japanese response has been to set up production within the EC to avoid tariffs or quotas and to take advantage of the artificially high prices produced by the anti-dumping duties or quotas. The cost to consumers has been considerable but EC firms may have lost out through the false sense of security arising from the belief that they could afford to delay entry into new product lines.

The amount of Japanese investment in the EC has exercised European minds. In one sense the Community had wanted Japanese companies to set up full-scale manufacturing plants in Europe to provide new jobs and state of the art technology. Many Japanese companies like Toyota, Sony and Nissan were glad to do so through most Japanese investment in the EC has been in services rather than manufacturing. However the nature of the manufacturing plants created in the EC has attracted criticism. Critics have dubbed the Japanese factories 'screwdriver' operations because all that the Japanese companies transferred to Europe was final assembly with many of the skilled operations and sourcing remaining outside the EC. Thus the Commission has insisted on local content rules, i.e. that for cars, for example, up to 80 per cent of the content of Japanese cars assembled in the EC should be composed of components bought within the EC. Such rules are however difficult to supervise and still enable Japanese companies to keep control of their know-how so that little technology transfer occurs.

EC-Japanese relations then seem destined to remain fractious though for the EC to impose a blanket restriction on all Japanese imports is inadvisable. It could damage European manufacturers whose reliance on Japanese components is higher than is generally realized as Mark Smalley of business advisers PA International Consulting has warned. British manufacturers alone buy from Japan up to 20 per cent of their component needs, with dependence particularly high in the electronics and car industries. Consequently a blanket limitation on imports could well damage Europe more than Japan. In any case Japanese exports prevented from entering the EC could well be deflected to Europe's own export markets in other parts of the world.

The real long-term solution is for Japan to open its markets genuinely to foreign competitors. With this in mind, possibly the best Community policy is one of severe selective controls on imports of Japanese consumer goods with the promise that such controls would disappear as soon as the way was cleared for increased European exports to Japan. Certainly by 1992 the severe recession in the EC combined with the huge EC trade deficit with Japan was helping to spread the view that more sanctions against Japan were necessary. Such views had long been held in more protectionist France but were now becoming prevalent in powerful German pressure groups such as the industrial association, the Bundesverebrand de Deutsche Industrie, formerly a keen supporter of free trade. Even a well known Commission free trader like Sir Leon Brittan commented in 1992 that he would not rule out the threat of reciprocity to force Japan to open up its home market. More extreme protectionists like Jacques Calvet, head of Peugeot and Citroen, wanted permanent restrictions on Japanese imports combined with much national and EC aid to European industry.

Analysts confirm the worst fears of industrialists like Calvet. Euromonitor Reports, a car research group, has stated that if the EC liberalizes car imports by 1999 only Volkswagen among European car producers was sure to survive with either Renault or Fiat likely to collapse or be taken over. With the six biggest Japanese carmakers planning to produce more than 1.5 million cars a year in the EC by the year 2000, the Euromonitor Report seems realistic though possibly on the optimistic side.

Given the difficulties in the way of EC firms exporting to Japan, the Community has put pressure on Japan through GATT to open up its markets in the field of pharmaceuticals, agricultural products, motor vehicles, medical equipment, cosmetics, wines and spirits. To encourage European firms to enter Japanese markets, the Community has set up a number of initiatives to assist them. Chief of these initiatives, dating from 1979, is EXPROM (Export Promotion Programme) which has provided management training, market studies and financial help for trade missions and other trade promotion services in Japan. A key element in EXPROM is the Executive Training Programme through which the Commission has sent over 200 young European executives to Japan for 18 months of intensive language and business training. Many graduates of this programme have since reached managerial positions in their companies' Japanese subsidiaries. EXPROM provides a directory of European firms in Japan who are able and willing to help newcomers and has prepared a checklist of major construction projects in Japan for which interested European firms may tender.

Relations with developing countries

The Community has a complex set of aid and trade agreements with various blocs of third world countries. At the top of this pyramid is the Lomé Convention which the Community has described as 'a pioneering model of co-operation between equal partners'. The negotiations for the first Lomé Convention began in 1974 with various countries from Africa, the Caribbean and the Pacific (the ACP states). The Community was moved to pursue such an agreement for mixed motives. The disparity in wealth between European countries and the Third World was growing but also a rapid increase in the price of Third World commodities like oil, coffee, copper and sugar made the Commission anxious to stabilize trade with the ACP countries.

The first Lomé Convention was signed in February 1975 between the Community and forty-six ACP states and ran from April 1976 to March 1980. Trade co-operation was a major feature of the agreement. Under the terms of the Convention, the ACP countries were not required to give preferential treatment to imports from the Community but practically all ACP exports had free access to Community markets.

The really novel feature was Stabilization of Export Earnings (Stabex). Where an ACP country found that its earnings from the export of one of the products covered by the scheme fell below its average earnings, it could obtain help from the European Development Fund (EDF) to meet the difference. The aim of Stabex was to help those countries which were heavily dependent on one or a handful of commodities and whose export earnings were at the mercy of sudden market fluctuations or, in the case of agricultural products, a disastrous climatic year. For any of the products to be taken into consideration, it had to represent at least 7.5 per cent of the value of the country's total exports in the previous year (the dependence threshold) and earnings from exports to the Community of the given product had to be less than the average of earnings over the four preceding years by at least 7.5 per cent (the trigger threshold)

The third main area of the agreement was over financial aid and technical co-operation. Total aid under the first Lomé Convention reached 3,446 million EUAs, the EDF distributing 3,056 million EUAs and the EIB allocating 390 million EUAs in loans to finance ACP projects.

Perhaps too much was expected of this agreement by the ACP countries and certainly it disappointed them in practice. Therefore when negotiations commenced in 1978–9 for a second Lomé Convention, they were undertaken in a less optimistic and less cordial spirit. Nevertheless Lomé II which ran from 1980 to 1985 did contain some improvements on Lomé I. The Stabex scheme was extended by the inclusion of new agricultural products, raising the number of commodities in the scheme to forty-four. The dependence and trigger thresholds were brought down from 7.5 per cent to 6.5 per cent.

A new scheme called Sysmin was introduced to protect the ACP countries against loss of earnings from exports of minerals in a manner similar to the Stabex operation for agricultural products and raw materials. However the Sysmin scheme operated on much higher dependence and trigger thresholds (15 per cent and 10 per cent respectively) than Stabex.

The ACP countries were particularly aggrieved over the amount of aid agreed under Lomé II. They asked for 10,830 million EUAs of aid but had to be content with a final figure of 5,692 million EUAs. They felt strongly that the negotiations had been carried on in a high-handed fashion by the Community.

The third Lomé Convention was signed in December 1984 only after 413 days of acrimonious negotiations between the Community and sixty-six ACP countries and was to run from March 1985 to 1990. Once again the ACP diplomats were disappointed at the Community's offer on aid and trade and even the former Community Commissioner for Development Policy, Edgard Pisani, who had spearheaded attempts to reform the Lomé agreement, admitted that Lomé III did not contain any revolutionary changes.

The ACP countries had asked for 12 billion ECUs of aid from the Community, more than double the amount given to the group by Lomé II. They justified this figure by pointing to the increase in the ACP population, to inflation and to the new areas of activity to be tackled under Lomé III. The Community states, especially West

Germany and Britain, were always opposed to such a large increase and after much haggling the Community offered 7 billion ECUs in October 1984 though this was raised to 7.4 billion ECUs in November. With the 1.1 billion ECUs in loans from the EIB, total Community aid under Lomé II was raised to 8.5 billion ECUs. The 7.4 billion ECUs of grants from the EDF were to be divided as follows:

(*a*) Aid for projects 5.77 billion ECUs
(*b*) Stabex transfers 925 million ECUs
(*c*) Sysmin transfers 415 million ECUs
(*d*) Exceptional aid for emergencies 290 million ECUs.

The ACP group was also angered by the Community demand for regular consultations on how the aid was being used by the ACP states. They saw this as a Community attempt to 'dictate and preach'. Though Community negotiations toned down the original texts, the principle of dialogue on the use of aid was ultimately accepted by the ACP group. Their acceptance followed discreet hints that a refusal to accept dialogue would mean even less European help. The Europeans pressed for such an arrangement because examples of fraud and misuse of EDF money had occurred in previous years.

The ACP group felt that the trade provisions under Lomé III were 'particularly weak'. They had demanded complete duty free access to European markets for all their products. The Community argued that the ACP group already had duty free access to Community markets for 99.5 per cent of their exports and would only agree to accelerate its consideration of specific ACP requests for preferential access. In the past such Commission deliberation often took two years and this was to be reduced to six months. ACP exporters were also promised that any concessions given by the Community to exports from other developing countries would be matched by similar preferences for the ACP group. The Community continued to claim the right to stop ACP imports if they endangered the survival of its own industry and quotas still existed on some food imports from the ACP group, for example, sugar, beef, rum and rice.

The Community insisted that it monitor more closely the use of the money spent on Stabex, obviously suspicious that ACP governments did not always use the Stabex transfers for the benefit of the sector concerned. A few new items like dried bananas and mangoes were added to the list of products covered by the system and the dependence and trigger thresholds were lowered by 0.5 per cent to 6 per cent.

The Community insisted that it monitor more closely the use of the Sysmin system. To help Zimbabwe, Botswana and Niger, uranium, nickel and chrome were now included in the list of minerals eligible for Sysmin aid.

The importance of increasing ACP food production was recognized as the top priority of Lomé III. This neglected sector will receive more funds in future years with the aim of reducing ACP dependence on food aid from Europe in the long-run. Such new thinking was prompted by the famines in Ethiopia, Sudan and other areas of Africa where drought, soil erosion and the cutting down of forests for firewood had led to the expansion of the deserts. In its anti-desertification drive the Community identified three priority targets – reafforestation, protection of livestock and game, and the efficient management of water. Help to local industry would be given with a view to servicing the needs of agriculture.

One important innovation in Lomé III was a decision to encourage European industrialists to invest in Africa. In the past they have naturally been wary of doing so out of fear of nationalization and political instability. The new convention included a framework for the conclusion of bilateral investment protection agreements between the Community and each of the ACP states. Such agreements included an undertaking to accord investors fairer treatment and to create a more favourable investment climate. A joint Community– ACP insurance and guarantee scheme was considered. Though it is likely to help the unstable investment climate only marginally in the short-run, it could augur a promising area of development in Community–ACP relations.

The background to the signing of Lomé IV in December 1989 was not propitious. Agreement was only reached after a bitter 14 month negotiation process with disagreements over the amount of aid, solutions to the problems of ACP states' debts and access into the Community market of ACP commodities. Apart from the debt issue, such disagreements were hardly new and cropped up with depressing regularity during all Lomé negotiations. However the context of the negotiations was less hopeful than ever for the ACP countries.

Firstly, the economic situation had declined even further. Besides being burdened with tremendous debts, the ACP growth rate was below that of 1970. Secondly, changes in the Community itself worried the ACP partners. In their view the single market programme might well put their exports to the Community in jeopardy if internal free trade within the Community was complemented by a Fortress Europe mentality. Moreover the single market was bound to be extended to EFTA countries in the effort to create a future European Economic Space. Above all the Community states were clearly giving more attention to the transformation of Eastern Europe and the ACP states feared with good reason that EC funding would be found for the economic restructuring of East European states instead of aid for Lomé IV. That the revival of Eastern Europe would in the long-run benefit the ACP states by increasing world demand for tropical products was small consolation.

Given these difficulties it was an achievement to complete Lomé IV at all but it did combine continuity with some innovation. The Community increased the volume of aid for the first five years (1990–5) from 8,500 million ECU to 12,000 million ECU, an increase in real terms of over 20 per cent. In an attempt to provide continuity the life of Lomé IV was doubled from five to ten years and it will thus expire in March 2000. The Financial Protocol will be reviewed in 1995 and the longer term of the Convention should increase investor security and confidence. The number of ACP states rose from sixty-six to sixty-nine, including Namibia.

Among new measures was an arrangement over economic aid. Facing severe budgetary difficulties in the 1980s, most ACP states had been forced into seeking financial assistance from the IMF and the World Bank but these institutions had imposed drastic economic reforms (structural adjustment programmes) as a condition for the credit. Under Lomé IV a new fund was set up to help the structural adjustment worth 1,150 million ECU, to be used for development projects.

Lomé IV also did something to dispel fears of a Fortress Europe. Not only was unrestricted access maintained for the vast majority of ACP exports but new concessions were granted on a number of agricultural products with access guaranteed after 1992 for ACP bananas and rum.

Some efforts were made to tackle ACP indebtedness itself. Stabex transfers which were to increase by 62 per cent on Lomé III were to be totally in the form of grants, not loans. Loans from the EIB were to be cheaper. To help the private sector there were increases in the risk capital and technical assistance available.

It would be easy to wax cynical over the Lomé Conventions. They were trumpeted as a model for relations with the Third World but they have not been replicated by the Community with other developing countries nor by other industrialized countries. It is even debatable whether such aid ever really raises the standard of living of poor countries. Peter Bauer has argued in '*The Development Frontier*' that aid often reduces poor people's income because the aid goes to corrupt government and distracts attention from the need to stimulate exports. Since the mid-1960s the Third World has become relatively less important overall for Europe in terms of trade, finance and military strategy. The LDC (developing countries) share of total EC imports has fallen since the oil price shocks from 23 per cent in 1975 to 13 per cent in 1988. The sharpest fall in trade share has, however, been experienced by the ACP states whose share of EC imports fell from 10 per cent in 1960 to 4 per cent in 1988. The ACP share of Community imports from LDC

Table 11.1   Lomé in brief

Lomé	ACP (No.)	Period	Finance (ECUm)
I	46	1975–1980	3,450
II	57	1980–1985	5,600
III	66	1985–1990	8,500
IV	69	1990–2000	12,000 (1990–95)

Table 11.2   The Lomé IV Financial Protocol 1990–1995 (ECUm)

Grants for national and regional programmes	6,215
Structural adjustment	1,150
Stabex	1,500
Sysmin	480
Emergency Aid	250
Refugee Aid	100
Interest rate subsidies	280
Risk Capital	825
EIB loans for national and regional projects	1,200

states even fell by a quarter from 20.5 per cent in 1975 to 15.1 per cent in 1987.

Christopher Stevens has pointed out that it is incongruous that the ACP should be both the most preferred and yet least successful trading partners with the EC. However he warns us against writing off the Lomé Conventions as valueless because the poor ACP trade performance reflected two factors. First, the Lomé Convention provided the ACP with either zero or very limited preference over their major competitors for the greater part of their exports. Second, ACP exports are more heavily concentrated than are those of other LDCs on commodities for which world demand is growing slowly. Without the Lomé Conventions the ACP trade performance would have been even worse and the peoples of those states even more impoverished (see Tables 11.1 and 11.2).

Aid to non-associated countries

In 1976 the Council adopted an aid programme for non-associated countries. Initially it had an annual budget of 20 million ECU and covered seven countries. By 1983 the programme had been extended to 30 recipient countries with a budget of 235 million ECU. For 1987

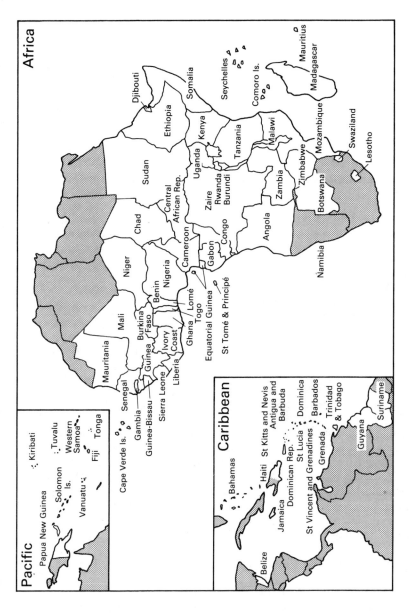

Figure 11.1 The Lomé link. The 68 countries joined to the European Community under the Lomé Convention

Table 11.3 The ACP states

Angola	Ghana	St Lucia
Antigua & Barbuda	Grenada	St Vincent & the
Bahamas	Guinea	Grenadines
Belize	Guyana	São Tomé & Principe
Benin	Haiti	Seychelles
Botswana	Jamaica	Sierra Leone
Burkina	Kenya	Solomon Islands
Burundi	Kiribati	Somalia
Cameroon	Lesotho	Sudan
Cape Verde	Liberia	Surinam
Central African Republic	Madagascar	Swaziland
Chad	Malawi	Tanzania
Comoros	Mali	Togo
Congo	Mauritania	Tonga
Côte d'Ivoire	Mauritius	Trinidad and Tobago
Djibouti	Mozambique	Tuvalu
Dominica	Namibia	Uganda
Equatorial Guinea	Niger	Vanuatu
Ethiopia	Nigeria	Western Samoa
Fiji	Papua New Guinea	Zaire
Gabon	Rwanda	Zambia
Gambia	St Kitts-Nevis	Zimbabwe

The ACP states have a total population of over 400 million, of which the largest are Nigeria (105m), Ethiopia (48m) and Zaire (33m).

the allocation was 284 million ECU, almost entirely for rural development. Aid is allocated on a project basis, hence not all countries receive aid every year. Since 1988 aid has been formally divided between Asia (65 per cent) and Latin America (35 per cent).

The 69 ACP states are shown in Table 11.3.

Further reading

Dykes, D (ed.), *The European Economy* (Chapter 10), Longmans, London, 1992.
The Economist, *World Trade*, 22 September, 1990.
Grilli, E R, *The European Community and the Developing Countries*, CUP, Cambridge, 1993.
Hindley, B in Minford, P (eds), *The Cost of Europe*, Manchester University Press, Manchester, 1992.
Nicolaides, P, *Trade Policy and Instruments of the European Community*, European Trends, Number 4, 1991.

Questions

1 Comment on the record of the EC as a free trading organization.
2 What problems faced the EC during the Uruguay Round of the GATT?
3 What tensions have beset EC–US trade relations in recent years?
4 Should the EC adopt tough measures to prevent further Japanese penetration of its home market?
5 Analyse the achievements of the Lomé Conventions in assisting the Third World.

12
Wider still and wider: the enlargement of the European Community

One constant theme in the development of the European Community has been the steady increase in the number of member states from the original six founder members to twelve members by 1986. In 1973 the Six became the Nine when Britain, Denmark and Ireland acceded to membership while in the 1980s the Community gained a veritable Mediterranean dimension when Greece joined in 1981 and Spain and Portugal in 1986 (see Figure 12.1).

Community membership is likely to rise again before the end of the century though EC leaders have been cautious to the point of obstruction in giving a firm timetable. There appear to be two chief reasons for their caution. Firstly, they are afraid of giving EC membership to poor states which would then be a heavy charge on the Community budget. Secondly, as Jacques Delors has stressed, such *widening* of membership might well hold back an objective dear to his heart as well as to that of others – the *deepening* of the Community's political and economic union. Therefore it was agreed at the Lisbon Summit in June 1992 that enlargement would not take place until the Maastricht Treaty had been ratified by all member states and agreement reached on the budgetary arrangements increasing spending on the poorer southern states.

Potential applicants for EC membership fall into three distinct groups. The first group comprising the prosperous EFTA states (Austria, Finland, Sweden, Switzerland and Norway) could be assimilated relatively easily and therefore a target date of 1995–6 could still be a realistic date for their accession to membership. The second group is made up of the new democracies of Eastern Europe (Poland, Czechoslovakia and Hungary) which signed association agreements with the EC in 1991. Possible future applicants from the region comprise Rumania, Bulgaria and the Baltic States of Latvia, Lithuania and Estonia. The third group are Mediterranean countries – Turkey, Cyprus and Malta. In contrast to the first group, the two latter groups have real hurdles to overcome if the EC is to consider their membership seriously, most notably the need to modernize their economies.

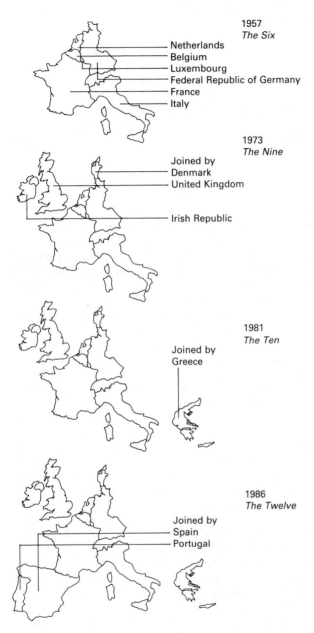

1957
The Six

Netherlands
Belgium
Luxembourg
Federal Republic of Germany
France
Italy

1973
The Nine

Joined by
Denmark
United Kingdom

Irish Republic

1981
The Ten

Joined by
Greece

1986
The Twelve

Joined by
Spain
Portugal

Figure 12.1 The evolution of the European Community

The motives behind enlargement

Under Article 237 of the Rome Treaty, 'any European state may apply to become a member of the Community'. The conditions of admission have to be negotiated between the Commission and the applicant state and the agreement reached must then be ratified by all contracting states. Since the Community was established, most European states have applied for membership or association and therefore the Community has been faced with the need for careful decisions over these issues. Although there were no guidelines in the Treaty as to how the founders of the Community imagined its membership would expand, in practice no enlargement has taken place without lengthy negotiations with each applicant state.

In general an applicant state must measure up to the test of three crucial principles: it must be a European state; it must be democratic to conform with the Summit declaration of October 1972 and the joint declaration by the European Parliament, the Council and the Commission of April 1977, a declaration endorsed in April 1978 by the European Council; it must be ready and able to accept not only the political and economic obligations of membership but also the major Community objectives as set out in Articles 2 and 3 of the Rome Treaty.

Given the problems over the accession of new members, the question must be asked why the Community should be enlarged and a number of general arguments have been made. The Community is committed by the Rome Treaty to remain open to new members. In the preamble to the Treaty, the signatories declared themselves 'resolved to preserve and strengthen liberty, calling upon the other peoples of Europe who share their ideal to join in their efforts'. A second argument is that enlargement would serve to consolidate democracy in the applicant countries. Recent successful applicants such as Greece, Portugal and Spain have all emerged from shorter or longer periods of dictatorship and arguably membership of the Community has helped to nurture their young democracies. For similar reasons East European membership should be encouraged. Strategic arguments have also been adduced. The strategic importance of Greece and Turkey is threefold. Together they constitute the southern flank of NATO, have influence on the important oil route from the Middle East to Western Europe and control the straits between the Black Sea and the Mediterranean, the only route which gave the former Soviet Union direct naval access to the Mediterranean and the Atlantic throughout the year. While these factors are of less importance after the demise of the Soviet Union, instability in the area or in Eastern Europe would harm the EC's economic interests.

Enlargement has proved that the Community is not just 'a rich man's club', and over time strengthens the Community's political, economic and commercial weight in the world. Spain is already the seventh industrial power in the world and Greek merchant shipping represents 13 per cent of the world merchant fleet. The historical, cultural and commercial links between Portugal and Spain on the one hand and the countries of Latin America on the other have helped to improve relations between the Community and South America, relations which deteriorated after the 1982 Falklands War.

The Commission has also pointed to specific economic advantages of enlargement. Though the level of development in Mediterranean and Eastern European states is lower than that in the Community, the growth rate is higher or potentially higher. A larger market would be opened up for the Community's industrial goods and also some farm produce (cereals, beef and pork, milk products) in a Community expanded from 270 million consumers in 1981 to approaching 400 million by the end of the century. Community industries in crisis might be helped if membership brought discipline and restricted production to the same industries in the applicant states.

Finally it has been argued that the difficulties which enlargement poses might be an advantage in that they could provide a stimulus for reforming important aspects of Community activity – the decision-making process and improved regional, social, industrial and agricultural policies.

The chief motives of the applicant states should also be considered. Broadly their governments have seen Community membership as offering the best opportunity to secure their somewhat fragile democracies. They have assumed that any renaissance of anti-democratic forces within their societies may be deterred by the fact that a return to authoritarianism would put at risk all of the political and economic ties which flow from Community membership. Secondly they have hoped that membership would help economic development and modernization through exposure to a large and competitive market. For example East European states hope that EC membership would complete the process of moving their economies away from a command model to a free market model. Also EFTA states were more enthusiastic applicants for EC membership after 1989 because the revolutionary developments there made Eastern Europe politically and economically unstable.

EFTA and the European Economic Area (EEA)

The European Free Trade Association (EFTA) was formed in 1959 between the 'Other Six' – Britain, Norway, Sweden, Denmark, Austria and Switzerland. Subsequently Finland, Liechtenstein and

Iceland became members. EFTA was purely a commercial arrange-ment – a free trade area primarily in industrial goods with little institutional machinery. Britain and Denmark left EFTA in 1973 but the remaining states were content within the association as a consid-erable liberalization of trade was achieved between the EC and EFTA.

It was the creation of the single market programme in 1985 which gave rise to fears that EFTA states might find access to the EC's internal market less easy than in the past. At the very least EFTA members felt that their relationship with the EC needed to be re-defined in such a way as would enable them to have some influence on Community decisions. Furthermore several EFTA states had begun to believe that full EC membership was a desirable long-term goal.

Discussions designed to promote a closer relationship began in 1984 when the two groups issued a joint declaration concerning the areas in which they wished to co-operate. The discussions soon gave rise to the idea of a European Economic Area (EEA), the central aim of which was to extend the 1992 Programme to the EFTA states. The event that really triggered the new development was a speech by Jacques Delors in January 1989 in which he proposed to EFTA 'a new form of association, with common decision-making and administrative institutions'. EFTA states welcomed the idea because they saw it as a good way in which to integrate into the EC's domes-tic market without becoming full members. Talks began seriously in December 1989 and were successfully concluded in October 1991. By then, however, several EFTA states made it clear that they accepted the terms of the new EEA only as a step to full EC membership. After some problems raised by the European Court of Justice over the legality of a proposed EFTA-EC court (the Special Court of Justice) the treaty setting up the EEA was eventually ratified in 1993.

The agreement on the EEA had almost imperial dimensions as it was a treaty between two blocs composed of 19 states in a market of 380 million consumers in a territory stretching from the Arctic to the Mediterranean and accounting for 46 per cent of world trade. Jacques Delors commented that the deal would provide useful experience for EFTA states which intended to apply for full EC membership while the External Affairs Commissioner, Frans Andriessen, who had been chief negotiator for the EC claimed that the new accord would give the Community a breathing space before embarking on enlargement.

The essential aim of the treaty was to extend most of the single market principles to the EFTA states. The agreement covered the free movement of goods, services, capital and people and enhanced co-operation between the two blocs on flanking policies such as R and D, the environment and social policy. The treaty therefore completed the process of abolishing import duties on manufactured goods from EFTA, and such goods now enjoy free circulation in the EEA on the basis of EC technical and safety regulations.

As the EEA is not a customs union, border controls and origins procedures still apply to goods arriving from EFTA countries though procedures have been simplified. Energy, coal, steel and food are to a large extent excluded from the agreement; for example, EFTA states retain their own farm policies rather than joining the CAP regime. Some greater free trade in fish has been achieved with the EC securing improved fishing rights for Community vessels in Norwegian waters (one of the most contentious issues). Public procurement is now for the first time opened up to all 19 countries on the basis of the relevant EC directives. EFTA states have also adopted the EC's competition rules.

As the previous EC–EFTA trading arrangements had not covered services, the treaty is a positive move away from highly protected markets to liberalization in accordance with Community rules on financial services, transport, audio-visual services and telecommunications. Now a credit institution licensed in the EC may set up operations in EFTA countries in line with the Community's Second Banking Directive (see Chapter 4).

The treaty's main impact on the free movement of capital falls in the area of foreign direct investment in EFTA states which have traditionally maintained very restrictive practices, for example in the purchase of real estate. Thus the EEA creates more opportunities for cross-border investment.

The agreement prohibits discrimination between EC and EFTA nationals in respect of pay, employment and working conditions. Therefore when an offer of employment is made EC and EFTA nationals may work in any of the 19 member states. EFTA states have adopted the main EC social provisions and professional people such as engineers and accountants can now seek employment throughout the EEA on the same basis of mutual recognition of qualifications as already exists in the EC.

Under the agreement EFTA states can now participate fully in the EC's R and D Framework Programmes (see Chapter 7). Co-operation is being increased on the environment, education, social policy, consumer protection and tourism. EFTA states have also agreed to establish and manage a fund to assist the EC's poorest regions. The fund comprises 500 million ECUs in grants over five years and 1.5 billion ECUs in soft loans. The beneficiaries of this largesse will be Spain, Portugal, Greece, Ireland and Northern Ireland.

The EC has reached a separate agreement with Switzerland and Austria on the transit of lorry traffic through the Alpine passes. There will be a limited increase in the number of EC lorries permitted to transit the two countries, with quotas largely based on historic shares. In exchange there will be measures to reduce pollution and encourage the use of alternative means of transport.

An EEA Council composed of ministers from the 19 states and a Commission representative provides political oversight for the functioning of the agreement, meeting once a month to supervise day-to-day business. This joint organization may reach decisions by consensus and provides a forum for settling disputes. Cases may be taken to an independent EEA Court consisting of five judges drawn from the European Court of Justice and three judges from EFTA. Their decisions will be binding.

The rapprochement between EFTA and the EC was prompted by a variety of political and economic motives. For the EC closer relations with EFTA states were desirable on commercial grounds because EFTA as a bloc is the EC's largest trading partner. In 1989 exports to EFTA constituted 26 per cent of the EC's exports to third countries (as against only 19 per cent to the USA). EFTA accounted for 23 per cent of the EC's imports whereas only 18 per cent originated from the USA. Moreover the EC enjoyed a trade surplus of over $4.5 billion with EFTA in 1989. In terms of communications, Switzerland and Austria hold the keys to the EC's full north-south market integration because they are located in the Community's geographical core.

The rapprochement with EFTA was also motivated by political and ideological factors. Denmark for example wished to avoid any separation from its traditional partners and neighbours in Scandinavia. Primarily the creation of the EEA was seen as a step towards returning EFTA states to the European fold. If EFTA states stay outside the EC the idea of a united Europe will remain unfulfilled for there can be no truly unified Europe without Vienna and Stockholm. With their more liberal external trade regimes and (farming apart) modest subsidies, EFTA states could also help to prevent the EC becoming too protectionist. Their arrival should tilt the EC towards higher environmental standards, stronger social policy and more open government.

For EFTA states the first incentive for rapprochement was economic – the fear of being excluded from the EC's single market. EFTA is very dependent on the Community for its foreign trade. In 1989–90 around 60 per cent of EFTA imports came from the EC and 58 per cent of its exports went to the EC. Most EFTA economies are already more integrated with the EC than are those of newer Community members such as Spain or Greece.

EFTA states reasoned that if the single market rules were not extended to them, then their exporters would continue to pay at Community borders for administration charges and delays. The non-opening of EC public procurement would also result in loss of sales for EFTA firms. The right of EFTA companies to compete on equal terms with Community firms for public sector contracts is crucial for Swedish firms such as Ericsson, the Swedish telecommunications giant and ABB, a Swiss–Swedish electrical engineering group because they sell much of their output to public utilities. Moreover, if they were excluded from the internal market, EFTA firms would not obtain the benefits of economies of scale or the effects of competition. Outside the single market, EFTA states would also become less attractive areas for foreign direct investment by Japanese and American companies.

EFTA states feared political isolation as the Community single market developed. A number of developments increased this feeling. They were naturally concerned by the turbulent development in Eastern Europe after 1989 but also by the signing of the Schengen Agreement in June 1990. This agreement between five EC states (the Benelux countries, France and Germany) ended border controls in advance of the 1992 programme but it increased the feeling of isolation of both Austria and Switzerland, countries bordering the signatory states.

A study in1991 by Victor Norman, a Norwegian economist, suggests that the gains from taking part in the single market for EFTA's industries could be two to three times bigger than the corresponding gains for Community industries. He argues that the main benefit to EFTA members arising from access to the single market will not come through greater exports but through fiercer competition within their home markets forcing efficiency gains.

The EEA treaty has important implications for business. Equally it may be seen as a significant step in the enlargement process. By February 1993 Austria, Sweden and Finland had opened negotiations with the EC over full membership and Norway was expected to join the group once the EC had finished a report on its application. The four countries had already covered much of the groundwork and hoped to sign treaties of accession by the end of 1993, hold referenda on the issue in 1994 and if their peoples agreed, join the EC in 1995.

However there were problems. Firstly the ratification of the EEA treaty ran into trouble. It was officially signed by the EC and EFTA in Oporto in May 1992 and was due to be implemented by 1 July 1993 but the rejection of the treaty by the Swiss in a referendum held in December 1992 created snags. The Swiss were to have contributed 27 per cent of the fund established under the treaty to boost the development of the four poorest EC states and the Spanish government feared that Swiss withdrawal would deplete the fund. The Spaniards intimated that they wanted the six remaining EFTA states to top up the fund with the implied threat that if they failed to do so then Spanish support for the treaty would be withheld.

Other specific difficulties threatened the enlargement timetable. Austria, Sweden and Finland are all neutral countries and Austria in particular is very attached to its 1955 neutrality law. There was reluctance therefore to be fully involved in the EC's ambitions over more defence and foreign policy co-operation which had been the subject of much debate at Maastricht in December 1991 (see Chapter 15).

Agricultural issues were difficult. Alpine and Nordic states subsidized their farmers even more than did the EC, partly because their climate was hostile to agriculture. They therefore wanted the CAP to support their farmers in the coldest areas.

The Nordic applicants also wanted the EC to change its regional policy so that Arctic areas qualified for aid, an objective opposed by the poorest EC member states. However as the applicant states (even after assistance from the CAP and ERDF) were likely to make a net contribution of between 2 and 3 billion ECUs a year to the Community budget, such opposition was hardly logical.

Each applicant state had its own special requests. The Swedes wished to maintain state alcohol monopolies, frontier controls, an opt-out of EMU and a monopoly on the husbandry of reindeer by the Sami people of North Sweden. The Finns wished to maintain free trade with the Baltic States and Austria wanted to maintain restrictions on the entry of EC lorries for 12 year and on the right of foreigners to buy property. The Norwegians wished to keep their oil and fishing rights.

The accession of these EFTA states would mean an increase in the number of small states in the EC with profound implications for voting procedures. If the new members were given three or five votes in the Council of Ministers (in line with current practice) then small states would then have 44 votes out of 92 despite having only 81 million out of the 371 million people in the EC. This would given them a disproportionate power to block Commission proposals or impose decisions on the larger states. Therefore either the current blocking majority of 23 votes would have to be maintained rather than being increased on a pro-rata basis or the larger states would have to be given more votes but with the definition of a qualified majority vote changed so that laws could be passed more easily. The larger states favoured the former option while the Commission favoured the latter solution, fearful that the arrival of new states would slow down EC decision-making across all Community institutions.

Finally there were concerns over public opinion in the applicant states where referenda would have to be held before EC membership could be fully ratified. In 1993 opinion in both Norway and Sweden was clearly against EC membership and it was very evenly balanced in Austria and Finland. However political parties and unions in Austria supported full EC membership. Austria's economy was already closely linked to the EC as 64 per cent of its exports went to the Community, especially Germany. Austria's business leaders hoped that membership would force an improvement in competitiveness while her political leaders saw in EC membership the completion of the process by which Austria would be free of any Russian tutelage.

Relations with Eastern Europe: the Community's ambivalent approach

Community relations with the states of Eastern Europe remained fragile in the years when these countries formed part of the Soviet orbit. Attempts in 1974 by the EC and COMECON (the Soviet bloc Council for Mutual Economic Assistance) to establish closer economic links had little success and the Soviet invasion of Afghanistan in 1979 effectively prevented the development of closer economic ties.

This limited relationship was revolutionized by the dramatic changes in Eastern Europe in 1989–90 which saw the reunification of West and East Germany and rapid political change in most East European countries. Former satellite states such as Poland and Hungary freed themselves from Soviet control and began to establish democratic government and free market economic management. The Soviet Union itself split into semi-independent republics, named the Commonwealth of Independent States (CIS) while Czechoslovakia divided into the Czech Republic and Slovakia in 1992.

These developments were greeted in the EC by a mixture of celebration and concern. The Commission's President, Jacques Delors, expressed his solidarity with the people of East Germany for their pursuit of self-determination though worries about the potential domination of Europe by the newly united Germany led to calls for fuller political and economic union within the EC. As far as the rest of Eastern and Central Europe was concerned, the EC recognized that it would need to develop a new policy towards Eastern Europe (Ostpolitik) and while publicly applauding the newly won freedom many EC leaders, like France's foreign minister Roland Dumas, privately felt less 'comfortable'.

Taken by surprise by the speed of change in the East, Community leaders were uneasy about the ending of the apparently stable world in which the division of Europe was the front line in the ideological and military Cold War, a world in which East and West rarely made contact. Therefore the changes were greeted with caution and Martin Holmes is right to dub the EC's political response to Eastern Europe as negative and unconvincing. 'Instead of embracing the countries of Eastern Europe by offering immediate EEC membership – or membership within a few years – Brussels has closed the door and prevaricated with talk of distant liaisons and association agreements.'

The EC's reluctance can be partly explained by administrative convenience. Administration in the Community is difficult with 11 languages, let alone 15 or 24. The upheaval involved in incorporating a number of new states is daunting. More significantly the EC has been determined to complete the key elements of the existing agenda created before the East European revolutions, especially the single market and moves towards EMU and greater political union. Such moves towards a federal EC would be diluted by the admission of East European states. For that very reason, among others, the British government warmly supported the notion of EC membership for all the countries of Eastern Europe!

Other factors explaining the general Community reluctance to give EC membership to East European states included a fear that East European migrants would flood into Western Europe and that low-cost producers in Eastern Europe would destroy companies in the West producing textiles, footwear, coal and steel. Rather unfairly the EC also argued that Central and Eastern Europe was not yet ready to meet the criteria of membership when, as *The Economist* pointed out in a survey of Eastern Europe in March 1993, several states had made real headway in establishing democracy and were moving faster than had been expected towards free market economies. More convincingly a final reason for EC reluctance is cost. Enlarging the EC to include East European states would add to the demands on the Community budget because these states would be eligible for help from the Structural Funds and the CAP to the tune of about £4 billion to £7 billion a year. Rich countries such as Germany balk at the extra which they would have to contribute while poorer members such as Spain dislike the idea of sharing subsidies with new claimants.

Even after the failure of the hardline coup in the Soviet Union in August 1991 which led to the temporary toppling of Gorbachev and the rise of Boris Yeltsin, the EC still demonstrated a cautious approach over Eastern Europe and little sympathy for the aspirations of the newly liberated states over Community membership. Indeed East European states came to suspect that EC foot-dragging over applications for membership from EFTA states and Turkey was partly motivated by a desire to delay still further the applications from Eastern Europe. A useful pretext for delay was to hand: the EC claimed that it had to push ahead with political and economic union *before* giving serious consideration to even the most promising of the East European applicants (Hungary, Poland and the Czech

Republic). Other East European states which only requested association, for example, Rumania and Bulgaria, were told that meaningful talks with the EC would have to wait until the talks with Poland,
Hungary and the Czech Republic had been finalized. Such blatant
delaying tactics did not augur well for co-operation in the wider
democratic Europe.

Nevertheless it would be overstating the case to suggest that the
EC has cold-shouldered the states of Central and Eastern Europe.
In 1991 the Community relented somewhat and signed 'Europe
agreements' which provided for associate member status for East
European states and at the Edinburgh Summit in December 1992.
EC governments committed themselves for the first time to the
principle of letting Central European states join. Where the EC still
disappointed Poland, Hungary and the Czech Republic was in its
refusal to fix a firm timetable for this process when the applicant
states wanted final negotiations to begin in 1996 for their accession
to membership by the year 2000.

Arguably this EC attitude is short-sighted. In its own interests it
should assist Eastern Europe because if the region falls into turmoil
then Community security itself is threatened. Additional members
from Eastern Europe would also dilute the influence of a united
Germany within the EC. Finally the region is likely to turn into one
of the fastest growing areas in the world, presenting Community
companies with immense opportunities for new business – especially
if the EC retains its influence in the region through positive policies.

To some extent such policies have at least been initiated by the
increase in trade and co-operation with Eastern Europe and by EC
help towards economic restructuring in the region. The improvement
in economic relations predated the collapse of Soviet control. In
June 1988 the signing of the Joint Declaration by the EC and
COMECON marked the formal recognition of the EC and enabled
the states of Central and Eastern Europe to develop bilateral
relations with the EC for the first time. Commercial and co-operation agreements were soon signed with Hungary (1988) and Poland
(1989) and after the fall of the Berlin Wall with five further states –
the USSR, Czechoslovakia, East Germany, Bulgaria and Rumania.
The agreements included a provision relating to the gradual abolition by the EC of quantitative restrictions on exports from the East,
a process to be completed by December 1994 for Hungary, Poland,
Rumania and Czechoslovakia and by December 1995 for the USSR
and Bulgaria. However these agreements provided safeguard
measures in case of special difficulties. Moreover, to prevent East
European goods being dumped in the EC, a price clause guaranteed
that exchanges would take place at market prices, i.e. in practice low-
cost East European goods would be likely to face an anti-dumping
duty or quota.

Community help to East European countries for the restructuring of their economies developed from an initiative decided by the 'industrialized countries summit' in Paris in July 1989 (the G7 states). The Seven asked the Commission to initiate moves to help the reform process in Hungary and Poland and the Commission duly responded by drawing up a number of programmes. August 1989 saw the launch of PHARE (Poland and Hungary; Assistance for Economic Restructuring) which developed five priority sectors:

1 Agricultural restructuring in Poland and Hungary.
2 Easier access for Hungarian and Polish exports to the markets of the Group of 24 (the 12 EC states, the 6 EFTA states plus the USA, Canada, Japan, Turkey, New Zealand and Australia).
3 Investment of 1 billion ECUs from the EIB, 200 million ECUs from the ECSC and a loan of 1 billion ECUs for Hungary.
4 Vocational training.
5 The environment.

Subsequently Bulgaria, Czechoslovakia, Rumania, Yugoslavia, Albania and the Baltic states were able to benefit from PHARE which had in 1992 a budget of 1 billion ECUs compared to 500 million ECUs in 1990. A recent emphasis has been help to promote small businesses and technical assistance, especially in the area of transport improvement.

To help the improvement of human skills in Central and Eastern Europe, TEMPUS (the Trans-European Mobility Scheme for University Students) was created in 1990. Essentially this programme opens up existing EC programmes like ERASMUS, COMETT and LINGUA to East European countries. It provides vocational training as well as retraining for young people and adults, including management training. The scheme is supported by Commission grants to encourage young people to study in universities and companies in Central and Eastern Europe and the EC. Teaching staff and industrial employees are also eligible for grants. For 1992–3 some 98 million ECUs were made available, a rise of 40 per cent on the previous year.

Since the break-up of the Soviet Union, the EC has forged ties with the new republic of the CIS. Emergency humanitarian food aid was given in the winter of 1991–2 but an ongoing programme of practical technical assistance was created through TACIS (Technical Assistance to the Commonwealth of Independent States and Georgia) to help the 11 CIS states and Georgia to build stable market economies. The Commission claimed that it was the world's largest aid programme of its kind with initial funding of 400 million ECUs in 1991 and 450 million ECUs in 1992. In 1991 TACIS funding provided advice, know-how and practical experience in the five priority areas of training, energy, transport, financial services and food distribution. Recipient states are closely involved with the Commission in the decision-making and management of TACIS programmes for their own country though the Commission is responsible for the actual selection of programmes which in 1991 numbered 350 projects. The biggest project supported was an educational programme giving advice to policy-makers in the 12 newly independent states on how to implement reform in addition to more down-to-earth training programmes and transport improvements, for example to the port and railways of St. Petersburg. In 1992 focal sectors were human resources, food production and distribution, commercial networks and energy, enterprise support services and nuclear safety.

In addition to these programmes the EC has created the necessary financial institution to assist the emerging democracies of Central and Eastern Europe. It is the European Bank for Reconstruction and Development (EBRD), located in London and the brainchild of President Mitterand. Negotiations for its creation began in 1990, involving many states outside the EC. It was agreed that the majority of the bank's capital stock should be held by EC states, the Commission and the EIB but about 40 states are involved in the bank's activities including the EC states, EFTA countries, the East European states as well as Japan and the USA. Article I of the EBRD's Articles of Agreement describes its chief purpose as 'to foster the transition towards open market-oriented economies and to promote private and entrepreneurial initiative in the Central and Eastern European countries committed to and applying the principles of multi-party democracy, pluralism and market economies'.

The EBRD was launched in April 1990 with a capital base of 10 billion ECUs under the presidency of Jacques Attali, a French socialist and professor of economics who is also a novelist. It makes loans and investments to help Eastern Europe's private sector enterprises (up to 30 per cent of its total investments). It has also made loans to individual projects in appropriate sectors such as agriculture, industry, communications and the environment, has helped the process of privatization of state-owned enterprises and has provided technical assistance.

The EC has also aimed at a more formal structured relationship with Eastern Europe now that the Cold War is over. Earlier agreements were merely commercial deals and clearly Eastern European states wanted treaties with a political dimension. Thus in 1991 Poland, Hungary and Czechoslovakia in signing an association agreement with the EC emphasized that they saw such an agreement as a real step towards eventual full membership. Such statements put the EC in the delicate position of having to establish a pecking order by which Eastern European states could move more closely towards

Community membership. One particularly difficult question in the future promised to be the precise status of the CIS.

Significant though the above developments are, the EC's overall response to Eastern Europe has had its distinct shortcomings. Given the aim of leading the region towards free market economies the choice of Jacques Attali as President of the EBRD was contradictory. He had been economic adviser to Mitterand and had supported the ill-fated nationalization in France between 1981 and 1983. According to Attali the free market took hundreds of years to develop in Western Europe and might take as long in the East. As Martin Holmes has dryly commented, such comments did not inspire confidence in the EBRD's President as a facilitator of free market reform in Eastern Europe. Bad publicity over mismanagement of EBRD funds led to Attali's resignation in June 1993.

In any case there is a danger that EC funding will merely be used by Eastern European countries to delay important and painful decisions over restructuring their economies. In a sense the funding provided the EC with a convenient human face to disguise its continuing protectionist trade policy towards Eastern Europe. In particular the areas where Eastern Europe enjoys a competitive advantage (in agriculture, textiles and steel) are subject to the greatest barriers in the form of quotas, duties and levies. The continuation of such protectionism has deeply disappointed Eastern European leaders. In April 1991 the Polish President, Lech Walesa, observed, 'We allow imports of all goods but the West is not buying ours. Why are we being punished. . . . We've handed Europe victory on a plate and the opportunity to link all Europe on a healthy basis yet just look at what Europe is doing. It does not want to get involved . . . it hums and haws'. Clearly Community trade policy was hindering East European progress towards prosperity. Mrs Thatcher was right to warn the EC in June 1991 that 'a new wall – a wealth wall – has arisen in Europe to replace the Berlin Wall. And the stability of Eastern Europe may be prolonged and aggravated as a result'.

EC business in Central and Eastern Europe

The newly democratizing states of the former Soviet empire have faced abundant problems since 1989. The move towards a free market economy has been a painful process in several states and the transition process has been made more difficult by religious and ethnic strife, tragically so in the CIS and Yugoslavia. It was also unfortunate that the liberation of Central and Eastern Europe occurred just when the EC economy was moving into a deep recession which increased protectionist leanings in the EC.

Yet Eastern Europe comprises some 140 million consumers, even before taking account of the 200 million former Soviet citizens west of the Ural mountains. Potentially then this area could become one of the most exciting regions in the world for business opportunities in the next 20 years. Nevertheless the opportunities will vary immensely within the region because the states are very different to one another. Some states such as Hungary, Poland and the Czech Republic (sometimes called the Visegrad states) have much more advanced economies than most other East European states and have already made genuine progress towards the free market. The situation in the former East Germany (the German Democratic Republic) is unique because it was united with West Germany in 1990, is now part of the EC and has been the recipient of vast sums invested in it by the German government. Other states such as Albania lack even the most basic of infrastructures.

Doing business in Eastern Europe is complicated because the situation in each state is changing quickly while at the same time there still remains the old culture of obstructive bureaucracy with officials still imbued with the old attitudes of the command economy. Thus EC companies have of necessity to carry out careful market and desk research before visits take place. There are few easy pickings in Eastern Europe: investment costs are heavy early on and profits usually lie some time in the future. In other words only long-term strategies are appropriate. At hand to help market entry are consultants and the embassies and trade missions from individual member states. The EC's own Business Information Centres (see Chapter 8) are being extended to Eastern Europe.

Even rich companies cannot enter all East European countries at once and there is a need to prioritize and take on board the unpalatable reality that the lack of managerial and technical skill in the area will require much investment in training. Given the natural reluctance of Western banks to give loans for risky projects, companies should consider EC programmes like PHARE. Many of the new East European companies, faced with limited funds, are eager to enter into joint ventures with Western companies.

Despite the problems, Western companies which establish a foothold in East European markets early on will be more likely to enjoy long-term success. Competition can only become stiffer over time as the vehicle sector has already demonstrated. In December 1990 Volkswagen was chosen by the Czech government to take control of its own carmaker, Skoda, defeating a rival bid by Renault. The success owed a lot to the investment strategies of Carl Hahn, head of Volkswagen, who has described Eastern Europe as the 'Wild East' with gigantic opportunities. The other European car company which was proactive early on in pushing into the emerging economies of Eastern Europe was Fiat which established links with car producers in the former Soviet Union and Poland where it hoped in time to make 1.4 million cars a year. Both investments are high risk but the rewards could be equally high. In that case Volkswagen and Fiat will have set an example to companies in all sectors on how to steal a march on their rivals, be they European, Japanese or American.

The Mediterranean perspective

Any decision by the EC to allow any of the East European states to join before Turkey would provoke a furious reaction from the Turkish government and also disappoint Cyprus and Malta. These three states have long harboured ambitions that they would eventually achieve full Community membership. They already enjoy close trading relations with the EC; Turkey signed an association agreement with the EC as long ago as 1963 and Malta and Cyprus followed suit in 1970 and 1972. Such preferential trading agreements mean that exports to, and imports from, the EC form a significant element in the trade of all three states. Close relations have developed between Turkey and the EC in other ways. Many Turkish workers are now employed in the EC and Turkey derives about 50 per cent of its foreign direct investment from the EC. Turkey was seen as an essential plank in NATO's defence until the demise of the Soviet Union and is still regarded as a vital pillar of relative stability in the Middle East, as the 1991 Gulf War demonstrated.

Nevertheless there are such huge problems barring the way to EC membership that it is hard to see these Mediterranean states acceding until well into the next century. For the two islands of Cyprus and Malta size is a difficulty. Although tiny Luxembourg as a founder member has full EC membership status, large EC states are reluctant to allow states such as Malta with a population of less than half a million and a 'city hall' mentality to have a similar position. Some appropriate status for small applicant states will have to be agreed before Malta and Cyprus can apply successfully, otherwise decision-making in the EC will become even more cumbersome as explained earlier.

Cyprus faces an apparently insoluble problem in its quest for EC membership. The island has been divided into a Turkish and a Greek zone after Turkey occupied the northern half of the island in 1974. Endless negotiations have not solved the reality of two divided communities. The impasse remains and it hardly seems possible that the EC could accept a divided Cyprus into the fold. Despite such difficulties both Cyprus and Malta applied for membership in 1990.

Above all other applications for Community membership it is that from Turkey which poses the greatest problems. To be sure, closer economic links have developed between Turkey and the EC. Over one million Turks are employed in EC states which supply 50 per cent of Turkey's foreign direct investment, 40 per cent of her imports and take 35 per cent of her exports. Turkey is potentially very rich in energy sources (coal and oil) and minerals (iron, copper, uranium, chrome and lead). The country is seen as important for Community interests in the Middle East and its stance during the Gulf War led to an offer of financial help from the EC in 1991 as it appreciated the strategic nature of Turkey's location in the region *vis à vis* Iraq.

However relations between Turkey and the Community have been soured by a number of problems. While Turkey does nearly half of its trade with the EC it has a large trade deficit with it and the Turkish government has protested at remaining restrictions on Turkish exports to the EC.

The size and relative backwardness of the Turkish economy also pose formidable difficulties. The Turkish GNP per capita is only about one third that of Greece. Turkey had a population of 40 million people by 1983 and owing to a high birth rate this population was expected to nearly double by early in the next century. A programme of aid, therefore, which would bring Turkey up to Community levels would have to be so vast as to be unthinkable.

The issue of Turkish migrant workers in the Community has also clouded relations. By 1980 there were 714,000 Turkish guest workers in the EC, a figure which did not include dependents. Some 591,000 were working in West Germany. By 1991 the total number of Turks in Germany alone (workers and dependents) numbered 1.5 million. For Turkey their continued stay in the EC was valuable because they sent much of their earnings home, thus providing income and foreign exchange. But the two recessions in the EC in the 1980s and early 1990s with the attendant high unemployment have led to strict controls on the influx of guest workers who are no longer wanted to do the unpleasant jobs. Through the offer of attractive 'leave packages' efforts have been made to persuade Turkish guest workers to return home. Many have nevertheless stayed and were a focus of racialist attacks in Germany in 1992. If Turkey were one day to join the EC, the implications of the right to free movement for EC workers across the Community would be immense. It would be politically unacceptable for Turks to possess the same rights of free movement enjoyed by other EC citizens.

Other obstacles in Turco–Community relations are also political and indeed psychological. On both sides there are doubts whether Turkey is in fact a European country and therefore eligible to accede to the Treaty of Rome. The aftermath of the Cyprus invasion of 1974 created a profound sense of estrangement for the West in Turkey and caused relations with Greece to deteriorate still further. The Community tried at the time to avoid becoming a party to the disputes between Turkey and Greece but the Greek entry to the EC in 1981 had serious impli-cations for Turkey. Greece has the right to veto decisions affecting Turkey, including Turkish application for full membership.

In the 1980s Greek hostility was counter-balanced by Turkey's close relations with West Germany, Turkey's largest trading partner which had pressed successfully for more aid to Turkey. However in 1992 Germany condemned Turkish military action against its Kurdish minority and suspended all arms supplies to its NATO ally. The Turkish president, Turgat Ozal over-reacted in accusing Germany of behaviour 'which corresponds to that of Hitler's Germany'.

The quarrel raised again the question whether Turkey could enter constructively into EC membership given its Islamic traditions and human rights record. The country's democratic pedigree is also uncertain. Democratic governments were overthrown in Turkey by military coups d'état in 1960, 1971 and 1980 and though the parlia-mentary system has been restored its chief feature has always been unstable coalitions which have been blamed for creating a cycle of economic crisis and urban violence leading to the imposition of martial law by the army. There is reason to hope that the new attempt to consolidate democracy in Turkey under Mr Suleyman Demirel's True Path Party will be more successful than its prede-cessors but time will be needed to prove to the EC that democratic government can work in Turkey. In any case the addition of East European states to the list of countries seeking EC membership has effectively ended Turkey's hopes, never very bright, of entry to the Community in this century.

Further reading

Dykes, D, *The European Economy* (Chapter 6), Longmans, London, 1992.

Hurwitz, L and Lequesne, C, *The State of the European Community* (Chapters 21–23), Longmans, London, 1991.

Minford, P, *The Cost of Europe* (Chapter 7), Manchester University Press, Manchester, 1992.

Swann, D, *The Economics of the Common Market* (Chapter II) Penguin, (Seventh Edition). Harmondsworth, 1992.

Tsoukalis, L, *The European Community and its Mediterranean Enlargement*, Allen and Unwin, London, 1981.

Questions

1 Examine the arguments in favour of the Community increasing its

present membership.
2 Why was the European Economic Area created?
3 Analyse the problems and opportunities for EC firms developing trading links with Eastern Europe.
4 Critically examine the EC's response to developments in Eastern Europe since 1989.
5 Why is it unlikely that Mediterranean applicants will accede to Community membership in the near future?

13
Company preparation for the European Market: a British model

Sources of information and services

More than 20 years after the UK's accession to the Community there are still many people who possess only a scant knowledge of how the Community works. Businesses in particular have been frowned upon for not making a bigger effort to penetrate Community markets or obtain more of the business generated by Community funds in the form of public supply contracts and overseas development projects.

One reason for any failure on the part of British business has been the fact that grappling with Community laws and practices has proved to be both confusing and difficult. In theory working within a Community framework ought not to be more difficult than working in Britain but in practice it certainly is; the Community is still evolving and it is tiresome for businesses to keep up to date with current developments when they have enough to do keeping their operations profitable. Also, obtaining information can be difficult because the sources are both numerous and awkwardly distributed throughout the country. In addition many businesses have not grasped that Community law on any particular subject is administered by the same authority that deals with that subject on the national level. Once this principle has been grasped, it then becomes a matter of knowing which division of the appropriate government department to turn to for advice and information. It is rarely necessary in the first stages of an enquiry to forge personal links with officials in the Commission though, of course, many companies do. The average business can obtain all information on day-to-day Community matters from government departments or trade associations.

In treating the sources of information and services at more length it is convenient to deal with them in three main sections: (1) sources of basic statistical information, (2) Community sources, (3) services for exporters from the British government and national organizations.

Basic statistical information

A firm commencing research into potential markets in Europe can do a lot of preparatory research by itself, i.e. desk research, but it needs sources of reliable information, particularly statistical data. Business people who feel that they lack absolutely basic facts about Western Europe should peruse supplements in the quality national dailies, particularly the *Financial Times* and weekly journals like *The Economist* which contain much up-to-date information.

The Overseas Trade Statistics of the UK (OTS) published monthly by HMSO give a detailed breakdown of the UK's imports and exports by product and principal countries of origin and destination. Studying them can give the exporter a real indication of the main West European markets for his or her products. All the West European countries publish series similar to the OTS which will help the exporter. For making direct comparisons between markets, the *Statistics of Foreign Trade* published by the Organization for Economic Co-operation and Development (OECD) are essential because these give details of trade between OECD member countries (which include all Community countries) broken down by product and trading partner. The International Monetary Fund (IMF) publishes an extremely comprehensive survey *International Financial Statistics* while the Community's own source of statistical information, Eurostat, in its monthly *External Trade Bulletin*, provides overseas trade data specifically for Community member countries.

Institutions worth consulting for statistical information include the Statistics and Marketing Intelligence Library (SMIL) of the British Overseas Trade Board (see p. 256). In addition foreign embassies and chambers of commerce keep trade directories, statistics and details of government legislation and some of the chambers of commerce have good libraries. Foreign embassies need to be approached tactfully and may appear unhelpful if the exporter asks for more than general information as naturally the embassy staff are there to promote their own country's exports. Specific information on the Community can be provided by the EEC Information Office in the Department of Trade which holds copies of Community publications.

A company can rarely expect to find ready-published material that provides exactly the information it requires on a defined market. Specific organizations exist to provide regular marketing reviews of specific product and service sectors in Community countries. Two of the best known are Euromonitor Publications with its bi-monthly *Market Research Europe* and its annual *International/European Marketing Data and Statistics* and the Economist Intelligence Unit with its monthly *Marketing in Europe* which covers three product groups:

(*a*) food, drink and tobacco,
(*b*) clothing, furniture and leisure goods and
(*c*) domestic appliances, household and chemist goods.

Other published sources worth considering are trade directories such as from Dun and Bradstreet. *Croner's Reference Book for Exporters*, amended monthly, is comprehensive and reliable and ought to be part of a firm's export library as should *Export*, the monthly journal of the Institute of Export.

Community sources

The *Official Journal of the European Communities* needs to be carefully vetted by businesses as it contains much important information on European trading opportunities, for example, on public tender. Central and local authorities in the Community are required to publish calls for tender for public contracts under rules discussed in Chapter 4. Such calls for tender are published in special supplements of the *Official Journal of the European Communities* and may also include calls for tender from the ACP countries.

The UK Offices of the Commission, at 8 Storey's Gate in London, offer general and specialized information about the work of the Communities. The Commission has press and information offices in most European countries, including ones at 4 Cathedral Road, Cardiff and 7 Alva Street, Edinburgh. The Commission itself at 200 Rue de la Loi in Brussels can be contacted easily as the telephonists speak English, though it would be prudent for someone to find out the name of the official dealing with their particular problem first.

In certain cases the Commission might be worth consulting over the possibility of financial assistance from one of the Community funds. For example, under Article 55 of the Treaty of Paris which set up the European Coal and Steel Community there are provisions for research grants. Financial aid may be granted to companies, research institutes or individuals who wish to carry out research of interest to the coalmining or iron and steel industries. Requests for such assistance should be addressed to the President of the Commission with details of the research project.

One exciting new development that British firms trading in Europe should now consider exploiting is Euronet DIANE (Direct Access to Information in Europe). This information retrieval system is fast, efficient and relatively inexpensive. Its data bases and data banks store all kinds of information on almost all subjects that businesses will be required to research. They are constantly updated so that the most complete data is always available. The system can often replace more traditional methods of market research and save a lot of time.

Services for exporters from the British government and national organizations

The most valuable source of information for British businesses wishing to strengthen their trading links with other Community countries is the Department of Trade and Industry which is based mainly at Export House, 50 Ludgate Hill in London. Its EC Information Unit, however, is located at Millbank Tower, London and it can help businesses of all types and sizes by answering questions on Community issues and guiding them where necessary to more specialized information sources. It is a good and free service, has six lines and a competent staff who work hard to answer queries.

As West European trade amounted to about 60 per cent of UK foreign trade by 1980, the Department of Trade decided in that year to carry out a reorganization to cope with this development. The Western and General Division (WEG) was set up in June 1980 to deal with bilateral commercial relations with Western European governments. Thus if businesses find that Community or national law has given rise to difficulties or if they feel that they have been victims of discrimination in their trade in Western Europe, WEG can make representations on their behalf to the government concerned. When requesting help of this kind, the exporter should give the fullest possible details.

Within the Department of Trade and Industry it is, however, the British Overseas Trade Board (BOTB) which provides the bulk of the services that help British exporters. It was set up in January 1972 with the following responsibilities:

(a) To advise the government on strategy for overseas trade.
(b) To direct and develop the government export-promotion services on behalf of the Secretary of State for Trade and Industry who is its president.
(c) To encourage and support industry and commerce in overseas trade with the aid of appropriate governmental and non-governmental organizations at home and abroad.
(d) To contribute to the exchange of views between government, industry and commerce in the field of overseas trade and to search for solutions to problems.

Its members are mainly business people with practical experience of exporting. Based at 1 Victoria Street, London, SW1H 0ET, it has ten regional offices. It offers a wide range of free information on specific markets and how exporters should tackle them. Its information is kept up-to-date as it is in close and constant touch with the commercial staff in UK embassies abroad.

One valuable service is its Statistics and Marketing Intelligence Library (SMIL) in Victoria Street. It carries the trade statistics publications of all countries and the full international range of United Nations, OECD and European Community statistics. It also stocks a wide range of trade directories and hints to exporters on specific markets. Access is free and the library is open Mondays to Fridays from 0930 hours to 1730 hours. Facilities for researchers are good with a document copying service. Most officially published tables may be copied while some other sources may not. SMIL has the most complete and up-to-date collection of economic statistics in the UK and one of the largest in the world.

The BOTB offers help for researching export markets through its Export Marketing Research Scheme. It offers free professional advice on how to set about market research in the most effective way. Then when a firm has decided on its own independent market research project, the BOTB can make a grant of up to 50 per cent of the cost but unfortunately grants are not normally given for European Community markets.

The BOTB also runs a Marketing Prospects Service to help firms gain a much clearer picture of the markets at which they are aiming. Here the report is drawn up by the commercial staff of the British Embassy in the selected country. They should be given as much information about the exporting firm as possible to evaluate its prospects in that market. The charge can in certain circumstances be refunded and the report is normally provided within ten weeks.

The market prospects or advisory service seeks to answer two basic questions: what are the prospects of selling exporters' goods or services in the market, and how best they can exploit the market. Where appropriate, the commercial department will provide the names of agents or distributors interested in working with the exporter. The report can indicate points to attend to before the exporter actually visits the market and this could well save an unproductive journey. The report will cover local demand, the strength of the competition from locally produced and imported goods, the likely competitiveness of the firm's product in terms of price, design and delivery, the characteristics of the local market and methods of selling in it.

When a firm has decided to operate in a particular market it will need to appoint a representative to handle its goods there. The BOTB runs an Export Representative Service to help in this respect. The exporter will give the BOTB a clear idea of requirements after which the BOTB will contact the commercial department of the British Embassy in the selected country. Commercial officers will compile a report on local business people who have been sounded out by the Embassy as being interested in representing the exporter's products or service. Complementing this service is the Overseas Status Report Service. The exporter may have come across the name of an agent or distributor from another source. They would be well advised to have the BOTB provide an impartial report on the potential agent's trading capability and commercial standing. Again the commercial department of the relevant British Embassy will draw up the report which could help the exporter reach a decision or avoid the costly mistake of appointing the wrong firm as agent.

It will be clear from what has been said that the commercial departments of British Embassies in Community countries give a lot of support to the BOTB efforts on exporters' behalf. The British Embassy in Paris, backed up by four consulates-general in Bordeaux, Lille, Lyon and Marseille is typical. Its commercial department is divided into two sections each led by a UK-based first secretary. Each section has three or four commercial officers all of whom speak French and have usually had some experience of exporting. Each commercial officer has responsibility for a given area, for example, food, drink, pharmaceuticals or machine tools. They have built up an extensive list of contacts in the world of French industry and commerce, so extensive that in 1982 an ICL computer was installed to remember them and marshall them in order.

Commercial officers must battle to maintain an up-to-date knowledge of the French market in their particular field by visits to French firms, trade fairs, the Franco–British Chamber of Commerce and Industry, regional chambers of commerce and conferences, plus study of the trade press. In the four consulates-general the commercial sections maintain a similar programme and may often have knowledge of a particular industry in their region which the Paris Embassy does not have, for example, the Lille consulate-general on the textile industry and the Bordeaux consulate-general on the wine trade. Given this depth of knowledge it is always worthwhile for British exporters to enlist the support of the commercial officers on all aspects of exporting and in this respect face-to-face conversations can be particularly fruitful.

New market opportunities may arise in the European Community without the exporter being aware of them. To cover this eventuality, the BOTB runs the Export Intelligence Service. It receives a non-stop supply of export opportunities from nearly 200 British diplomatic posts worldwide. It is a computerized service which distributes export intelligence to subscribers each day. Each item is given a computerized coding and if it matches the type of information which the firm has requested, an immediate print-out is posted. The firm will receive this information within two or three days. Membership is open to eligible firms situated in the UK who manufacture or promote exports of British goods or services and to British chambers of commerce, trade associations and similar organizations. About 8,000 firms currently subscribe. A subscribing firm can request information on specific countries or a specific group of countries like the Community. The information or profile contains three elements: the type of information required, the geographical market, and the product or service to be covered. The BOTB claim that over £1,000 million per year of UK export sales follow directly from information provided by this service.

Much of the information received comes from the commercial departments in Embassies overseas and covers immediate business opportunities, pointers to future business and background market information. A typical selection of notices from France in 1982 included a market report on the French computer industry, a public supply contract inviting tenders for the supply of plastic receptacles for washing and storage and a specific export opportunity for British manufacturers of component parts of electronic amusement machines to create links with a potential French distributor. There was also a market pointer to the potential market in France for fast food such as the American-style hamburger or traditional French bakery products. The growth of the fast-food restaurants, it was argued, would give British manufacturers export opportunities in disposable packaging, catering equipment, restaurant design and the food items themselves.

All exporters should take note of the BOTB's Market Entry Guarantee Scheme (MEGS) which is designed to help smaller and medium-sized firms deal with the financial risk and problems associated with developing a new market. Even when a firm has done its homework it has to expect high costs and low returns in the early stages with profits only starting to come by perhaps the third year. MEGS is designed to help the firm through the early loss-making period. It covers 50 per cent of the cost of on-the-spot office accommodation, staff training and sales promotion. This funding is repayable with interest through a levy on actual sales. If the venture is unsuccessful, any shortfall at the end of the agreed period will be cancelled.

Firms sending representatives on trade missions abroad can be helped by the BOTB. Such missions are composed of selling-groups of British business people, often sponsored by their trade association. They enable firms to explore at first hand the prospects for their products and services and to reinforce their marketing efforts. A new exporter can benefit from meeting more experienced members of the mission. Most missions are run by Chambers of Commerce or Trade Associations but an exporter does not have to be a member to take part. Members of a BOTB-supported mission may qualify for travel grants but such grants are rarely given to trade missions to Community countries as West European routes are frequently travelled by British businesses.

British firms wishing to exhibit abroad at trade fairs can be assisted by the BOTB which can provide an exhibition stand and display equipment at reduced rates. First-time exhibitors receive generous treatment. An exhibitor will be part of a British group at such fairs which are usually run by trade associations though the firm does not have to be a member. Where a trade association wishes to put on a specialized seminar to bring products or services to the attention of a specific audience the BOTB is willing to share a wide range of the costs involved, from hire of the auditorium to the printing of programmes. The amount of financial assistance varies with the market but the closer to home the fair is, the lower the financial contribution of the BOTB.

On occasions, representative bodies like trade associations will wish to organize business visits to the UK by groups from Western Europe. These groups will be made up of business people, journalists and others in a position to influence the future purchase of British goods. Consequently such visits also receive financial support from the BOTB through its Inward Missions scheme.

The activities of the BOTB both with fairs and inward missions often help to give more bite to the UK's export drive into Europe. On the eve of Spain's accession to the Community, in November 1984, the Electronic Component Industrial Federation (ECIF) with support under the BOTB's Inward Missions Scheme organized a visit to the UK for a group of Spanish buyers. Both the visitors and British companies who took part were surprised by the business potential that existed and a return visit to Spain took place in November 1985. Twenty-six British manufacturers of electronic components mounted a successful presentation of their products at the Holiday Inn in Madrid. They felt that they had met many potential customers and for some of the manufacturers it was the first time that the Spanish market had been seriously considered. Clearly the task-force concept of a joint industry–government attack on an overseas market had proved its worth in Madrid.

For help with details of safety and technical regulations the exporter should turn to Technical Help to Exporters (THE). Set up in 1966, it is a service run by the British Standards Institution (which has connections with the BOTB) and its function is to assist exporters in overcoming technical obstacles. The UK was the first country in the world to set up such a service, an example that has since been followed by France, New Zealand and Sweden. It is a non-profit organization and receives a government grant to finance its work. It can supply an exporter with detailed information on foreign regulations, assist in their interpretation, provide translations and assist in obtaining foreign approval for the firm's products. The fees charged vary with the complexity of the problem and whether or not the firm is a member of THE. Its engineer will examine equipment to determine whether or not it will meet the relevant Community country's requirements and if not will suggest appropriate modifications. THE has an extensive library available for members for reference purposes. Here as in other sectors of its operations, THE is particularly strong on Western Europe. Of increasing importance is the provision of translated key foreign regulations and by 1984 over 6,000 translations were available off the shelf.

Documentation is a nightmare and a minefield for British exporters. Apparently nearly 70 per cent of all presentations made by companies for documentary letters of credit contain errors the first time round and in 1984 *British Business* put the cost of all errors in export documentation at £1 billion per annum. Documents are a vital element in many methods of obtaining payment for export orders and if the documents contain omissions or errors or are not available at the time and place of customs clearance, the consequences can be deadly. Errors in the procedure will damage not only the immediate contract, resulting in delayed payment and perhaps the imposition of fines, but may damage the longer-term prospects in the market. Only by demonstrating the ability to deliver the goods without hitches is a firm likely to build up confidence in the minds of its European customers.

Banks, chambers of commerce and freight forwarders can advise on documentary requirements and simpler ways of preparing documents and perhaps the exporters should first contact their trade association for help. Its documents section is the nearest body with the professional touch as it validates many documents each day. However, many exporters, freight forwarders and others have pooled their experience of the demands of documentation and this is available to business people through a BOTB activity, the Simplification of International Trade Procedures Board (SITPRO). It has three main objectives:

1 To expose and reduce the hidden costs of international trade. These costs are often not appreciated by businesses. In a 1986 SITPRO survey over 92 per cent of respondents did not know their company's export documentation overhead costs. Perhaps too many companies regard such costs as unquantifiable and unavoidable. In fact, some costs like the high error rate in letters of credit mentioned earlier can be significantly reduced and this is a worthwhile exercise because documentation preparation can cost as much as 6 per cent of the value of the goods traded.
2 To work for a simpler system of international trading. SITPRO is a research organization which gathers together highly experienced people from all sectors of international trade to investi-

gate the root causes of complexity in international trade, identify appropriate solutions and negotiate for the removal of obstacles and where removal of these obstacles is not possible, develop and implement solutions which allow exporters to surmount the problems. Many solutions introduce simplified options in documentary and customs procedure that can halve paperwork costs. Well over 3,000 documentary systems are now used by over 7,000 British exporters and freight forwarders at an estimated annual saving to them of over £100 million. Simplification of documentary procedures at a Community level is now SITPRO's most important task and the European Community itself is beginning to give the issue the degree of attention that it deserves.

3   To maintain a lead in applying information technology to international trading. It believes that many difficulties facing the international trader have been caused by the failure of export/import practices to keep up with change – change in transport technology and information technology. The very nature of international trade with its mixture of international law makes it far more difficult to apply new information technology to the process of international trade than domestic trade. SITPRO has begun to tackle this problem by making its range of paper-based export documentation methods capable of being used with a wide range of microcomputers by means of its own software. It hopes that in time there will be a real quantum leap into paperless exporting where data is transmitted directly from one computer to another instead of using paper documents as the link.

Help for business people on the documentation requirements of particular Community countries can also be obtained from the BOTB's Exports to Europe Branch (EEB). It was set up in 1980 to provide a single focus for the co-ordination of trade promotion in Western Europe and a single point of inquiry for all information about the national markets of Western Europe. The EEB works closely with the BOTB's European trade committee which advises the BOTB on trade with Western Europe and is made up of business people with practical experience of the West European markets. As a result of this liaison the EEB can provide general information and advice about the markets of Western Europe, including background economic information, details of trading patterns as well as specific information covering customs regulations, tariffs, taxes and other legislation affecting British exporters. Finally, it offers a number of useful publications for exporters in particular its *Country Profiles, Marketing Consumer Goods in Western Europe* (with separate editions for Italy, West Germany, Belgium and France) and *Selling to Western Europe* which covers the research and choice of markets, visiting markets and advice on how to sell and distribute exports in Western Europe.

Government departments other than that of Trade and Industry also offer information and services. HM Customs and Excise based at King's Beam House, Mark Lane in London will provide essential information for the commencement of market research. Before starting work on this an exporter needs to know the appropriate classification number of the product. This can be extracted from the *Guide to the Classification for Overseas Trade Statistics* published annually by Her Majesty's Stationery Office (HMSO) but in case of any difficulty the full Customs Co-operation Council Nomenclature (CCCN) can be obtained from the classification section of HM Customs and Excise.

Other government departments worth consulting are the British Standards Institute for checking out technical details and the Department of Transport, worth consulting over the rules relating to freight. Getting goods to Community countries from the UK will inevitably involve a sea or air journey though the use of roll-on, roll-off ferries makes it possible to deliver anywhere in Western Europe without transferring goods between vehicles. Unless the vehicle is cleared at the point of first landing on mainland Europe it is better to cross intermediate frontiers under the security of the Community Transit System but any exporter considering the use of his own lorries to deliver to mainland Europe should contact the International Road Freight Office at the Department of Transport for advice on requirements. The Department publishes a pamphlet summarizing the main requirements.

In addition to government departments, a number of specialized trade organizations exist that can give an exporter valuable advice. As exporters become more involved in the exporting process, they will need to be proficient in complex and detailed negotiations with European customers. These will be more successful if the local language is used. Some European business people speak excellent English, especially Germans, Dutch and Danes, but many do not. Some, like the French, do not wish to and even fluent speakers of English may prefer to do business in their native language. Therefore, if no member of the firm's staff speaks the local language, someone should be trained to do so or the use of an interpreter should be considered, despite the expense. The British may rest assured that their competitors in Europe will speak the local language. Advice on translation and other language services is available from the Institute of Linguists as well as from the BOTB and chambers of commerce.

If exporters do not have or wish to use their own lorries for exporting goods, they can choose from a number of road hauliers who operate direct services to Community countries. The names of

hauliers operating such services and who are members of the Road
Haulage Association are available in the directory which can be
obtained free from the Road Haulage Association. If the exporter
wishes to use rail, British Rail offers an international service linked
to its internal freight network and can handle specialized wagons,
tankers and containers and low temperature transport. Information
on this can be obtained from the European Rail Traffic Manager.
For small packets and parcels an exporter should not discount the
use of ordinary postal services and information on this can be found
in the Post Office Guide.

Perhaps the best way for new exporters to ensure that their goods
are shipped safely to their European customers is to use the services
of a freight forwarder. Freight forwarders are fully conversant with
all export procedures and know the special requirements of the
particular countries to which the goods are being consigned. They
can advise the exporter on all packing, marking and labelling
requirements and find the most suitable mode of transport for the
exporter's goods. They can reserve shipping space, prepare the
necessary documents and arrange insurance, thus saving the exporter
a lot of potential headaches. Information about their services and
the names of members may be obtained from the Institute of Freight
Forwarders.

Further advice may be needed on packing. It is obviously crucial
that goods arrive at their final destination in the condition in which
they left the factory and full allowance should be made for very
rough treatment indeed during transit. The science of good packing
is, however, complicated. There are minimum standards to be
observed and special regulations applying to certain goods. Labelling
and shipping marks on the outer package must be right. For technical advice on these issues, the Research Association for the Paper
and Board Printing and Packaging Industries (PIRA) is most useful.

Consulting even a fraction of this bewildering variety of sources
will inevitably result in the use of a number of precise terms and
these must be clearly understood by exporters. Take, for example,
the task facing them when they prepare a document like an invoice.
This needs to provide a detailed description of the goods including
unit prices, totals, weights and other specifications as well as the
packing details and shipping marks. The invoice should also specify
the terms of sale which will most commonly be CIF (Cost, Insurance
and Freight) though a variety of other terms may be used. Exact
definitions of such international trade terms and the responsibilities
which they impose on the buyer and seller are given in Inco terms.
These are definitions which have been classified by the
International Chamber of Commerce and they can be obtained
from the British National Committee of the International Chamber
of Commerce.

Even in a small exporting firm it is advisable to have a member of the staff who is fully trained to deal with the whole question of documentation. In this respect the firm should try to employ someone who has taken a good course of study in export practice and documentation, for example, the course for the Institute of Export examinations or the foundation course on overseas trade which is available at various teaching institutions.

Lobbying in the European Community

This subject concerns many companies in the United Kingdom, even those which do not trade with companies in other member states. Community policies in a number of areas have direct effects within each member state and consequently upon the whole range of a company's domestic activities. As a result, almost any firm in this country should have an interest in keeping informed about developments in Community policies and knowing how to influence them.

Some companies have ignored the Community almost completely and some have paid dearly for this neglect. Costly mistakes continue to be made by companies that have failed to appreciate that Community legislation can seriously affect their operations. For example, heavier and heavier fines have been imposed for infringements of Community competition law and these fines can amount to as much as 10 per cent of annual turnover and single market legislation will continue to have a greater impact over time.

There are ten major channels through which an individual company can put over its point of view in a European context in the hope that favourable changes may take place:

(*a*)   national trade associations;
(*b*)   the British government;
(*c*)   the Commission;
(*d*)   the United Kingdom Representative in Brussels (UK Rep.);
(*e*)   foreign embassies;
(*f*)   the European Parliament;
(*g*)   the Economic and Social Committee;
(*h*)   European trade associations;
(*i*)   the Court of Justice; and
(*j*)   the media.

National trade associations

National trade associations can perform a significant role in assisting their members, particularly smaller firms, to understand the implications of the development of Community policies. Though many are poor in terms of money or staff, some are powerful lobbies for the interest of their members, for example, the Food and Drink Industries Council and the Society of Motor Manufacturers and Traders. Sometimes a company might not need to go any further than informing its trade association of its problem. The trade association will then investigate the problem thoroughly.

In addition to trade associations, there exist national employers' organizations such as the Confederation of British Industry (CBI), the British Institute of Management (BIM) and the Institute of Directors. The CBI is a particularly powerful organization.

The British government

In most sectors, any action taken by the Commission is subject to the final approval of the Council of Ministers, since any one member state has the power to veto a proposal if vital national interests are deemed at stake. The Commission generally consults member governments as a matter of course throughout the evolution of a policy proposal. It therefore follows that if firms are concerned about possible or existing Community law they should in the first instance make their views known to the government (normally through the Department of Trade and Industry) in order that those views may be taken into consideration by officials in discussion in Brussels.

In each government department there are a number of senior civil servants whose main function is responsibility for Community affairs. Business people can telephone, write or arrange meetings with these officials. The EC information unit at the Department of Trade and Industry will often be able to solve a problem if it is merely one of information.

If government departments do not solve the problem, the lobbying of local members of parliament can be an effective way of influencing the Community. An MP has the power to ask questions and obtain answers from the government department concerned and usually such pressure elicits a rapid response.

The Commission

The Commission itself can be approached directly and indeed it has indicated that it welcomes lobbying by industry as this can lead to an awareness of problems which might otherwise have slipped its notice. There may be situations where individual firms wish to contact the Commission but normally regular and established contacts, particularly those by bodies representing European-wide industry, carry more weight and are more likely to have established effective channels of communication. The Commission, in fact, usually expects and prefers a single contact for individual sectors but will consider any reasonable case from a single firm as well.

The offices of the Commission in the UK may be approached first by companies rather than trying to contact Brussels. Commission officials based in the UK can then take the matter on from there. Normally, however, the Commission office in London will advise businesses to take up the matter directly with the Commission.

Commission officials are, in fact, approachable. The first step for a company to take is to find out the names of the officials dealing with its particular problem. About three times a year the Commission produces a directory of its senior officials. It can be obtained from Commission sales agents in many countries as well as from the office for official publications at Boîte Postale 1003, Luxembourg.

For businesses in constant touch with the Commission, it would be worth obtaining an internal Commission telephone directory through a contact. The phone call can be as effective a way as any of obtaining a meeting with the officials able to help. Alternatively the Commission office in London can be asked whether they can arrange such a meeting. This is a sensible way if the nature of the enquiries necessitates meeting several officials or if the company does not know the names of the appropriate officials. Enquiries, particularly technical ones, should be put in writing to enable the officials to be better prepared for the meeting. The Commission could be invited to visit the Company in the UK to meet people from the industry. Such officials have good travel allowances and often readily accept such invitations.

The United Kingdom Representative in Brussels

The United Kingdom Representative in Brussels (UK Rep.) may be another useful channel. Probably the best person to contact in his or her office is the first or second secretary who is likely to be the expert on the particular problem. He or she may also suggest people to contact in the Commission or elsewhere and will perhaps arrange a meeting with the UK Rep. counsellor responsible for the area of business in question.

Foreign embassies

If a problem is connected with bilateral Community trade, the foreign embassies in London may be of some use. Each of Britain's Community partners has an embassy in London which has sections attached to it dealing with bilateral trade matters. Sometimes trading problems may be more open to solution by a national government than by the Commission. Contact with the appropriate embassy is relatively easy through a visit, phone call or letter.

The European Parliament

European members of parliament have seen their influence grow slowly over the years and should not be left out of the lobbying process. They can be contacted individually or through the parties to which they belong. Meetings with company representatives can usually be arranged in the member's constituency or in London. The European member of parliament is usually well informed about Community affairs and can ask both oral and written questions on behalf of the business concerned.

The Economic and Social Committee

The Economic and Social Committee (ECOSOC) has very limited power but its individual members can still on occasions give useful support to a company seeking a solution to Community-created business problems. As about one-third of the Committee come from the world of business, they will normally be sympathetic to a company's difficulties. A list of members can be obtained from the Committee Secretariat.

European trade associations

Companies can make their views known through well-established channels within Europe which are regularly consulted by the Commission. These are the European trade associations. Over the years the national trade associations in the Community and sometimes other European countries have developed close connections with each other. The Union des Industries de la Communauté Européenne (UNICE) brings together national confederations of employers' associations including the CBI and the Patronat of France. The directors of UNICE have regular meetings with the President of the Commission and other commissioners and maintain close contacts with the individual directorates of the Commission. There are standing arrangements to consult UNICE, even though the Commission is under no statutory obligation to do so. The exchanges between the Commission and UNICE are two-way and UNICE can take the initiative in putting forward its views which may be based on a survey by one of its expert committees.

The permanent conference of the chambers of commerce and industry is composed of the national associations of chambers of commerce and industry within the Community. Like UNICE it is consulted by the Commission as a matter of course. The conference tries to influence the development of Community policies, formulates views and passes them on to the Commission and member governments. It holds regular conferences with the President and the individual commissioners.

At a sectoral level, a number of committees represent broad areas of activity such as the Permanent Committee for Agricultural and Food Industries (CIAA), the Committee of European Associations of Insurance Companies (CEA) and the Committee of Nationalized and Public Utilities (CEEP).

In addition to these broad organizations, there are organizations representing forty more specific sectors. Approximately half of them are industrial and half commercial. Some of the most important, such as COMETEXTIL which represents the textile industries, carry considerable weight with the Commission because they present a common view on behalf of a very fragmented industry. There are over one hundred European federations covering particular product groups.

The Court of Justice

If all the above means of tackling the problems fail to result in a solution, a company has the option of approaching the Court of Justice though it would be best to approach the Commission first. The Court of Justice can be petitioned by any country, company or individual on matters relating to Community law and it is obliged to respond to petitions.

The media

Finally, a company which has a problem which is newsworthy may find the media useful in giving publicity to its case.

This long list of pressure points does, however, illustrate a key problem for the lobbyist in the Community. Power is diffused, crystallizing at times in the meetings of the Council of Ministers (the principal decision-making body) or in a committee where the Commission (the executive body) sits with representatives from the twelve member states. The Commission puts forward most policy proposals in the first instance but the Council of Ministers makes the final decision. Only then can the Commission implement its own proposals. As a result the lobbyist is not dealing with one centre of power but thirteen altogether.

Even where the Commission has the power to act on its own, notably under the competition rules, the same diffusion exists. There is an elaborate system of consultation which reduces the chances of the Commission doing anything that would offend the national governments.

The other side of the coin is that because the Community market remains fragmented, industry is fragmented as well. When, therefore, there is an industry grouping, it can move only at the pace of the slowest if it wants to maintain any unity. A good example of this industry fragmentation occurred in 1985 when Robert Lutz, chief of Ford in Europe, worried at the Community motor industry's loss of competitive edge compared to the Japanese, approached Jacques Delors, President of the Commission, with a plan to block Community motor manufacturers signing up joint ventures with Japanese companies. Such a move, Lutz hoped, would stop the spread of Japanese manufacturers in the Community market. But while this high-level lobbying suited Ford, it did not suite several other motor companies, like Austin Rover in Britain or Alfa Romeo in Italy because they already had joint ventures with Japanese manufacturers.

In cases like this a company would probably do better to lobby nationally, rather than in the Community, its own government being its most likely effective protector. In 1985 the Central Electricity Generating Board (CEGB) disliked Community proposals for controlling the amount of pollutants which can be emitted from large industrial plants like power stations because of the capital cost involved in complying with the regulations. Its main defender, naturally, was the British government.

Firms then have to consider a two-layer system of lobbying, one by which they seek to influence the Commission and Council of Ministers and the other by which they bring pressure to bear on their national governments. When consumer electronics firms such as Philips were worried about low-tariff levels on goods from Japan, they engaged in discussions with the Commission on ways to increase the tariff levels. But they also enlisted the French government's support to argue the case for a higher tariff at the political level.

The Commission is open to lobbying because it is anxious to establish a genuine rapport with the people who are creating the wealth to make the Community economy expand. Significantly the most imaginative R and D programme adopted by the Community (ESPRIT) was demanded of the Commission by top companies in the high technology sector. On that occasion the Commission responded to a need expressed from outside but it also invites lobbying under the guise of consultation as a device to quicken the pace of the economy. One of the most interesting examples of this strategy was the creation of the Round Table of European Industrialists in 1983 with the Commission's active encouragement. Its chief objective was to galvanize European governments into action on industrial issues. By 1986 it contained the heads of twenty-four European corporations including the bosses of Siemens, Philips, Pilkington Glass and the National Coal Board. They are powerful men, able as one Community official put it, to pick up the telephone and get straight through to their own prime minister. They have the power to get things done and have promoted initiatives in high technology, venture capital and employment measures. It has established a

Dutch-based venture capital outfit called Euroventures, has a plan to create a European institute of technology akin to the Massachusetts Institute of Technology and has played a key role in the Eureka advanced research project.

Other successful lobbying groups include that of the chemical industry – CEFIC – which has often managed to persuade the Commission to investigate complaints of dumping carried out by American chemicals firms. The model for other lobbying groups is, however, COPA (Comité des organisations professionelles des pays de la Communauté Economique Européenne) which is the federation of all farmers' unions and the representative of the farming lobby. Over the years it has been the most successful lobbying group of all, drawing to its members three quarters of the Community budget. It has managed both to keep its links with the Community institutions in Brussels and to create a strong political niche inside the member states. It has not been averse to violent agitation and only in 1985 did the Commission begin to rein in its power by putting a ceiling on farm spending. Most other lobbying groups are of the opinion that the reins need to be drawn a good deal tighter yet!

Further reading

Anderson, C, *Influencing the European Community*, Kogan Page, London, 1992.

Ellis, J and Williams, D, *Corporate Strategy and Financial Analysis*, Pitman, London, 1993.

Hogan, J, *The European Marketplace*, Macmillan, London, 1991.

Lynch, R, *European Business Strategies*, Kogan Page, London, 1990.

Morris, B et al., *Business Europe*, Macmillan, London, 1992.

Welford, R and Prescott, K, *European Business*, Pitman, London, 1992.

Questions

1 In what ways may a failure to keep abreast of Community developments damage a firm's prospects in the European market?
2 Describe the chief sources of information which are of value to British exporters.
3 How may a firm seek help in solving its documentary problems in its European business?
4 Why is lobbying a crucial aspect of a company's activities in the European context?
5 What are the major channels by which a company may seek to influence EC legislation?

14
The new European market

The survival of cultural diversity

Increasingly, as a result of the single market programme, the countries of Community Europe have a number of broad features in common. Most have good transport systems, good retailing systems, effective media and a considerable degree of technological and financial development. They may therefore appear to be comfortingly similar to the home market apart from language and a few social differences. However exporters should be on their guard; there are real differences between the cultures of the Community member nations, and these differences have practical effects on business prospects that exporters would be foolish to ignore. No Community market really resembles another and ignorance of the differences has led to loss of orders. As John Harvey-Jones has warned, there is as yet no pan-European homogenized taste. In three areas in particular such differences need to be borne in mind by exporters:

(a) product preferences,
(b) advertising and sales promotion styles, and
(c) business practices which obtain in the Community market of their choice.

In addition to ensuring that a product is functionally sound for the user, an exporter to Europe has to cater for buyers' preferences in certain aspects such as colour, aesthetic qualities, physical taste, size, weight and volume which make up the physical core of the product. Colour preferences influence the sales of both industrial and consumer goods. A British aircraft manufacturer once lost an order through refusal to conform to an airline's planned interior colour scheme. Recently textile companies in Lyon competing for scarce skilled labour wished to offer better working conditions rather than increased wages. They therefore insisted that suppliers of sewing machines should provide them with frames in colours matching the decor of their workrooms.

Opinion on what is aesthetically tasteful varies immensely from one Community country to another. The British, for example, like symmetry in the design on china dinner services and in lounge suites. The Dutch in contrast do not appreciate symmetry so highly and prefer to buy individual pieces of furniture which they hope will give an individual style to their living rooms. Therefore British furniture manufacturers who have concentrated on making suites of furniture have had to rethink their overall strategy for the rich Dutch market.

Physical taste preferences vary widely throughout the Community. Worcestershire sauce sells well throughout Western Europe except Italy. Most Germans think that British chocolate is too sweet whereas most Spaniards are of the opinion that British beer is too bitter. Many taste preferences are hard to overcome and the exporter has the difficult job of judging whether heavy advertising will overcome them as indeed it can on occasions.

The varied size, weight and volume requirements for consumer goods throughout the Community, determined by local incomes, shopping habits and physical characteristics, have important implications for exporters. If they are in the shoe business they need to know that French women's feet tend to be bigger than those of English women and that Italian men tend to have narrower feet than Englishmen so that the appropriate range of sizes and widths can be supplied. Greeks and Spaniards are on average smaller than the British and exporters of clothing need to offer different ranges of clothing sizes for those markets.

The precise use to which a product is put will be significantly different on occasions in Western Europe to the UK. The bike is a good example of this phenomenon. In the UK it is mainly a means of recreation but in the flatter territories of the Netherlands and Denmark it is a common means of transport for running errands and going to work. What will be required in these countries is a more durable utility machine with a stout frame rather than a trendy machine with all the latest extras. This difference of function has implications not only for the actual design of the bike for the Continental market but also for its marketing. The bicycle manufacturer will tend to emphasize the links between physical fitness and cycling in the UK but will rely more on competitive pricing in the Netherlands and Denmark with a stress on the robustness of the product.

When exporting to other member states care must be taken to ensure that the right packaging, nomenclature and symbols are used because what works well in the one state will not necessarily work well in the rest of Europe. One British firm experiencing poor sales in France found that whereas in the UK the owl, its chosen mark, symbolizes wisdom, in France it is regarded as an ordinary bird of limited intelligence. When Rolls-Royce launched its 'Silver Mist' model in Germany, it created the impression that it was selling luxury lavatories rather than luxury cars, a prime example of how careless use of model names can have unfortunate consequences.

Despite the general rule that most European nations prefer local products, sales of goods with a national charisma can benefit from the retention of the language of origin on label and packs. To emphasize the 'Scottishness' of a whisky, for example, underlines its genuineness and quality. Sometimes the actual choice of language can be difficult as in Belgium or Luxembourg. In Luxembourg most people speak Luxembourgish but the language of education is French and the language of business is German. One solution may be to use Luxembourgish for headings on packets and French or German for the general text.

Finally instructions for use and protective packaging need to be tailored to the market in question. Consumers in Southern Europe will be less familiar with, for example, food mixes than British consumers and instructions for use should therefore be much more explicit than in the UK. Similarly the hot climate in Southern Europe can cause trouble to exporters. A British pharmaceutical manufacturer angered many Italian customers who had bought tablets loose-packed in bottles. As a result of the hot Italian climate the tablets soon became a useless coagulated mess when they should have been individually foil-wrapped.

The influence of the local culture on advertising or the effectiveness of advertising is immense. As pointed out above, it can sometimes be hard even to choose the appropriate language in which to advertise and translation from one language into several European languages, for example Spanish, tend to take up more space. The advertiser is then faced with the decision whether to use smaller type, making reading tiresome, reducing the content at the risk of omitting important points or taking a larger space at an unacceptably higher cost. Another solution would be to recast the whole advertisement but this could destroy its visual appeal.

A more fundamental problem is vested in the saying 'To kill a message, translate it'. Esso's 1960s 'Put a tiger in your tank' could be translated directly into Dutch but had to be changed for Italy and France (where there is no directly translatable word for tank) into 'Nett un tigre nel motore' and 'Mettez un tigre dans votre moteur'. Careless translation can lead to disaster for the firm and hilarity for others. Chrysler's 'Dart for power' was used in Spain where in translation it meant 'Dart is an aphrodisiac'.

In addition to the basic translation problems there is the perennial danger of projecting a message which is unsuitable for the European market, however well it has succeeded in the domestic campaign. It is easy to make errors through misjudgement of local perceptions and culture. Maxwell House's appeal 'America's finest coffee' angered the Dutch who felt that they had centuries of experience of roasting coffee, far more than the parvenu Americans. In contrast, firms who researched local perceptions of their products' country of origin were able to advertise more effectively. Guinness researched the West German market and learned that it was possible to emphasize the Irishness of its product since Ireland's image in West Germany was that of a country of rural charm and wholesome food. Italians, however, did not appreciate the difference between Ireland and the UK and therefore the Irishness of Guinness was not worth emphasizing in the Italian market.

Finally, the style of advertising varies from one Community country to another and usually conformity with the local style is advisable in the early stages. French advertising tends to have more panache and Italian advertising more sentimentality than is normal in the UK. With this aspect as with all other elements of advertising, insensitivity to the diversity of national cultures will endanger the advertising effort. Local advice and careful audience research are essential.

The variety of business practices within the Community is surprisingly wide and is particularly evident in larger firms where barriers are often erected between departments. These obstacles to collaboration tend to force decisions upwards to senior management who prefer to take the decisions anyway. Such realities have important implications for exporters within Europe. They should be aware that often only minor issues can be conducted with junior or middle managers. Senior management should be approached if any important business is being discussed.

This is a large generalization and is less true of Germany as illustrated by a comparative analysis of business organization in France and Germany carried out by the Laboratoire d'Economie et de Sociologie du Travail of Aix-en-Provence. The researchers found that compared to French companies German firms contained far fewer bureaucratic barriers both between departments and between management tiers. German managers were also given far wider areas of responsibility. As a result, business people trading with German firms found negotiations with them much swifter than with their French counterparts.

There are many other ways in which business practices vary within the Community. The Germans insist on punctuality; the Latins, particularly the Spanish, spend as much time with a visitor as is courteous but regard punctuality and courtesy as quite unrelated. The British regard business negotiations as completed when a contract has been signed. In Greece the contract is often regarded as merely a stage in negotiations which only end when the work involved has been concluded, an attitude that British business people may feel smacks of sharp practice.

Such differences in approach impose pressures on exporters but understanding the cultural mosaic will enhance the prospects of export success.

Particular European markets: some considerations

A low growth Community?

European integration after 1958 was assisted by a startling and unique economic recovery in Western Europe which, even bearing in mind its variations in pace, was steeper and smoother than at any period in modern history. Even the oil crises of the 1970s did not permanently prevent further strong growth after 1983 and the last years of the decade witnessed a business boom partly provoked by high investment from companies preparing for the single market.

The Europe of the 1990s presents a very different picture. The Community has gone into a recession that is both deep and long-lasting. The Paris-based organization of the rich industrial economies, the Organization for Economic Co-operation and Development (OECD) has been forced on several occasions to reduce the growth projections for its 24 members. By June of 1993 it was forecasting negative growth for that year in the EC with only a 1.8 per cent growth rate in 1994. Unemployment seemed set to rise from a 9.9 per cent rate in 1992 to 11.9 per cent in 1994. The OECD felt that Germany, the locomotive of the European economy, would be particularly affected. Growth in Germany was expected to fall by 1.9 per cent in 1993, only recovering to 1.4 per cent in 1994, while Germany's jobless rate was forecast to jump from 7.7 per cent in 1992 to 11.3 per cent in 1994 (see Table 14.1).

For business such figures make gloomy reading and from it two obvious lessons may be derived. Firstly European companies should not rely overmuch on the European market and should consider markets overseas where the growth prospects are brighter. In the USA and Japan growth was expected to exceed 3 per cent in 1994 and strong growth was also expected in Australia, Canada, Asia and Latin America. Secondly the task of winning orders in a more competitive but recession-hit Europe will be even harder than in the past.

Germany; the locomotive economy

Germany, Italy, France, Spain and Britain form the core of the European economy, accounting in 1990 (including East Germany)

Table 14.1 *OECD forecasts June 1993*

	GDP, % change (DEC 1992 forecasts in brackets)			Unemployment rate, %		
	1992	*1993*	*1994*	*1992*	*1993*	*1994*
United States	2.1	2.6(2.4)	3.1(3.1)	7.4	7.0	6.5
Japan	1.3	1.0(2.3)	3.3(3.1)	2.2	2.5	2.6
Germany	2.0	–1.9(1.2)	1.4(2.9)	7.7	10.1	11.3
OECD Europe	1.0	–0.3(1.2)	1.8(2.5)	9.9	11.4	11.9
Total OECD	1.5	1.2(1.9)	2.7(2.9)	7.9	8.5	8.6

for 89 per cent of total Community GDP and for 84 per cent of its population. Yet the prospects of the other four as well as those of the smaller member states have depended very much on a strong Germany acting as a locomotive for the rest of Europe and until 1991 Germany fulfilled this role. It was politically stable and enjoyed harmonious labour relations as German unions were usually willing to practise wage restraint in the interests of controlling inflation and retaining jobs. The small number of unions contributed to an absence of demarcation disputes. The postwar years saw an economic miracle based on the efficiency and hard work of its managers and workforce although by the 1980s German industrialists had to concede that they had fallen behind in some of the industries of the future like microelectronics, and the old powerhouse of the German economy, the Ruhr, suffered as heavy industries declined.

Nevertheless the economy still seemed basically strong as growth rates of 3 per cent were enjoyed in the mid-1980s, based on strong exports. German industry was powerful in a number of sectors. The motor vehicle industry employed 700,000 people with over 60 per cent of production exported by six major car producers. The German aerospace industry expanded to rank third in Europe behind those of the UK and France, dominated by two concerns, Messerschmitt-Bölkow-Blohm (MBB) and Daimler-Benz. The chemicals industry was a major propellant of growth, employing over 500,000 people and dominated by three giants – Hoechst, Bayer and BASF.

The dynamism of the West German economy in the late 1980s was symbolized by two related developments, one geographical and one organization. Southern Germany, especially Bavaria, expanded its industrial base, Bavaria becoming the heartland of the country's microelectronics development. Small companies contributed to the expansion but multinationals with household names like Motorola and Hitachi located in Bavaria and the great German company, Siemens, built a huge complex on the outskirts of Munich to implement a crash R and D programme designed to put the company in a leading position in microchip production. Baden-Wurttemberg also enjoyed success as big automotive and electrical companies including IBM, Bosch, Porsche and Daimler-Benz located there.

The second factor which appeared to point to the dynamism of the German economy was merger mania with 600 mergers in 1985 alone. Leading industrialists like Hans Vogel of Messerschmitt and Karl-Heinz Kaske of Siemens along with state premiers like Othar Spaeth of Baden-Wurttemberg believed that companies with traditional engineering skills needed to be linked with high technology companies. These leaders were acutely aware that they had a long way to go before they could compete with Japan and the USA because they did not yet possess the critical mass in R and D that leads to research breakthroughs. One of the most notable mergers was the seizure by Daimler-Benz of the ailing AEG electrical group and the Dornier aerospace company, the latter coup provoking a business feud as dramatic as anything in Dallas or Dynasty.

The two developments, linked to traditional strengths, seemed likely to change the country's role in the world economy. No longer an imitator adapting to trends originating in the USA, Germany was expected to grasp a world leadership role. Certainly other member states became dependent on Germany as a key export market, Britain for example exporting well in the fields of office machinery, data-processing equipment and the provision of financial services. Well over 1,000 British companies had set up subsidiaries in Germany by the end of the 1980s. Selling there was no easy option: German business expected punctuality and efficiency with meetings well prepared in advance. Given the division of Germany into five areas (now six with East Germany) – the north, the Ruhr, Frankfurt, Bavaria with Baden-Wurttemberg, and West Berlin, regular exporters were well advised to have two agents. Orders were won only where quality, reliability, competitive pricing and good back-up services were assured. Then the rewards were great.

The price of German reunification

In October 1990 the two postwar halves of Germany were formally reunited after a treaty on monetary, economic and social union had been signed in the previous July. The East German currency, the Ostmark, gave way to the West German Deutschmark as East Germany's legal tender and the Bundesbank became the central bank for all Germany. However early euphoria about this historic event soon gave way to virtual despair because the process of reunification brought new problems to the German economy and revealed some of its underlying weaknesses.

Basic flaws in East German industry

For many years before reunification the Soviet authorities had trumpeted to the world that East Germany was a model of what could be achieved by the command economy. Consequently it had not been fully appreciated in the West just how badly run down East Germany had become. If it were a model, it was as an example of how a Soviet control had ruined a potentially prosperous region. A massive failure to invest had led to an appalling situation in housing and infrastructure while industry had been fatally held back by bureaucratic red tape. Mr Horst Sindermann, formerly number three in the Politburo, conveyed the full effect of East German planning in an interview in *Der Spiegal* in 1990. 'I found in Berlin a giant bureaucracy that I was, as government leader, quite helpless against. Everything was controlled down to the smallest detail. Everything depended on everything else, but lots of things didn't work and nobody could say why not. Before every meeting of the council of ministers there was a mountain of paper – several hundred pages high. Nobody could work through it all, but it was there that the planning bureaucrats had laid their traps.'

Many areas of business had received no investment; where investment was undertaken much of it was wasted. For example 140 billion Ostmarks were spent on the development of a four megabit memory chip by Carl Zeiss, the struggling optical and microelectronics concern but in the end production was abandoned. The consequence of inadequate investment was that East German workers achieved 40 per cent of the real output of West German workers and living standards were far lower in the East. East Germans owned only half as many cars per household (and cars like the Trabant were a joke), only half as many colour televisions and only 7 per cent owned a telephone. It was clear that the cost of restoring the East German economy, especially given the horrendous pollution from the country's heavy industries, would be huge. The East German transport minister opined in 1990 that 200 billion marks would be needed to renew the infrastructure alone.

Rising unemployment in East Germany

In 1990 the East German economics minister, Gerhard Pohl, stated that his ministry had reviewed 3,000 East German companies and found that 30 per cent would be capable of converting to the open market, 50 per cent would need overhauling to survive and 20 per cent were doomed to bankruptcy. Perhaps even this gloomy view was optimistic: 30 per cent of the companies should have been placed in the last category because East German companies had no experience in marketing as their products had been distributed by the state. Many companies like Carl Zeiss with old-fashioned methods and over-large workforces had relied on captive markets in the former COMECON states. Many, about 8,000, had been state-owned and had to be privatized by the giant trusteeship (Treuhandenstalt) set up for that purpose.

Such companies could not stand the full blast of competition from West German and other EC companies. Thus East Germany rapidly began to appear an industrial graveyard with official unemployment rising to 800,000 and a further 1,900,000 on short-time by 1993. Nearly one third of the workforce was effectively idle and forecasts suggested that the total of official and disguised unemployment would double by 1995. This social catastrophe led to a wave of suicides and more street violence.

Inflation

In the move to one currency East Germans swapped their Ostmarks for Deutschmarks. The Bundesbank, ever mindful of inflation, fought a rearguard action over the conversion rate, pressing for two Ostmarks for every Deutschmark. The Kohl government preferred an arrangement more generous to East Germans. The basic swap rate for an asset or liability denominated in Ostmarks was two for one into Deutschmarks but 4,000 Ostmarks per head (6,000 for people over 60 and 2,000 for those under 15) could be exchanged on a one for one basis. The concessions added 170 billion marks to West Germany's money supply. It was hoped that this would not be inflationary because the 14 per cent rise in the money supply corresponded closely to estimates of the ratio of East German to West German real GDP. However an inflationary impulse was felt as East Germans, deprived of quality consumer goods for so long, indulged in a spending spree.

The conversion had two other direct consequences: it immediately put up the real cost of East German labour because the former black-market value of the Deutschmark had been over five Ostmarks and this was compounded by East German workers, now with union power, demanding wage increases to bring their wages closer to those in West Germany.

The combined effects of increased consumer spending, increased wage costs and more government expenditure on the East led to an inflation rate of 5 per cent in 1992 in a state which had been the model of a low inflation economy. Accordingly the Bundesbank raised interest rates to 9 per cent but this imposed deflation on an already recession-hit West Germany.

Immigration problems

This battery of problems went beyond economic considerations; a real fear gripped German life as attacks on immigrants escalated whether those immigrants were East Germans, East Europeans or Turks. Germans from one region of the country had traditionally little affection for fellow countrymen from other regions. The Prussian Bismarck, contemplating his southern compatriots, remarked dismissively, 'the Bavarian is a cross between an Austrian and a human being' while Adenauer, a Rhinelander drawn more to the west than to Prussia in the east, once remarked with distaste, 'You can smell Prussia when you cross the Elbe'. The flood of East Germans to the west of the country was thus viewed with alarm by West Germans.

However the core of the immigrant problem was the estimated six million foreigners in Germany, nearly one third of whom were Turkish. The Turks became a particular target for tragic racially motivated attacks from neo-Nazis. Many Turkish families had lived in Germany for over 20 years but were still regarded as gastarbeiter (guest-workers), the assumption being that one day they would go home. No easy solution seemed feasible even when the government tightened Germany's asylum laws or even if it were to offer dual citizenship to the guestworkers. The recession had led to two large groups of unemployed – East German youths made redundant from ex-communist companies closed down due to their unprofitability and young male immigrants unable to find work or laid off from recession-hit plants in West Germany. The circumstances were a recipe for growing violence.

Weaknesses in the West German economy

The first four factors discussed hit an economy which was by 1990 already showing signs of strain. Many small and medium-sized German companies had had their competitive edge eroded during the 1980s by high wage settlements, a strong mark, government policies and perhaps complacency. In that decade the productivity of factory workers grew faster in America, Japan, France and Britain than in Germany. By 1991 German labour costs per unit of output were 36 per cent higher than in Britain and Japan and 45 per cent higher than in France. German workers had become pampered with a six week annual holiday plus public holidays (14 days in Bavaria); a short working week and early retirement. Consequently the industrial base in industries like agriculture, coal, and shipbuilding could only be safeguarded by large subsidies. But large subsidies meant heavier taxation and by 1993 the tax burden was a national record of 43.7 per cent of GDP. When higher interest rates restored the strength of the mark in the ERM, German exporters experienced a decline in orders after 1991.

The cost of subsidies in the West allied to spending in East Germany (150 billion marks a year) led to a near-crisis in Germany's public finances with the public sector borrowing, officially at 5 per cent of GDP, in reality approaching 8 per cent and well above the 3 per cent upper limit criterion set at Maastricht for European Monetary Union. Yet action to cut the deficit by more taxation or reductions in government expenditure only threatened to push Germany further into recession.

The recession hit many famous German companies. Mercedes-Benz experienced a 45 per cent slump in profits in 1992 and along with Volkswagen had to take drastic action through enforced redundancies to cut production costs. Some companies felt compelled to move to cheaper foreign locations: BMW planned to locate in the USA, furniture and textile companies moved to Eastern Europe and a cutlery company set up in China.

Whether Germany recovers quickly from the recession depends partly on the Bundesbank which has refused to cut interest rates sharply. It has argued that inflation has been double the target rate of 2 per cent and is likely to remain at around 4 per cent. Such inflation, it has insisted, was not its fault but that of the government (which raised taxes and prices for government services instead of cutting spending) and the unions which demanded wage parity between east and west much too quickly. However the high cost of borrowing in Germany has held back recovery.

Yet if Germany is no longer the booming economy that it once was, it still remains a huge market. Government spending in East Germany is immense and that region promises to be a springboard to other markets in Eastern Europe. The actions of West German companies after 1989 demonstrate the range of opportunities available. In the vehicles sector, Volkswagen, Opel and Daimler-Benz have invested in joint ventures with East German companies. In engineering AEG and Thyssen have built links with East German companies to manufacture a range of products from railway wagons to measuring equipment. In electricals, Standard Elektrick Lorenz has gained contracts to modernize East Germany's telephone system and Siemens has contracts to develop East Germany's telecommunications and electrical tools. Opportunities have arisen in tourism, banking and insurance: Allianz, Europe's largest insurance company based in Munich gained a large stake in East Germany's monopoly insurer in 1990.

In the long-run high levels of investment will make East Germany a growth area. The danger for non-German companies is that many of the most lucrative opportunities have already been seized by West German firms with foreign companies virtually excluded. But foreign companies that do make the effort have succeeded in winning business in East Germany, as French firms have proved. Elf Aquitaine, France's leading oil company, has made the biggest investment in East Germany so far. With Thyssen, its minority

German partner, it agreed in July 1992 to invest 6 billion marks between 1992 and 1996 in a chain of filling stations and a giant oil refinery at Leana. Renault has snapped up distributors across East Germany, raising sales there from 16,000 vehicles in 1990 to 73,500 in 1992, becoming Germany's top supplier of foreign cars. The French have also invaded Germany's financial services. Crédit Lyonnias for example acquiring German companies to create a network of 200 branches across Germany. By 1993 French firms owned about 1,000 subsidiaries in Germany.

Other Community markets

If Germany no longer possesses the potential that it once had, where is business to expand? Certainly it was possible to point in Chapter 12 to market opportunities in states applying to become members of the EC, especially the richer EFTA states. Finland and Sweden offer opportunities in vehicle components, Finland, Iceland, Sweden, Switzerland and Austria in clothing, Austria and Sweden in electrical components, Finland and Switzerland in computers, Austria, Finland, Norway and Switzerland in medical equipment, Austria, Norway and Switzerland in security equipment and Austria, Switzerland, Sweden and Norway in telecommunications.

Yet these markets are small and most companies would be wise to concentrate on the large European states. Many would agree with Uwe Specht, a member of the management board of Henkel, a German company with large French operations, when he said that German business increasingly sees France and the Benelux countries as the core European market. France is a large market of 55 million rich consumers and under the Fifth Republic enjoys stable democratic government. The 1993 elections created once again the special French phenomenon of 'co-habitation' (a French socialist president and a right-wing cabinet). Dissatisfaction with Mitterand reached new heights in 1992 because unemployment had risen sharply and some groups such as the farming interest had special grievances. However inflation was low, the franc stable despite strains within the ERM and French economic growth among the highest in the EC.

There are some particular difficulties facing exporters to the French market. The French are a nationalistic people and visiting businesspeople would do well to bear French wishes and habits in mind. It is, for example, usual in France for personal acquaintances to shake hands on meeting and parting and failure to do so may give offence. Of much more importance is the French preference to do business in their own language and French businesspeople can be unresponsive to approaches in other languages. A knowledge of German may also be an advanvantage when doing business in French districts near the German border.

This point about language is fundamental and indeed legal. In 1975 the French government passed a law on the use of the French language. Article 1 lays down that advertisements, instructions for use and terms of guarantees for all goods and services used in France must be in French. Foreign businesses would do well, therefore, to ensure that all their literature is in French, with prices quoted in French francs and weights and measures quoted in metric terms.

Another problem facing the exporters to France relates to investment. Though foreign investment is welcomed in France, procedures can be rather cumbersome and obligations onerous. In certain fields, for example, public utilities, stockbrokerage, road transport, travel agencies and life insurance, there are severe restrictions.

In general, unless prior authorization is granted by the Ministry of Finance, all capital movements and payments between French residents and non-residents must be transacted through approved intermediaries (commercial banks). For most direct investment which increases foreign control over French enterprises, the application for approval must be sent to the Ministry of the Economy, giving full details of the investing company and the impact of its investment plans on the area concerned. Also various local regulations must be observed when investing in France. A zoning certificate (certificat d'urbanisme) is needed, indicating the kind of construction permitted. This is obtaining from the Directeur Départemental de l'Equipement in the relevant district. There is also a need for a building permit which can only be obtained by furnishing full details of the plans to the local major or prefect. Local building regulations are now being made more rigorous in France. A law of 1977 obliges a company planning new plant to make a study of its environmental impact. Finally, all firms employing fifty people or more must have workers' councils and firms with more than one hundred employees must have profit-sharing schemes.

The most serious potential obstacle for the exporter is the attitude of the French government to imports. At the time Mitterand's government came to power in 1981, France was running a huge trade deficit of fifty billion francs. As a result the prime government objective was the reconquest of the domestic market, a controversial phrase for would-be exporters as it seemed to imply favourable treatment for home industry and went against the intentions of the Rome Treaty. In 1982 the then minister for the economy, Jacques Delors, even said that importers in France would be encouraged to buy French goods.

It is important, therefore that exporters appreciate the sensitivity of the French on this question. Disputes on the import of Italian or Spanish wine or British lamb (la guerre de mouton) into France underline the fact that exporting to France can have unexpected complications. France can react more quickly than most to what it regards as unwanted imports because of its centralized administrative system based on Paris. If Paris so indicates, all sorts of people from customs officers onwards have to take note and make life difficult for exporters. This can be done quite discreetly, for example, by restricting the availability of credit to distributors on certain goods which they import.

The network of regulations is in any case a real barrier. While import licences are not required for most imported goods, the importation of some classes of goods is prohibited and others subject to special formalities such as second-hand goods, pharmaceuticals, dietary specialities and biological products. Import arrangements for agricultural products and certain foodstuffs are particularly complicated.

However, the problems of the French market must not be overstated. If French officialdom can be obstructive, there is also a wide range of incentives offered to companies investing in the country's less developed regions or areas of high unemployment while at the same time further commercial activity is discouraged in crowded conurbations like Paris. The overall development of the regions is administered by the Délégation à l'Aménagement du Territoire et l'Action Régionale (DATAR). DATAR officials will advise on suitable sites, arrange meetings with appropriate parties, help to obtain government approval and prepare the necessary applications. Foreign-controlled companies are well represented in petroleum products, agricultural equipment, electrical equipment, machinery, chemicals and pharmaceuticals.

Foreign firms with the right approach and product do well in France. In the 1980s the computer market in France grew at the rate of 15 per cent and ICL achieved some successes there. Its DRS small multi-micro intelligent terminal was sold to the tune of 470 systems worth £1.5 million to Crédit Agricole and a private technical company offered 130 of ICL's PERQ design computers at £25,000 each. Another British firm Rowntree Mackintosh, taking care to sell under a French name (Lanvin Rêve Noir) became the biggest chocolate manufacturer in France, its sales growing at a rate of 30 per cent a year.

Noteworthy successes have been gained by Portakabin, especially since 1976 when this York-based firm's accommodation units were used in the building of the new Lille metro. 30 per cent of the company's trade has been with the government because of the amount of state involvement in major projects. When the French government announced its intention of reconquering the home market, Portakabin was quick to point out how it used European steel, French electrical products, French cars and French equipment where possible. The nuclear power project at Gravelines used six hundred Portakabins but the firm was also a market leader at the luxury end of the instant accommodation business where most of its European competitors made cheaper, less well-equipped units. As its units could be linked together to form a large instant building, it gained business from local authorities wishing to enlarge schools and hospitals. The Mitterand government's decentralization policy has helped such regional business because regional authorities can now decide how to spend resources whereas in the past Paris made the decision.

The company also ensured rapid delivery of units. It took only two days to get a unit from the factory in York to Dunkirk and therefore the French-based subsidiaries could offer two weeks' delivery for most orders.

The household products group Reckitt and Colman which makes goods ranging from Brasso to Disprin also set up in Lille. However, whereas Portakabin set up merely to market its goods, Reckitt and Colman created a plant – Reckitts Colours – to manufacture paints. It was the Lille plant which provided the blue and white paint for Concorde. To meet competition from Spanish and Belgian competitors, the firm installed high-technology machinery to reduce manufacturing time from three months to six weeks. It also increased its range of colours, for example, violet and pink for the cosmetic trade and deep maroon and red for the plastics, ceramics and car paints industries.

Identifying sectors in the French market where demand is growing is not easy but opportunities exist in energy conservation, electronic and car components, scientific instruments especially medical equipment, industrial machinery, for example knitting and printing machinery for the textile industry, and in consumer goods with quality and style.

Exporters to France should consider concentrating their efforts in areas other than the obvious one of the Paris conurbation. Lyon is a promising centre, under three hours journey from Paris, thanks to the TGV (Train à Grande Vitesse). It is at the hub of a motorway network which provides access to southern France, Switzerland, Germany, Italy and Spain and it has a potential market of 150 million consumers within a radius of 800 kilometres. The area has a rich diversity of industry including metal-working, chemicals, textiles and hydro and nuclear power. The financial services sector has grown quickly as a result of the general development of the region.

Finally, in this analysis of the French market, it is worthwhile taking on board the advice of Peter Abberley, a sales engineer for John Marshall Engineers, a private company manufacturing specialist machine tools for the tube and bar industries. The company is export orientated and in 1983 was awarded two gold awards by the International Export Association. In 1983 in his book *Exporting to France: a Small Firm's Experience* published by the BETRO Trust,

Mr Abberley stressed the following key hints to bear in mind if exporting to France was to be successful:

1   The most important factor in selling to France is finding a good agent to work for you. It is worth waiting until the right person is found.
2   French buyers are usually loyal to their suppliers so initial market penetration may be slow. However, once sales start, these buyers will also be loyal to you.
3   All verbal and written contracts should be in French and sent promptly. The French respond to any effort made by foreigners to speak and write their language. As interpreters now cost about £100 a day, this could also save money!
4   Be prepared to back up your agent with frequent visits, especially in the early stages. Do not underestimate costs in France, especially the cost of entertaining. Advise of any delays well in advance. The French are generally sympathetic to genuine problems.
5   Do not be put off by tales of French insularity.
6   If there is any aspect of the French market which you do not fully grasp, ask for help from the many sources available. Their help could save you a lot of time and frustration.

Most business will be continued to be done in the core markets of the EC but the markets in states which have relatively recently gained membership should not be neglected. Starting from a low, base growth rates in Greece, Portugal and Spain have been high in recent years compared to those in the more mature industrialized economies.

Spain for a number of years enjoyed the highest growth rate in the EC. It has successfully completed a transition from Franco's dictatorship to moderate socialist government under Felipe Gonzales. Despite facing high inflation and high unemployment it still promises to be a high growth area. The agricultural sector is a massive producer of cereals, vegetables, fruit, wine and olive oil while some industrial sectors especially vehicle production have experienced rapid expansion. Tourism remains an important source of foreign exchange with about 40 million foreigners a year visiting Spain.

Entry to the Community marked an important moment in Spanish history. For centuries Spain had let Europe pass it by, cultivating an image of splendid isolation. For many Spaniards, therefore, Community membership was a psychological matter, the moment when their country became part of Europe again and not merely a kind of backward outcrop. Adapting to membership was not easy for Spain because its markets had been heavily protected but the elimination of tariffs was carried out over a transitional period from 1986 to 1993 and the country became a major beneficiary from the EC budget. The Spanish government was keen to modernize its major industries (steel, shipbuilding and vehicles) and its programme provided much business for foreign companies supplying flexible manufacturing systems (FMS), computer-aided design and manufacture (CAD/DAM) and robotics.

The government was also concerned to develop information technology including the modernization of its telecommunications systems. The financial services sector in Spain also wished to exploit modern technology and therefore a number of computer companies – Apple, Olivetti and Philips – have sold well in Spain.

Foreign firms have moved into Spain's financial services sector. The country is the second most intensively banked state in Europe and foreign banks like Barclays have created a presence there against local banks which tend to be slow and expensive. The Spanish insurance industry was underdeveloped and big insurance companies, like the Royal which took a 60 per cent stake in the Spanish company Velasquez, have moved in on a long-term basis. Spanish people have in the past not used life insurance as a form of saving as frequently as have the British. However as wealth in Spain has increased, more individuals have become aware of the advantages of insurance while the growing number of international companies operating in Spain has increased requirements for commercial cover.

The supply of car components remains a promising sector because Spain is now Europe's fourth largest car producer after investment there in the 1980s by Volkswagen, Fiat, Renault, Ford and General Motors. For such companies it is still common practice to have multiple sources for bought-in components such as carburettors and generators. The modernization of Spanish agriculture may still provide some business for firms manufacturing agricultural machinery while the continuation of hotel building provides a market for building materials and construction work. Other sectors with growth potential include energy conservation, marine equipment, hospital and medical equipment, offshore oil and gas equipment, printing machinery and, given the rising crime rate, security equipment.

The need for a coherent European strategy

This chapter has concentrated on the difficulties facing European business but the EC nevertheless remains as one of the three dominant economic blocs in the world. With a GDP of 4,729 billion ECUs in 1990, the EC surpassed the USA with a GDP of 4,311 billion ECUs and Japan with 2,264 billion ECUs. Nevertheless the

New Europe is now a more challenging place to do business than a few years ago. Companies that flourished in relatively protected markets now face severe difficulties in surviving in a more competitive Europe.

In a recent article Gerry Blanchard highlighted seven factors creating turbulence in the European business scene – the globalization of most industrial sectors, deregulation, the unremitting pace of technological change, demographics (the ageing population and an increasing shortage of skilled young people in Western Europe), the Single European Market, the opening up of Central and Eastern Europe and, finally, the recession. To this list could be added an eighth factor creating more business pressure, the turbulence in the ERM since September 1992.

Companies need to make an appropriate response to such challenges and preparation to meet one challenge also helps a company to fend off other dangers. For example a company preparing well for the single market will become more competitive globally.

Pointing to ICL as a model, Blanchard pinpoints the areas where a strong business response is required. Firstly a company must create a genuine European strategy to focus effort and resources on the changes needed to make itself more competitive. ICL set up a European Strategy Panel to advise the ICL Chief Executive, Peter Bronfield, on single market opportunities. A second priority was lobbying the EC institutions on behalf of its customers and itself to ensure that single market legislation was beneficial. A third priority was for the company to tell its own staff what was going on and to help them assess the relevance of changes for their own work through an awareness programme which included in-house magazines, conferences and roadshows.

A fourth priority for the European Strategy Board was to measure progress against objectives in its evolving European home-base especially in the development of core competencies, the gaining of market niches, the development of pan-European distribution channels, the exploitation of technological changes, managing the supply/value-added chain and adopting a European mindset.

The actions taken by ICL has affected all its functions – business policy, marketing, R and D, information systems and training. The changes have included more use of the ECU in payments and loans, new product conformance to European standards, collaboration with public bodies such as the Andalucian Regional Authority in Spain and with companies like Skoda in software ventures, and the acquisition of foreign firms like Nokia Data in Finland.

Thus ICL achieved a co-ordinated strategy as seen in the launch of the DRS 6000 computer simultaneously across Europe in 1991 with the first sale to the Commission, a new warehouse near Utrecht to stock spares for distribution across frontiers and prices denominated in ECUs. By then ICL staff could dial their colleagues directly from desk to desk from country to country as the internal voice and data network developed.

Mistakes were made but the overall lesson was clear. Speed was of the essence and a proactive approach examining all aspects of the company's operations essential. As Blanchard concludes, 'Think in European terms before thinking in national terms. Ostriches and blinkered donkeys have no future in the new Europe. Open-eyed competitive companies have everything to gain'.

Further reading

Drew, J, *Doing Business in the European Community*, Whurr (Third Edition), London, 1992.

Gibbs, P, *Doing Business in the European Community*, Kogan Page, London, 1990.

Morris, B et al, *Business Europe*, Macmillan, London, 1992.

Randlesome, C (ed.), *Business Cultures in Europe*, Butterworth-Heinemann (Second Edition), Oxford, 1993.

Rouffignac, P D, *Europe's New Business Culture*, Pitman, London, 1991.

Somers, F (ed.), *The European Economies*, Pitman, London, 1991.

Questions

1 Explain why the survival of cultural diversity in the EC has profound implications for business.
2 Critically examine the consequences of German reunification for European economic growth in the 1990s.
3 In which sectors are there export opportunities in France and Spain?
4 What factors have been creating turbulence in the European business environment? How may companies respond to the challenges involved?

15
Political and economic union in the 1990s, or the great Maastricht fiasco

The visionary splendour fades

The aim of political and economic union is not fully spelt out in the Rome Treaty because the founding fathers committed themselves only in general terms to 'an ever closer union'. The first firm decision to move towards monetary union and a more co-ordinated Community foreign policy only came at the Paris Summit in 1972. The heads of government affirmed 'the determination of the states of the enlarged European Communities irrevocably to achieve economic and monetary union'. With what in hindsight may be viewed as wild optimism, the governments hoped that the process would begin in 1973 and be completed in 1980. As explained in Chapter 10, early attempts at creating a zone of monetary stability through the Snake failed and only in 1979 was further progress made with the creation of the EMS.

The goal of a more federal united Europe was revived in the 1980s by two factors. Firstly, the Single European Act of 1986 committed the EC to effecting a true single market and some of the chief figures involved in the process, for example Lord Cockfield, argued that a full single market required a single currency. In June 1988 at the Hanover Summit, Jacques Delors was asked to produce a report which duly provided the foundation on which to set up an intergovernmental conference (IGC) on economic and monetary union in April 1989.

The second factor was the fall of the Berlin Wall in 1989 and the consequent reunification of Germany in October 1990. From this developed a new momentum for a more federal Europe. German politicians like the German Chancellor Helmut Kohl and senior politicians from other states like Mitterand and Jean-Pierre Cot in France feared that a powerful united Germany might look East and become more independent of the EC. In their view some way had to be found of locking Germany permanently into the Community through the creation of a more politically integrated Western

Europe. Accordingly Kohl and Mitterand put political and economic union firmly on the agenda at the Rome Summit in November 1990 despite the opposition of the British Premier, Margaret Thatcher, and a second IGC was set up to examine the question of political union.

The work of the two IGCs culminated in December 1991 with the signing of the Treaty on European Union, known popularly as the Maastricht Treaty as the treaty was signed in the small Dutch town of Maastricht. The text of the treaty was involved and long (61,351 words) but at the time it was hailed as a turning point in the history of the Community even by politicians who had never read the treaty! Each country's leaders tended to read what they wanted into the treaty and its results. Mitterand returned home claiming that he had prevented Britain from stifling the movement towards a federal Europe while John Major told the House of Commons that the treaty was 'a good agreement for Europe and for the United Kingdom' because he had been instrumental in creating a framework for co-operation between member states as opposed to allowing EC powers to get out of hand on issues like foreign policy and workers' rights.

During 1992 and 1993 the euphoria felt at the time of the Maastricht Summit evaporated as the dream of a more united EC began to appear more and more unrealistic. The tragedies involved in the civil war in Bosnia cruelly exposed the incapacity of the EC to mount a coherent response to the problem of the former Yugoslavia. The near collapse of the ERM in September 1992 and the move to a 15 per cent band in August 1993 destroyed the possibility of a smooth and orderly transition to a single currency. Above all Maastricht became almost a pejorative term because the politicians had signally failed to win the hearts and minds of their publics over the concept of European unity. Disillusioned by the arrogance of their leaders and by rising unemployment, ordinary people throughout the member states evinced a deep degree of scepticism towards the ideas symbolized by Maastricht. The Danish people rejected the Maastricht Treaty in June 1992 and needed a second referendum in May 1993. The French referendum of September 1992 led to a tiny majority in favour of the treaty though to be fair French voters took the opportunity to display their discontent with the French government. In Germany serious newspapers like *Der Spiegel* and popular newspapers like Der *Bild* expressed considerable worries about the desirability of 'chocolate' currency, the ECU, replacing a strong currency like the mark.

The struggle required by the British government to achieve ratification of the Maastricht bill in the House of Commons (achieved in August 1993) became a veritable chapter of delay and accidents which infuriated Britain's partners. At the heart of the British problem over Maastricht was a fear of the 'F' word, federalism, which the British had insisted should not be included in the text of the Maastricht Treaty. To continental Europeans the word did not arouse fear and loathing because it represented a form of government which left the regions and local governments with considerable powers as in federal Germany where the länder (the state governments like Bavaria) remained significant. To the British federalism represented the danger of a radical shift of power to the centre which would infringe British sovereignty and the status of the British parliament. Opponents of Maastricht referred to 'a conveyor-belt to federalism', hinting darkly that if the Maastricht Treaty was ratified Brussels would continue to gather more and more power over the member states. This view was most succinctly put by one of Britain's leading Europhobes, Lord Tebbit, in June 1993 during the debate in the House of Lords on the Maastricht bill. In a trenchant speech he claimed that Maastricht would undermine Britain's national institutions to the extent that Britain would become a province of a federal Europe as Saxony was a province in Germany, the British parliament would be a provincial assembly and the Chancellor of the Exchequer would have the same powers as the treasurer of a rate-capped local authority.

Maastricht survived such criticism only in a bruised and bloody state. Far from uniting Europeans it had become a cause of more disunity. Quite simply the conditions required for its successful advance were not present in the two years after its signing. Recession is never a good time to attempt bold new ventures because nations turn inwards and seek to protect their narrower interests. Even more fundamentally the error of the political elites in seeking to impose Maastricht on the people of Europe without much real consultation had at last provoked a strong reaction. Maastricht was 'a treaty too far' in its effort to promote too much change too quickly.

Despite such setbacks, the treaty does provide a framework and an agenda for the 1990s though chastened European politicians would do well to concentrate on winning more public approval for its crucial elements.

The key elements of the Maastricht Treaty

The Maastricht Treaty is titled 'The Treaty on European Unity', reflecting the ambition of its creators to move the Community towards 'an ever closer union among the peoples of Europe'. In Article B of the treaty are enshrined the following objectives:

> To promote economic and social progress which is balanced and sustainable, in particular through the creation of an area without inter-

nal frontiers, through the strengthening of economic and social cohesion and through the establishment of economic and monetary union, ultimately including a single currency; to assert its identity on the international scene, in particular through the implementation of a common foreign and security policy including the eventual framing of a common defence policy.

This quotation from the treaty refers to what have been termed its three major pillars: (1) European Monetary Union (EMU), (2) Home affairs and justice, and (3) Security.

European Monetary Union (EMU)

In Chapter 9 the potential advantages and costs of EMU were discussed and arguably it is in the sections covering economic and monetary union (Article 2 and Articles 102–109) that the Maastricht Treaty is most wide-ranging and radical. Here is set out a clear timetable for sweeping away national currencies to create the European Currency Unit (ECU) as a rival to the dollar. According to this timetable the ECU will become a currency in its own right in the period 1997 to 1999. Preparing the way for the move to a single currency is the technical process known as convergence. At the moment economic indicators vary widely between the member states. Under the terms of the Maastricht Treaty, it is hoped that the differences in each country's inflation, interest rates, exchange rate fluctuations and budget and public sector deficits will be reduced and converge with the record of the best-performing economies. Then in principle it will be relatively easy to lock the exchange rates of member states irrevocably and merge the currencies into one.

It is considered that the ECU would have to be as strong as the mark has been and that therefore there will have to be a central bank to impose monetary discipline as strongly as has the Bundesbank in Germany. This new institution is to be the European Central Bank which would have real powers to impose monetary discipline on the member states to maintain low inflation.

The road to EMU has *three* stages. In Stage 1 governments must implement policies to achieve the desired convergence. The Council of Finance Ministers, in the shape of Ecofin, has the duty to give strong advice to member states whose national economic policies are 'inconsistent with the guidelines or present a risk to EMU'. The Commission, too, has a new role, that of monitoring each government's debt, and if a member state's debt rises too rapidly the Commission will prompt Ecofin to order that remedial action be taken in the offending state. If a state fails to comply then tough and escalating sanctions may be imposed. Firstly the EIB can 'reconsider its lending policy' to the member state concerned. Then the EC can call in interest-free loans from that state or even impose fines if the Council of Ministers so decides by a two-thirds majority vote on a proposal from the Commission, the vote not including the member state concerned.

Once a member state has achieved economic convergence, it will be eligible to join the monetary union. However the five criteria for achieving this convergence are tough if they are adhered to in practice. Low inflation was deemed vital to maintain European competitiveness and therefore the treaty emphasizes that member states must reduce their annual inflation to within 1.5 per cent of the average of the three lowest inflation nations. Secondly member states must also have long-term interest rates no greater than 2 per cent above the average of the three states with the lowest interest rates. Thirdly member states must keep their budget deficit within 3 per cent of GDP and fourthly public sector debt must be no higher than 60 per cent of GDP. The fifth and final criterion for joining the monetary union covers exchange rates. Member states must have kept their currencies within the narrow band of the ERM for two years without any unilateral devaluation of their currency in that period.

It will readily be appreciated that such stiff criteria might be difficult to attain and events since the Maastricht Summit have confirmed this. In December 1991 only France and Luxembourg met all five criteria; ironically even Germany could not meet the third criterion after high government borrowing to finance spending in East Germany. The Southern states (Spain, Greece, Portugal and Italy) find much difficulty in meeting the inflation and interest rate criteria, and Britain, Belgium, the Netherlands, Italy and Greece have much to do to meet the debt criteria. As to the exchange rate issue, Britain and Italy now reside outside the ERM altogether with no plans for an early return while further collapse of the ERM in August 1993 threatened the whole single currency enterprise (see Chapter 9).

Stage 2 should begin in 1994 with the establishment of the European Monetary Institute (EMI) whose members are the national central banks. The role of the EMI will be that of creating the right conditions for Stage 3 by strengthening co-operation between the national central banks, co-ordinating monetary policy throughout the EC, to reduce inflation, expanding the use of the ECU and monitoring the EMS. It will prepare the way for the establishment of a European System of Central Banks (ESCB), the creation of a single monetary policy and the implementation of a single currency in the third stage.

Under this timetable a key date is December 1996. By then the EMI will specify the framework of the ESCB and the Council must decide whether a majority of states meet the four convergence criteria of inflation, interest rates, budget deficits and exchange rates. If the answer is in the affirmative then the EC can launch the third stage of monetary union by setting a date for the move to a single currency. If there is not a sufficient majority the aim will be to establish the ESCB by July 1998 and a date for the move to a single currency by 1 January 1999 at the latest.

When Stage 3 begins the ECU will be a currency in its own right. States participating in EMU will agree the conversion rates at which their currencies will be irrevocably fixed and exchanged for ECUs. From the first date the ECB will take over from the EMI and will have more freedom than national central banks to take independent decisions, 'not taking instruction from anyone whether EC institutions, governments or any other body'. The ECB will have exclusive right to authorize the issue of ECU bank notes by itself or by the national central banks. In conjunction with the national central banks it will implement monetary policy with control of inflation a prime objective.

Both Britain and Denmark have refused to be bound by Maastricht's strictures on EMU, winning opt-outs. Britain is not obliged under the treaty to move to the third stage of EMU without a separate decision to do so by its government and parliament. Britain may notify the Council whether it intends to move to the third stage before the Council makes its assessment on when EMU begins. If no date is set for the beginning of the third stage before 1 January 1998, Britain must notify its intention by that date. If Britain decides not to move to the third stage, it will retain its powers in the field of monetary policy but lose its voting rights in the Council concerning convergence criteria, have no right to participate in appointments to the ECB but still pay its subscription to the capital of the ECB as a contribution to its operational costs. If at any time in the future Britain wished to join EMU it could move to the third stage providing that the Council was satisfied that the convergence criteria were met by Britain.

Whether Britain will choose to exercise its opt-out if and when the moment of decision arrives is difficult to judge. There could be a decision to stay out of EMU on political grounds if the British people did not wish to be part of a federal superstate in which important powers over economic decisions would be lost. Economic policy could be more tailored to Britain's needs and, as to economic costs of staying out of EMU, it could be argued that many successful economies, for example Switzerland and Japan, have never linked their economic policies closely with those of other countries.

The opposing view is that staying out of EMU would be injurious to British interests in at least five ways. Firstly Britain would lose much influence in decision-making within the EC. Secondly rival companies in Europe would gain a commercial advantage over British companies which would still be burdened by transaction costs when exporting to the EC. Thirdly Britain would be less attractive as a home for foreign direct investment and thus jobs and new technology would be lost. Fourthly the position of London as a financial centre might well be affected if Britain remained outside the single currency zone because a number of financial institutions could well re-locate in Paris or Frankfurt. Finally, it is argued, the pound outside EMU would be even more weak and volatile than in recent years as it would be put under pressure by three big world currencies – the ECU in addition to the yen and the dollar.

Home affairs and justice

The second major pillar of the Maastricht Treaty concerns home affairs and justice. For the first time many areas of interior policy become a matter for intergovernmental co-operation between the member states. One reason for this development was an appreciation that attempts to eliminate borders under the single market programme could lead to a growth in international crime unless more co-operation offset the loss of border controls. A second factor made increased co-operation more urgent – the fear of waves of immigrants entering the EC from Southern and Eastern Europe. Such immigration had already become a critical problem in Germany where a combination of liberal asylum laws and growing unemployment had put immigration at the top of the political agenda. German leaders were anxious for a Community-led policy to impose some overall control on immigration in the EC as a whole.

Accordingly Article K of the Maastricht Treaty raises a number of issues related to immigration as a matter of concern for member states, for example asylum policy, immigration policy, customs co-operation and policy regarding nationals from third countries crossing into the EC. A number of clauses refers to criminal matters – the combating of drug trafficking, terrorism and international fraud. It is hoped to create a European Police Office (Europol) to act as an EC-wide information exchange system on serious international crime as well as more judicial co-operation. Arguably only co-ordinated action bringing together the police and judicial authorities across borders can counter the increased problems of immigration and crime though some member states are concerned that ultimate control should still lie with the individual national governments.

Security

The third pillar of the Maastricht Treaty embraces the concept of security – the creation of a coherent Community foreign and defence policy. Federalists have argued that the EC needs such a policy, given crises in the Middle East and Eastern Europe combined with a reduction by the USA of its global commitments. However it is in this area that Maastricht is a fudge, with the little progress that has been made disappointing small states like Belgium and the Netherlands.

Article J of the treaty states that a common foreign and defence policy will be implemented, but the actual proposals for implementation do not make it a Community competence because too many member states were unwilling to cede such matters to supranational control. Instead, Maastricht brings in a more developed form of the political co-operation which had already been evolving in the 1980s (see Chapter 1). A more highly institutional system of co-operation has been agreed but one which may be difficult to operate. Where member states agree in principle unanimously that a joint stance on an international crisis would be helpful they will meet and vote on the appropriate Community response to the crisis and how such a response will be implemented. The details of such implementation will be decided by qualified majority. For example, if there were a crisis in the Middle East, the decision to take action there (the principle of the matter) would require unanimity but the details of the operation (numbers of troops etc) would be decided by qualified majority. However it is easy to see that the distinction between the issues of principle and implementation will be difficult to draw in practice. It is also likely that member states will resent being overruled on matters of foreign policy and the end result may be a more incoherent political co-operation rather than a genuine Community foreign policy.

A similar fudge seems to threaten over defence. Article J of the treaty points to the aim of 'the eventual framing of a common defence policy which might in time lead to a common defence', i.e. a European army. To start off the process in earnest it is suggested that the Western European Union (WEU) should 'elaborate and implement decisions and actions of the union which have defence implications'. The WEU is to move its secretariat from London to Brussels, set up a planning unit and invite member states which are not members of the WEU (Greece, Denmark and Ireland) to join.

These vague arrangements reflect the divisions in the EC over defence. Some member states – Germany, France and some smaller states – were anxious to make European Defence Policy a reality and the French and Germans have symbolized their belief in it by creating a Franco–German Brigade based in Bavaria. Other members dislike the whole concept; Britain and the Netherlands believe an EDP could undermine NATO, Ireland does not wish to end its tradition of neutrality and many Danes dislike the prospect of conscription in a European army, a possibly decisive factor in their rejection of Maastricht in the June 1992 referendum.

On important decisions over defence, unanimity is to remain the rule and the WEU's role is seen as strengthing the Atlantic alliance which is specifically described as 'the essential forum for consultation among its members on politics bearing on the security and defence commitments of allies in NATO'. Quite how the WEU will co-operate with NATO is not clear. Some states like Britain wish to forge strong links between the two bodies; other states, for example Ireland and France, prefer to link the WEU more closely with the EC itself. The clauses on defence appear a recipe for confusion and it may not be too cynical to suggest that this incoherence was deliberately encouraged by some member states that desire a toothless rather than a strong EDP.

Other important elements in the treaty

Among other important elements in the treaty is the idea of Euro-citizenship. All individuals holding the nationality of a member state will also be citizens of the European Union. The new citizenship is not intended to weaken existing national identities but will confer under Article 8 of the treaty new rights, three of which are clearly specified in the Treaty. Firstly, as far as local and European elections are concerned, a Community citizen living in another member state will be treated as a national of that state. Thus Community citizens will be able to stand as candidates and vote in these elections (NB not general elections). Secondly, citizens of the Union will gain the right to take cases of alleged maladministration to a new Community ombudsman who will investigate the complaint and publish the findings although there is no legal obligation for the report to be acted upon. A third right will improve the diplomatic protection of Community citizens outside the EC. Any Community citizen travelling in a part of the world where his own country is not represented will be able to use the diplomatic and consular facilities of other member states.

Supporters of this new European citizenship emphasize that the concept will promote a sense of European identity, demonstrate that the Community has a human face and prove that it is not remote from the concerns of ordinary people. Cynics would counter this view by stigmatizing the concept as largely a propaganda exercise.

As explained in Chapter 8 the Commission has attempted to temper the rigours of the single market by introducing measures through the Social Charter to protect workers' rights. At Maastricht attempts were made to build on this through the *Social Chapter.* However extending Community powers over social policy legislation proved to be one of the most divisive issues at the Summit. While eleven states supported Community-wide laws on improved living and working conditions, terms of employment, employee consultation and social security, Britain firmly asserted that these were areas best left to national governments. The issue threatened to prevent any agreement on the treaty as a whole until Britain won an opt-out on the Social Chapter which became a separate protocol to the treaty, signed by the other states.

The protocol confirms that determination to implement the 1989 Social Charter and sets out areas for action. Article 1 of the protocol points to the aims as 'the promotion of employment, improved living and working conditions, proper social protection, dialogue between management and labour and the development of human resources with a view to lasting high employment and the combating of exclusion'. Specific areas highlighted in Article 2 are the protection of workers' health and safety, information and consultation of workers, equality between men and women in job opportunities, worker representation and social security matters.

The British opt-out was much resented by the other member states because they believed that Britain would gain an unfair competitive edge over other states by having lower labour costs. Britain would consequently attract more FDI and in practice export unemployment to the rest of the EC – social dumping.

The real worth of the British opt-out was soon shown, however, to be of dubious value. Under the Rome Treaty and the Single European Act many social provisions can still be proposed under health and safety legislation which, because such legislation is subject to qualified majority voting, Britain cannot veto. Indeed for two reasons the British opt-out on the Social Chapter can now be seen as disadvantageous for Britain. Firstly it has led to more Commission determination to impose such laws on Britain as a form of Euro-revenge. Secondly the opt-out has backfired because Britain has excluded herself from discussion on social policies in the Council of Ministers and is thus unable to exert any moderating influence on social measures passed.

By June 1993 the reality was unavoidable. Britain was outvoted in the Council of Ministers over new EC laws governing working hours, the only consolation being that the new provisions would only become mandatory for industry in nine years. The laws provided for a maximum 48 hour working week, including a minimum daily rest period of 11 hours in each 24 hour period, a minimum weekly rest period (which 'should in principle include Sunday') of 24 hours and paid annual leave of at least 4 weeks with no facility for payment in lieu.

At the same time another measure under consideration would require companies with more than 1,000 employees in more than one Community state to establish a newly elected layer of worker consultation called 'works councils'. The councils would have to be consulted on everything from employment conditions, new technology and relocation plans to 'any proposal creating serious consequences' for the interests of workers. After Maastricht's full ratification eleven member states would implement the directive on councils and British companies would be under great pressure to set up such councils in their subsidiaries in other Community states and then have to grant them to their British workers as well.

Business pressure groups in Britain like the Confederation of British Industry and the Institute of Directors fiercely oppose such measures because in their view they threaten to disrupt efficient working patterns and lead to increased costs.

The threatened imposition on British elements of the Social Chapter despite the opt-out casts doubt on another alleged British triumph as the Maastricht Summit – the emphasis on the concept of *subsidiarity.*

This much misunderstood word has an honourable purpose and history. It originates from the Latin word 'subsidium' meaning reserve troops and was first used in Pope Leo XIII's 1891 encyclical Rerum Novarum. It was later adopted by Pope Pius XI in his 1931 enclycical Quadragesimo Anno which defined the principle that decisions affecting people's lives should be taken as far down the chain of command as possible. Community officials, including Delors, began to use the term often in the 1980s, insisting that the principle played a part in decision-making well before Maastricht in two ways. Firstly officials would only legislate at Community level where necessary and secondly they would feel an obligation to explain why such legislation was necessary.

Community leaders seized on the concept in the period before the Maastricht Summit though for varied motives. The German chancellor, Kohl, saw subsidiarity as synonymous with German-style federalism and its proper distribution of power between local communities, the regions, the German central government in Bonn and the Community. The British saw in the concept a golden opportunity to erect a barrier against the increasing powers of the Commission. Thus the subsidiarity principle is now enshrined in the treaty, Clause 3B of which states:

> In areas which do not fall within its exclusive competence, the Community shall take action, in accordance with the principle of subsidiarity, only if and in so far as the objectives of the proposed action cannot be sufficiently achieved by member states and can therefore, by reason of the scale or the effects of the proposed action, be better achieved by the Community.

To give the concept some flesh a Committee of the Regions was established under Article 198 to represent the regions of Europe with, in theory, some real status as it must be consulted by the Council of Ministers and the Commission and can meet on its own initiative to consider specifically regional issues. But such clauses are vague; the right to be consulted usually entails the right to be ignored and the treaty fails to make clear whether members of the Committee of the Regions will be nominated by governments or elected.

The doctrine of subsidiarity carries with it a larger problem: nobody agrees on what the word means. In a cogent analysis of the term, the House of Commons Foreign Affairs Committee concluded in May 1993 that while in one sense subsidiarity could be a powerful decentralizing concept, in other definitions it would allow for precisely the centralizing tendencies identified by Jacques Delors in a speech to the European Parliament in January 1990 in which he referred to 'the natural tendency of the centre to accumulate power'. British lawyers tend to agree that this latter interpretation of subsidiarity is more realistic. Leolin Price QC commented in January 1992 that the treaty definition of subsidiarity, far from offering protection to member states, was proposing 'a massive new transfer of additional governmental power to the Community'. Lord Mackenzie-Stuart, President of the European Court of Justice from 1984 to 1988, called the treaty definition 'a rich and prime example of gobbledegook embracing simultaneously two opposed concepts of subsidiarity. To regard the chosen formula as a constitutional safeguard shows great optimism'.

Certainly attempts to provide a more concrete definition of the principle and practice of subsidiarity, for example at the Edinburgh Summit in December 1992, have so far failed. For British and other Community employers faced by new Brussels directives on everything from technical standards to workers' rights, subsidiarity has seemed a sick joke. One company chairman returning in June 1993 from a bruising week in Brussels during which he found Commission officials in buoyant confident mood after the second Danish referendum was forced to comment, 'For them it's full steam ahead towards a fully federal Europe'.

The treaty's proposals on the powers of the *major institutions*, largely treated in Chapter 2, are not very radical but are significant. Maastricht attempts to address the so-called 'democratic deficit' by granting greater powers to the European Parliament through the Co-decision Procedure, a consequence of which was some reduction of the powers of the Commission in the decision-making process. However the Commission remains the 'guardian of the treaty' and retains all its principal functions. Under Maastricht several new policy areas are opened up to it under Articles 126 to 130. The new areas of Community 'competence' include education, especially vocational training, and cultural matters, for example the encouragement of cultural exchanges between member states. Public health, trans-European transport networks and the environment also fall more firmly within the Community remit. Arguably only co-ordinated action at a Community level can deal with problems like pollution, training and trans-European transport networks but the clauses do represent a further advance in Community power to inter-fere in areas of national life better handled by national governments.

The Council of Ministers remains the most powerful of the insti-tutions with the treaty extending qualified majority voting to about 70 important policy areas with specific mention made of capital flows, transport, the environment, education and cohesion funding. The British were gratified to gain more powers for the European Court of Justice to fine member states failing to comply with Community law.

It was recognized at the Maastricht Summit that meeting the convergence criteria necessary to join EMU would impose a heavy burden on the poorer states. Consequently they demanded and gained a promise of help in facing this burden under Article 130. Here the Community promises action leading to 'the strengthening of its economic and social cohesion' and the reduction of 'the dispar-ities between the level of development of the various regions and the backwardness of the least-favoured regions, including rural ones'. In addition to the Structural Funds, the Council was charged with setting up a *Cohesion Fund* by the end of 1993 to give financial help to environmental and transport projects in the four poorest states. As explained in Chapter 8 such a fund worth 2.6 billion ECU a year was agreed at the Edinburgh Summit in December 1992.

Finally the treaty reinforces the principle of *enlargement* – that membership is open to all democratic European countries (see Chapter 12). Under Article O it is stated that 'any European state may apply to become a member of the Union'. Negotiations with potential new members like Sweden and Austria began in earnest in 1993.

An evaluation of Maastricht

Whether the many clauses of the Maastricht Treaty will be fully implemented by the end of the century is doubtful. In a number of areas, for example in security and regional proposals, the clauses are so anodyne that they will change little. Some other areas, notably subsidiarity, are couched in such highly ambiguous language that the effect could cut both ways.

On the positive side decision making should certainly be helped by the greater use of qualified majority voting and the democratic deficit narrowed by the greater powers accorded to the European

Parliament. If EMU is ever implemented, then the single currency should integrate European business by eliminating transaction costs and allowing the ECB to contain inflation.

Against this, a more jaundiced view of European progress towards political and economic union is feasible. Much remains to be done to make European government democratically accountable. The chief law-making forum in the EC remains the Council of Ministers which is highly undemocratic in its procedures. The Foreign Affairs Committee of the UK parliament commented in 1993 of the Council: 'It is accountable to no one. It is more of a cabal than a cabinet, more of a diplomatic conference that a senate. And yet it legislates profusely'. Clearly its activities and voting ought to be much more open but Maastricht does not tackle this omission. Decision-making may be made slower by the virtual veto power given to the European Parliament under the co-decision Procedure.

More crucially for business, the Social Chapter, if implemented, could well add to business costs, an especially damaging factor in states which are already uncompetitive in the single market. Even more worrying are the convergence criteria; several states will fail to meet them and a two-speed Europe seems inevitable on the road to EMU. But weaker states attempting to meet the criteria will have to embrace the deflationary monetary policies of the Bundesbank. Yet the EC is already in deep recession and urgently needs policies for economic growth. It is in this area that Maastricht is so lacking. It promises more regulated labour markets and an attack on inflation but makes little or no mention of measures for growth and job creation. As Brian Reading has stressed, Europe needs flexible labour markets, low taxation and social security contributions, high profits in finance investment in high technology products and growing economies with buoyant tax revenues from which better education and training can be afforded. The task is urgent because competition from abroad, already strong from advanced industrial countries (AICs) and newly industrialized countries (NICs) will become ever more formidable as newly exporting countries (NECs) from the Third World develop their industries. These NECs are not small countries; they include large states like Malaysia and China and their competition is likely to erode still further Europe's industrial employment. It is therefore difficult to see anything but a harsh period of transition ahead in which much of the Maastricht Treaty may have to be jettisoned or amended.

Further reading

Bangemann, M, *Meeting the Global Challenge*, Kogan Page, London, 1992.

Barrell, R (ed.), *Economic Convergence and Monetary Union in Europe*, Sage, London, 1992.

Crawford, M, *One Money for Europe: the Economics and Politics of Maastricht*, Macmillan, London, 1993.

The European, *Maastricht Made Simple*, Milton Keynes, 1992.

Maclay, M, *Multi-speed Europe: the Community Beyond Maastricht*, RIIA, London, 1992.

Questions

1 Is European monetary union by the year 2000 now a realistic objective?
2 Why did European leaders set such store on furthering European political and economic union at the Maastricht summit?
3 Why did the Maastricht Treaty provoke a hostile reaction in Denmark and Britain?
4 In what ways would an implemented Maastricht Treaty have an impact on European business?

Index